# DAILY DEVOTIONS FOR A
# WOMAN OF PRAYER

# DAILY DEVOTIONS FOR A
# WOMAN OF PRAYER

365 Readings to Deepen
Your Communication
with God

BARBOUR
PUBLISHING

Print ISBN 978-1-63609-423-6

Member of the
Evangelical Christian
Publishers Association

# INTRODUCTION

Experience an intimate connection to your heavenly Father every day of the year. This beautiful daily devotional will encourage your soul and enhance your spiritual journey with 365 refreshing devotional thoughts. Read on, daughter of God—and come to know just how deeply and tenderly the King loves you.

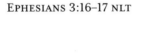

*I pray that from his glorious, unlimited resources he will empower you with inner strength through his Spirit. Then Christ will make his home in your hearts as you trust in him. Your roots will grow down into God's love and keep you strong.*
EPHESIANS 3:16–17 NLT

# DAY 1
# A BOLD REQUEST

*When they had crossed, Elijah said to Elisha, "Tell me, what*
*can I do for you before I am taken from you?" "Let me inherit*
*a double portion of your spirit," Elisha replied.*
2 KINGS 2:9 NIV

What a bold request.

Elijah filled the role of leader, prophet, and miracle worker. Why would Elisha want the heavy responsibilities and difficulties involved in this type of work? He did not ask to have a larger ministry than Elijah—he was only asking to inherit what Elijah was leaving and to be able to carry it on.

What might God give us if we asked boldly for the impossible? God deeply desires to bless us. If our hearts line up with His will and we stay open to His call, He will surprise us. God takes the ordinary and, through His power, transforms our prayers into the extraordinary—even double-portion requests.

* * * * * * * * * * * * * * * * * * * * * * * * * * * * * * * * * * * *

*Bless me, Lord. When my heart aligns with Your will and*
*when I ask for the impossible, bless me. Show me beyond*
*my expectations that You are my God. Amen.*

# DAY 2
# DWELLING ON THE IMPORTANT THINGS

*Set your mind on things above, not on things on the earth.*
Colossians 3:2 nkjv

Andrea spent the morning cooking and baking, getting ready for a family get-together at her sister's house. She worked hard on each of her dishes, especially the pie, then loaded the food into the car and drove to her sister's. Delicious food covered the kitchen counter and Andrea added her contributions to the bounty. When it came time for dessert, Andrea sliced into the pie she had spent time carefully putting together. To her dismay, the filling had not set like it should have. Disappointment clouded her day. In spite of the good time she had visiting with everyone, she felt her time and money had been wasted on the pie.

Sometimes we worry about little things and forget to look at the big picture. If all we see are the things that go wrong or the trouble around us, we have missed what's important. Instead of focusing on spending time with her family, Andrea fretted about how long it had taken her to fix the pie and how much she had spent on the ingredients.

As Christians, we can focus on our problems and the little things that frustrate us or we can keep our minds on heavenly things and know we have hope beyond what troubles us here. Christ is bigger than anything we may have to endure here on earth.

*Lord, help us to keep our minds fixed on You so that the problems we face are seen through Your grace in our lives. Amen.*

# DAY 3

## PRAYERFUL CONSIDERATION

*Trust in the Lord with all your heart and lean not on your own understanding;*
*in all your ways submit to him, and he will make your paths straight.*

PROVERBS 3:5–6 NIV

Have you ever had to make a decision but didn't know what to do? As Christians, we have a reliable resource for counsel. When decision-making poses a threat to our serenity and peace, Proverbs 3:5–6 provides sound advice.

God provides the solution to decision-making with a promise—namely, if we take all our concerns to God, He will direct our paths. When we're tempted to act on our own wisdom, the Lord tells us to stop, reflect, and prayerfully consider each matter. He gives us uncomplicated advice for our major and not-so-major decisions. The question is *Will we listen?* That's the most important decision of all.

* * * * * * * * * * * * * * * * * * * * * * * * * * * * * * * * * * * * * * * *

*Often, Lord, I run on ahead of You and make decisions on my own. Help me*
*to remember that even with small decisions I need to seek Your will. Amen.*

# DAY 4
# A BIT OF A TOAD

*"I no longer call you servants, because a servant does not know his master's business. Instead, I have called you friends."*
JOHN 15:15 NIV

A good friendship takes time, effort, and sensitivity, but a healthy friendship is not one-sided. For instance, how would you feel if you had a friend—let's call her Amelia—who only comes around when she wants to borrow something—like your fondue pot, your designer sunglasses, or your car with a full tank of gas? Amelia asks, "Could you babysit while I get the polish freshened on my toenails? Oh, and I need to unload big-time since my boss has become this miserly, manipulative, and mean-spirited mule of a man. Oh, and would you mind helping me with my daughter's costume for the school's talent show? This year she's a singing toad."

These might not be outrageous things to ask of a buddy, and yet if that's all Amelia ever came calling for, wouldn't you think your friend was a bit of a toad too? Why? Because you want a relationship in which someone not only needs you but loves you. Wouldn't you think that Amelia's brand of friendship wasn't intimate, wasn't real?

Christ would like to be our friend—a real one. And if we only go to Him in prayer begging for a better job, better health, and a bigger house, might we not be sending the same message, that we're more interested in the "getting" than the loving?

* * * * * * * * * * * * * * * * * * * * * * * * * * * * * * * * * * * * * * * *

*Lord, please help me love You as a real friend*
*and not just for what You can give me. Amen.*

# DAY 5
# HE WILL ANSWER

*I waited patiently for the Lord; and he inclined unto me, and*
*heard my cry. He brought me up also out of an horrible pit.*
PSALM 40:1–2 KJV

David found himself trapped in a "horrible pit" with no apparent way out, and he cried loudly to the Lord to rescue him. Then he waited. It took time for God to answer. David undoubtedly learned more patience in the process and probably had to endure doubts, wondering if God cared about the dilemma he was in.

Even Jeremiah didn't always get immediate answers to prayer. One time he and some Jewish refugees were in a dire situation and were desperate to know what to do. Yet after Jeremiah prayed, the Lord took ten days to answer (Jeremiah 42:7). But the answer *did* come. . .in time.

Today we sometimes find ourselves in a "horrible pit" as well, and we pray desperately for God to bring us up out of it. He will. We often just need to be patient.

. . . . . . . . . . . . . . . . . . . . . . . . . . . . . . . . . . . . . . . . . . .

*Why is patience so hard? It's because Your timing is perfect*
*and beyond my understanding. Help me to be patient with*
*You, God. I know that You will answer me. Amen.*

# DAY 6
# STILLNESS

*Be still, and know that I am God.*
PSALM 46:10 NKJV

David wrote, "Meditate within your heart on your bed, and be still" (Psalm 4:4 NKJV). Many of us have lost the ability to meditate on God. We either tell ourselves that meditation is something only Buddhist monks do, or else we cry out frantic prayers while distracted by the careening roller coaster of life. When we lie down in bed at night, instead of meditating calmly and trusting in God, we fret and toss and turn.

When we learn to trust that God can protect us and work out our problems, then we can lie down peacefully and sleep (Psalm 4:8). That same trust gives us the strength to face our days with confidence.

*Dear God, quiet my mind. Remove from it all the worldly thoughts that come between You and me. Create stillness within me, and turn my thoughts toward You. Amen.*

# DAY 7
# RENEWING THE MIND

*Don't copy the behavior and customs of this world, but let God transform*
*you into a new person by changing the way you think. Then you will learn*
*to know God's will for you, which is good and pleasing and perfect.*

ROMANS 12:2 NLT

We are surrounded by technology that introduces us to new ideas all the time. No matter what your choice of electronic device, you have the world at your disposal. Sometimes the information isn't acceptable for Christians. We may not have asked for these bits of information, but they invade our world every day. No matter where we turn, evil is present on all sides. Paul wrote to the Roman church, telling them not to be conformed to the world around them but to allow God to transform them and renew their minds. Can we as twenty-first-century Christians do the same? Yes, we can.

1. Don't allow yourself to view or read everything that comes across the screen in front of you. If it appears suggestive or impure, it probably is.

2. Take time to read your Bible every day. Don't let the cyber world be your only source of information. Hear what God has to say to you personally.

3. Ask God to renew your mind and show you what is profitable for you as a Christian.

4. Don't accept something just because everyone else does it even if it's "politically correct." Choose today to be transformed by the renewing of your mind.

*Father, help me not to conform to the world's ideas. Renew my mind*
*and help me to know Your acceptable will for my life. Amen.*

# DAY 8

# THAT LITTLE INNER MECHANISM

*"Do not let your hearts be troubled.*
*You believe in God; believe also in me."*
JOHN 14:1 NIV

There is something wonderful about a music box—that treasure chest of sweet and melodic tranquility—and if one believed in enchantment, it might be called the music of fairies. What if that music box were wound up over and over and over without ever letting it wind back down again? What if the little winding key got tighter and tighter until the inner mechanisms—like the cylinder, the comb, and the flywheel—could no longer work? It would no longer be able to play its beautiful music.

Well, when our hearts become troubled with the cares of this world, we can no longer play the music we were created to play. We are essentially broken. So, how does one undo, unravel, and slow down when our own winding key has been wound too tightly and our inner mechanism—our soul—can no longer function properly? We should take all our troubles to the Lord in prayer. Every heartache. Every disappointment. Every sorrow. He will let us rest in Him and disentangle ourselves from the human stresses so that we can rise again. So that we can once again play our music to a world that needs to hear it.

. . . . . . . . . . . . . . . . . . . . . . . . . . . . . . . . . . . . . . . .

*Lord, when I am feeling anxious, help me to remember*
*that You hold me in the palm of Your hand. You have the*
*power to restore and refresh my weary soul. Amen.*

# DAY 9

## GOD'S GREAT MERCY

*"We do not make requests of you because we are*
*righteous, but because of your great mercy."*
DANIEL 9:18 NIV

When Daniel "understood from the Scriptures, according to the word of the LORD given to Jeremiah the prophet, that the desolation of Jerusalem would last seventy years" (Daniel 9:2 NIV), he prayed a long prayer of confession for his people, who had sinned so badly and persistently against God that He had allowed heavy punishment to fall upon them. And in that prayer, Daniel uttered one of the great truths of scripture, the verse we know now as Daniel 9:18.

Let's understand, with Daniel, that we bring absolutely nothing to God. But let's also know, like Daniel, that in God's great mercy, He chooses to hear, love, and forgive us.

- - - - - - - - - - - - - - - - - - - - - - - - - - - - - - - - - - - - - - - - - - - -

*Oh mighty God, Your great mercy is beyond my understanding.*
*I have nothing to bring You, yet in my sinfulness You hear me,*
*love me, and forgive me. Thank You, Father. Amen.*

# DAY 10
# SUCH AS I HAVE

*Then Peter said, "Silver and gold I do not have, but what I do have I*
*give you: In the name of Jesus Christ of Nazareth, rise up and walk."*
Acts 3:6 nkjv

Have you ever been asked to fill a position for which you felt unqualified? Your first thought is to say no. Surely there is someone better qualified than you for the job. Satan doesn't make your decision any easier. He whispers negative thoughts into your ears. "You can't do that; you're not good at it." "Everyone's looking at you and thinking what a bad job you're doing." "You're making a mess of this. Let someone else do it." All his thoughts are lies, of course. Maybe you aren't as experienced as the last person who had the job, but you're the one God chose. You may not have the abilities or talents of others, but you have something God can use.

When Peter and John approached the lame man at the gate of the temple, Peter didn't hesitate to tell him they didn't have any silver or gold for him. But he had something the man could use. He said, "What I do have I give you." God is looking for those who are willing to give what they do have. He knew before He called you what you could do, and He also can qualify you to do whatever He requires. Give God what you have, and allow Him to use it.

. . . . . . . . . . . . . . . . . . . . . . . . . . . . . . . . . . . . . . . . .

*Lord, use me and whatever I have for Your glory.*
*Help me to surrender all I have to You willingly. Amen.*

# DAY 11
# MINDING YOUR OWN BUSINESS

*Make it your goal to live a quiet life, minding your own business
and working with your hands, just as we instructed you before.*
1 Thessalonians 4:11 nlt

In the 1960s, there was a popular TV sitcom that had as one of its characters a nosy lady named Gladys Kravitz. She spent her time peering out her windows at all the neighbors to see what they were doing. Any little incident had her shrieking for her husband, Abner, to come and see what was happening.

It's easy to judge the Gladys Kravitzes of the world and feel we're above those acts. We might not feel that eavesdropping on a coworker or family member is wrong. We're only concerned for them. Wanting to hear the latest gossip doesn't mean we're nosy, does it? Snooping on our neighbors is okay; we're a part of the neighborhood watch, after all.

Paul wrote to the members of the Thessalonian church that they should live a quiet life and mind their own business. In this day of cell phones and computers, we can know everything that's going on and pass it to someone else in a matter of seconds. If we are attempting to live by God's Word, we must be careful about our texts and emails. It's tempting to pass on that juicy tidbit about someone else, but it can be hurtful to others and destroy our testimony for Christ. Paul's advice to the Thessalonians is good advice for us also.

. . . . . . . . . . . . . . . . . . . . . . . . . . . . . . . . . . . . . . . . . .

*Lord, help me to mind my own business and
live a quiet life according to Your Word. Amen.*

# DAY 12
# TUMBLING THE STONES

*But just as he who called you is holy, so be holy in all you do.*
1 PETER 1:15 NIV

If you've ever spent time beachcombing, you know that the stones that get trapped in between the big rocks often get tossed and whirled a great deal. So much so that the edges get worked off, making them the smoothest of all. The colors and nuances and unique markings are accentuated. In other words, their beauty is brought out by the process of the constant stirring and abrasion—rock tumbling against rock. When you pick them up and roll them around in your palm, they feel like the shell of an egg. It's those stones that become part of your trove of little beach treasures.

God uses the tumbling turbulence of our lives to work off our edges—those jagged sinful, rebellious edges that keep us from being all that we were meant to be.

Being tumbled can be painful—stone hitting stone can't be all that fun—but the outcome will be holiness and a loveliness of spirit. We will be treasures, brighter than diamonds and more precious than gold.

Pray that God can use your tumbling trials to bring out the beauty of your soul.

. . . . . . . . . . . . . . . . . . . . . . . . . . . . . . . . . . . . . . . . . . .

*Dear Lord, please use the turbulent times of my life to*
*help make me beautiful in my spirit so that I can glorify*
*You and be all that You created me to be. Amen.*

# DAY 13
# GOD ALREADY KNOWS

*"As soon as you began to pray, a word went out, which I
have come to tell you, for you are highly esteemed."*
DANIEL 9:23 NIV

In the middle of pouring out his heart to God one day, Daniel's prayer was interrupted by the appearance of the angel Gabriel. Bringing insight and understanding (v. 22), Gabriel's message contained the interesting concept that in the instant that Daniel began to pray, the answer was already on its way.

Before Daniel got past his salutation, God knew Daniel's heart and had already set in motion the response to Daniel's unfinished prayer.

As He did for Daniel, God knows our needs even before we give voice to them in prayer. We can rest in the knowledge that even before the words leave our lips, God has already heard them, and He has already answered them.

. . . . . . . . . . . . . . . . . . . . . . . . . . . . . . . . . . . . . . . . . .

*Thank You, God, for answering my prayers. Before the words leave my lips,
You already have the answer. How great You are, God! I praise You. Amen.*

# DAY 14
# KEEP YOUR EYES ON JESUS

*I keep my eyes always on the LORD. With him*
*at my right hand, I will not be shaken.*
PSALM 16:8 NIV

A recent news story told of a young man in a truck who took his eyes off the road to text on his phone. He didn't realize the traffic ahead of him had stopped. He ran over the top of the car in front of him and crushed to death a woman and her mother who were sitting in the backseat. Charges were filed against him. Chances are he will serve prison time for the accident. Had he kept his eyes on the road in front of him, two people would still be alive today.

The young man on his phone may have thought the text message was of extreme importance, but he probably realizes now that nothing was more important than watching the road ahead. As Christians, we must keep our eyes always on the Lord. Taking our eyes off Christ and looking at the world around us can result in spiritual death for us and others as well. When we have Christ at our side, He will alert us to those obstacles that could cause us to get distracted in our Christian walk. Nothing is more important than keeping our eyes on the Lord. As we do so, life's priorities fall into place, and we aren't apt to have a spiritual wreck.

* * * * * * * * * * * * * * * * * * * * * * * * * * * * * * * * * * * * * * * * * *

*Jesus, keep me alert to the path ahead, and help me to walk in*
*Your footsteps, knowing they will guide me to safety. Amen.*

# DAY 15

# THE RADIANCE OF HIS SPLENDOR

*In the year that King Uzziah died, I saw the Lord, high and exalted,*
*seated on a throne; and the train of his robe filled the temple. Above him*
*were seraphim, each with six wings: With two wings they covered their*
*faces, with two they covered their feet, and with two they were flying.*

ISAIAH 6:1–2 NIV

Society has used the words *awesome* and *incredible* and *glorious* so loosely for so long that the words no longer fill us with pause or wonder. Perhaps we mentally shrug when we hear those words batted about in conversation. People might say they had an incredible trip or they bought some awesome stilettos or they had a glorious day at the spa. Despite this misapplication of these expressions, there are things that do fulfill the authentic meaning of these words.

The book of Isaiah tells us that the Lord is exalted, seated on a throne, and the train of His robe fills the temple. Isaiah also talks about the angels who attend Him and worship Him—that their wings cover their faces, surely because of the radiance of His splendor. How fearsome and humbling and magnificent that sight must be!

In fact, this holy scene in the heavens should remind us that one day every knee shall bow and every tongue confess that He is Lord. Why wait until that final day? Why not give praise to the One—the only One—who is worthy of our raised hearts and hands? The One who is truly incredible and awesome and glorious!

. . . . . . . . . . . . . . . . . . . . . . . . . . . . . . . . . . . . . . . . . . . .

*Lord God, help me to comprehend Your magnitude*
*and glory. I want to be awestruck by You. Amen.*

# DAY 16

# BEYOND WORDS...
# TO THE HEART

*And so the Lord says, "These people say they are mine. They honor
me with their lips, but their hearts are far from me. And their
worship of me is nothing but man-made rules learned by rote."*
ISAIAH 29:13 NLT

From God's perspective, the actions of our hearts speak louder than our words. And if our worship consists of mindlessly repeating words and going with the flow, we are missing out on connecting with a God who fiercely loves us and desires to be in an unscripted relationship with us.

This verse carries a sobering reminder that God looks beyond the words of our mouths and considers the heart that utters them. Creeds and prayers are familiar ways to connect with God and serve as wonderful reminders of His steadfast character. The next time an opportunity arises to recite from memory, consider how to bring the well-known words to life in a new and fresh understanding—spoken from the heart.

* * * * * * * * * * * * * * * * * * * * * * * * * * * * * * * * * * * * * * *

*Father, when I read the Bible, I will savor each word and consider its meaning.
And when I pray a familiar prayer, I will pray from my heart. Amen.*

# DAY 17
# LIVING WATER

*The woman said to him, "Sir, give me this water so that I won't*
*get thirsty and have to keep coming here to draw water."*
JOHN 4:15 NIV

The Samaritan woman who came to draw water from Jacob's well didn't know she would meet Someone who would change her life drastically. Her life had been filled with relationships that didn't work. She may have felt worthless and used. That day may have started out like every other day in her life, but when she approached the well, Jesus was waiting. He asked her for a drink. When she questioned His reason, He in turn offered her water—living water. If she drank of it, she would never thirst again. She was all for never having to come to the well again to draw water, not realizing Jesus was offering her spiritual life, not a physical refreshment. As they talked, she found living water that gave her a new lease on life.

Some days our life can seem like one endless task after another; it exhibits a sameness that makes us weary. We thirst for something better or maybe just different. Maybe it's time for a trip to the well. As we come to Christ in prayer, seeking a much-needed drink, we will find Him waiting at the well, offering the same living water to each of us that He offered to the Samaritan woman. Are there any among us who don't need times of spiritual refreshing in our lives? Grab a bucket and go to the well. Jesus is waiting.

. . . . . . . . . . . . . . . . . . . . . . . . . . . . . . . . . . . . . . . . .

*Jesus, help me to drink from Your well of living*
*water so I will never thirst again. Amen.*

# DAY 18

# RESTORING THE BROKEN PIECES

*And the vessel that he made of clay was marred in the hand of the potter; so he made it again into another vessel, as it seemed good to the potter to make.*

JEREMIAH 18:4 NKJV

Marcia enjoys restoring old furniture, giving it new life. She strips away the old finish that is scratched and ugly, sands the wood to a beautiful sheen, and covers it with a coat of new varnish or paint. Sometimes she replaces old, worn fabric with a new piece of cloth. When she's finished, she has a "new" piece of furniture. But it doesn't happen overnight. It takes patient, loving care to get it just right. If you were to visit her home, you would find it full of beautiful furniture lovingly restored by Marcia.

Jeremiah went to the potter's house and saw the potter at work on a vessel of clay. While the potter was working on the piece, it became marred. The potter didn't toss the clay away but kept working, fashioning it into another vessel. God wants to restore lives scratched and marred by sin just as Marcia restores furniture and the potter molds clay into usable vessels. No matter what has stained or disfigured our lives, God can mold us into the person He wants us to be. To become a usable vessel, we must allow the Potter to knead and work the clay. Even if we fall off the Potter's wheel by our own choice, He can pick us up and remold us into a new creation.

*Father, help me to stay on the Potter's wheel*
*until You are finished with me. Amen.*

# DAY 19
# THE MOST BEAUTIFUL WORDS

*So God created mankind in his own image, in the image of
God he created them; male and female he created them.*
GENESIS 1:27 NIV

Flowers—bluebonnets, Mexican primrose, and Indian paintbrush—picked in delight on a spring day are sometimes pressed inside the pages of a book. When time passes, and one revisits the flowers, they are dried and flat and lifeless, mere shadows of what they were. The vibrant colors are gone, the perfume no longer enchants, and the wonder of their beauty is only a distant memory. Yet there lingers an endearing essence of what once was.

That is so much like humans in their fallen state.

We were made in the image of God, but because of sin, we became shriveled and faded. Yet with the sacrifice Jesus made for us with His very life, mankind has hope to return to the beauty that once was ours. When those who belong to Christ die and pass into eternity, they will be given glorified bodies renewed with life and color. Not for a short time like the flowers of the field, but for all eternity.

If you've never asked the Lord to be yours, acknowledged your sin, and taken Him into your heart—well, what has been stopping you? They will be the most beautiful words you will ever speak and the most life-changing prayer you will ever pray.

. . . . . . . . . . . . . . . . . . . . . . . . . . . . . . . . . . . . . . . . . . .

*God, restore, refresh, and reconcile me to Yourself.
Help me to become all You have created me to be. Amen.*

## DAY 20

# ACCORDING TO HIS PURPOSE

*With this in mind, we constantly pray for you, that our God may make*
*you worthy of his calling, and that by his power he may bring to fruition*
*your every desire for goodness and your every deed prompted by faith.*

2 THESSALONIANS 1:11 NIV

God's sovereignty and our free will clash in a glorious kaleidoscope of grace in the second letter to the Thessalonians.

Here, Paul prayed for the church at Thessalonica that God would make them worthy of His calling. God calls; then God makes them deserving of that calling.

Elsewhere, Paul commanded believers to *live* lives worthy of God and His calling (Ephesians 4:1). Our effort, our choice.

Here, Paul prays that God will fulfill *our* purposes and actions prompted by our faith.

But God is the One who calls us "according to His purpose" (Romans 8:28 NIV; 2 Timothy 1:9). In fact, Paul goes so far as to say that call is "irrevocable" (Romans 11:29 NIV).

Let's rest in the fact that all the things we live and plan and believe, God will fulfill for us.

. . . . . . . . . . . . . . . . . . . . . . . . . . . . . . . . . . . . . . . .

*By faith I believe that You will fulfill the plans You*
*have for me. Right now, You are working on my behalf,*
*enlightening me to Your will. I thank You, Father! Amen.*

# DAY 21
# BE STILL

*Be still, and know that I am God; I will be exalted*
*among the nations, I will be exalted in the earth!*
PSALM 46:10 NKJV

Vanessa stepped outside into the blistering August heat to take out the garbage. She couldn't wait to get back inside where it was cool. When she tried to open the door, it was locked. Panic seized her for a moment, but she realized there was nothing she could do about it. They lived miles from town, and her husband wouldn't be home from work for a while. She searched for a place to get out of the sun and spotted a large shade tree. She sat down under the tree and looked around. For the first time in a long time, she noticed the beauty of God's creation that surrounded her home. God's blessings were apparent everywhere she looked. By the time her husband arrived home, she felt rested and refreshed despite the heat. She realized God had probably been trying to get her attention for some time. She just hadn't been listening. It had taken getting locked out of her house to make her stop and listen.

Has God been trying to get your attention lately? If you're rushing around, buried in responsibilities and tasks you feel are important, what will it take for God to make you stop and listen to His voice? What will it take for you to "be still" and acknowledge Him?

• • • • • • • • • • • • • • • • • • • • • • • • • • • • • • • • • • • • • •

*Father, help me to slow down so I can hear You speaking to me. Amen.*

# DAY 22
# AS EASY AS BREATHING

*Pray continually.*
1 Thessalonians 5:17 NIV

*Pray continually?* Don't those two words in the Bible seem a bit foreign to us? In fact, the words stand alone—looking rather stark. We stare at them, wondering how anyone, no matter how holy, could accomplish such a command. There would be no time left for working or playing or eating or resting.

Perhaps the scripture means that to pray without ceasing is when we are in natural conversation with Him during the day—as if we were chatting with a friend on and off while taking a long, pleasant walk together.

For instance, you might thank God when you wake up to a new morning. You might ask Him to bless your breakfast and invite Him to guide you through the day. You might feel compelled to breathe a prayer of thanksgiving when you have a near-miss with another car on your way to work. Perhaps you'd want to praise Him for the project you successfully completed and then request that He help your boss who's having a bad day or heal a coworker who's having some health issues. This kind of day does reflect the 1 Thessalonians scripture—that is, to stay so close to God that one finds praying as easy and comfortable as breathing.

. . . . . . . . . . . . . . . . . . . . . . . . . . . . . . . . . . . . . . . . .

*Father, please be present in my heart and thoughts always. Never let our communion and fellowship be severed. I want every area of my life to be committed to You through sincere, continual prayer. Amen.*

# DAY 23
# CALL ON HIM IN FAITH

*"Call to me and I will answer you and tell you great
and unsearchable things you do not know."*
JEREMIAH 33:3 NIV

Jeremiah 33:3 teaches that if we pray to God, He will answer us with wisdom. In the King James Version of the Bible, the word *pray* is used more than five hundred times. God wants us to pray. When we call on Him in prayer, we know that He hears us (1 John 5:15).

Proverbs 2:6 (NASB) says, "For the LORD gives wisdom; from His mouth come knowledge and understanding." God knows us fully, and He is able to direct us in wisdom and guide us through the works of His Holy Spirit.

Just as God gave Jeremiah wisdom when he prayed, He will do the same for you if you call on Him in faith (James 1:5–6).

*God, I need Your help. I've sought counsel for my problem,
and still I'm not sure what to do. But You know! Please,
God, guide me with Your wisdom. Amen.*

# DAY 24

# WATCH WHERE YOU'RE GOING

*Your word is a lamp for my feet, a light on my path.*
PSALM 119:105 NIV

Vickie had her mind on her husband, who was in the hospital, and didn't notice the concrete parking space barrier. She hung the toe of her shoe on it. Without warning, she fell forward, landing on her left knee. She stood and examined her wounds. Her hand was scraped and her knee hurt but nothing life threatening. She went on to the hospital to visit Sonny even though she could tell her knee was swollen. Later, the evidence of her fall showed in ugly black and blue bruises. She placed ice on her knee and kept it elevated as much as possible. The injury wasn't serious, just painful.

Sometimes we hang our toe on obstacles in our Christian walk. We may stumble around spiritually and even fall sometimes, but we don't have to remain on the ground. We can pick ourselves up and begin walking again. It may be painful at first, and we may even sustain a few scrapes and bruises and feel swollen from our fall, but God offers us healing. All we have to do is reach for His Word. God has given us a lamp through His Word, which shines light on our path as we walk day by day. Turn on the lamp by reading your Bible daily.

* * * * * * * * * * * * * * * * * * * * * * * * * * * * * * * * * *

*Father, open my understanding as I read Your Word,*
*that I may clearly see the path I need to travel. Amen.*

# DAY 25
## SEEN BY OTHERS

*"And when you pray, do not be like the hypocrites, for they love to pray standing in the synagogues and on the street corners to be seen by others. Truly I tell you, they have received their reward in full. But when you pray, go into your room, close the door and pray to your Father, who is unseen."*
MATTHEW 6:5–6 NIV

Have you ever heard a beautiful prayer in a large cathedral, and the words echoed and sang with a stirring rhythm and spiritual uplift of their own? Some people are gifted at praying in public. They know how to move and excite their audiences with an eloquent presentation. Unfortunately, humans must be careful not to enjoy the admiration of the crowd too much, since it would be easy to forget to whom the prayers are intended and begin to seek the approval of man over God.

Jesus encourages us to have a humble attitude when it comes to prayer by finding a quiet place to talk to Him, away from the attentive crowds. Does that mean we cannot pray in public? No, but it would be wise to be watchful of our motives, since a heartfelt closet prayer would surely be more welcome than a prayer raised up to impress the masses.

Where is your favorite quiet place to talk to God?

*Lord, give me a spirit of humility and sincerity when I pray in front of others. Help me to remember that prayer should not be used to show others how godly and well-spoken I am, but to connect with You, the living God. Amen.*

# DAY 26
# NO LIMITS

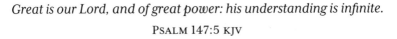

*Great is our Lord, and of great power: his understanding is infinite.*
PSALM 147:5 KJV

When you're praying for wisdom in a complex or desperate situation, fix this thought firmly in your mind: You may have no clue as to the right answer, but God certainly does! His understanding is without end.

At times, we don't understand why God allows us to go through troubled times, but He certainly knows—and He cares deeply for each one of us. He not only knows every star by name, but He knows *your* name too.

Psalm 147:5 is one of the most powerful scriptures in the Bible. When we meditate deeply on its words, they can fill our minds with peace and assurance.

· · · · · · · · · · · · · · · · · · · · · · · · · · · · · · · · · · · · · · · · · · · ·

*God, who am I among all the stars in the universe? But You*
*know their names, and You know mine too! You know me,*
*You understand me, and that brings me peace. Amen.*

# DAY 27
# QUIET TIME

*He says, "Be still, and know that I am God."*
PSALM 46:10 NIV

As you were growing up, how many times were you told to sit or stand still? And honestly, they were "tells" even if the adult added a "please." It may have seemed like you were merely being asked to be quiet, or not fidget, or not bump into another child, or not kick the seat in front of you. Could we as children have misread these dictates to be still? Were we actually being told to calm ourselves so that we might hear or learn something important rather than just as a control of our outward behavior?

Our earthly parents told us to be still just as our heavenly Father has instructed us to be still. When we calm ourselves physically and mentally, we are better able to focus our minds and listen with our hearts. We become open to hearing the Lord's direction for our lives. We allow ourselves to feel the peace that comes with the presence of the Holy Spirit within us.

Quiet time is a precious commodity. With mobile electronic devices, it seems we are constantly communicating via phone, text, or social media. Consider making time to put the electronics down and give yourself the gift of being still.

. . . . . . . . . . . . . . . . . . . . . . . . . . . . . . . . . . . . . . .

*Lord, in all the busyness I call my life, please help me to heed Your command to be still. I know You are my God and will direct me when I make quiet time to focus on You. Amen.*

# DAY 28
# WHY FASTING?

*"But when you fast, put oil on your head and wash your face, so that it will not be obvious to others that you are fasting, but only to your Father, who is unseen; and your Father, who sees what is done in secret, will reward you."*
MATTHEW 6:17–18 NIV

Eating has become a sport in our country, a mania—perhaps even a god. So, to commit to giving up a meal or two occasionally or giving up solid food for a little while to spend more time with the Lord seems impossible.

It isn't.

What is the purpose of fasting? First of all, planning meals, buying food, cooking, and cleaning up are time-consuming, and when we give them up even for a day, it allows us more time to turn our hearts toward heaven. Secondly, fasting along with our prayer can be powerful as we hear the Lord more clearly, sense His presence more keenly, and see the work of the Holy Spirit moving in our lives. Fasting can give us a new perspective, one that is more God-centered, peace-filled, refreshing, freeing, healing, and life-changing.

If you have health issues that keep you from traditional fasting, you might try fasting TV shows or desserts. If you do fast and pray, the Gospel of Matthew says not to grandstand about it but to do it quietly, and then God will reward you.

. . . . . . . . . . . . . . . . . . . . . . . . . . . . . . . . . . . . . . . . .

*Father, give me the desire and the discipline to seek You*
*in prayer in a more devoted and focused way. Amen.*

# DAY 29
## PRAYER SCHEDULE

*Seven times a day I praise you for your righteous laws.*
PSALM 119:164 NIV

The Bible tells us to pray without ceasing. A fixed-hour prayer ritual is called "praying the hours" or the "daily office." Hearts and minds turn toward God at set times. We try to create a space in our busy lives to praise God and express our gratitude throughout the day.

We can create any kind of prayer schedule. Each stoplight we pass, the ring of the alarm on our watches, or a pause during television commercials can all serve as simple reminders to pray. We can be alert during the day for ways God protects and guides us.

Seven moments a day—to thank the Lord for all the moments of our lives.

· · · · · · · · · · · · · · · · · · · · · · · · · · · · · · · · · · · · · · · ·

*Sometimes I forget to pray; busyness gets in the way. But I can change that! I will set aside specific times throughout my day to pray and praise You, Lord. Amen.*

# DAY 30
# MIND AND HEART

*"Accept instruction from his mouth and lay up his words in your heart."*
JOB 22:22 NIV

Although they were sisters, Alice knew she and Sally were as different as day and night. Alice liked to be organized and methodical. She always kept a to-do list and tried to have an overall plan to reach goals. Alice was comfortable evaluating opportunities, determining requirements, and translating everything into a written plan. If something changed, Alice tried to be flexible and revise her plan as needed.

Sally, on the other hand, appeared to plan only when all else failed. To Alice, it seemed like Sally put off deciding until the decision literally made itself. Alice loved her "big sis," but she couldn't understand how Sally had survived, let alone successfully balanced marriage, motherhood, and a career.

At a family reunion, their aunt put things in perspective for Alice. She said, "I am so pleased that you and Sally have both become the women that God intended. It's remarkable how similar you are. It's wonderful to see you both use your minds to listen for God's direction and then act from your heart. It's as evident as the noses on your lovely faces that your hearts for Jesus rule your lives."

. . . . . . . . . . . . . . . . . . . . . . . . . . . . . . . . . . . . . . . . .

*Lord, thank You for making each of Your children different*
*and unique. Help me to listen to You with my mind and then*
*follow the path directed by my Christian heart. Amen.*

## DAY 31
# ONE SOUL AT A TIME

*"If my people, who are called by my name, will humble themselves and pray and seek my face and turn from their wicked ways, then I will hear from heaven, and I will forgive their sin and will heal their land."*

2 CHRONICLES 7:14 NIV

If you have the courage to watch the evening news, you know that we live in perilous times. We also live in wicked times. People don't seem to care anymore about watching out for their neighbors. About lying and cheating a bit here and there. About living together first to see if that marriage thing might be for them. About honoring the sanctity of life and family and worship and God. In fact, the word *sin* has gone out of vogue, but just because a nation hides its transgressions doesn't mean they are getting away with them. Sound familiar? Just as Adam and Eve hid in the garden after they sinned, we as a nation are trying to hide our shame.

What can we do? It starts with one soul at a time. If we will humble ourselves and pray and seek His face and turn from our wicked ways, then He will hear us, forgive us, and heal our land. Let this be our personal petition, our greatest ambition, and our heart prayer as a nation.

*Lord, You have the power to guide and restore nations. Please help the people of this country to acknowledge their sin and their need for You. Amen.*

# DAY 32
## PRAYING GREAT PRAYERS

*And the sun stood still, and the moon stayed, until the*
*people had avenged themselves upon their enemies.*
JOSHUA 10:13 KJV

As Joshua prepared his men to fight, God promised him that He had already delivered the enemy into Israel's hand and that none of them would stand before the Israelites (v. 8). After they had smashed the overwhelming foe in battle and watched God drop bombs of hailstones on them, Joshua asked God to stop the clock. The sun and moon paused, and Joshua's men had another day of light to erase the menace.

The longest day in history was also a day for believing in the Lord for victory. Joshua went against the combined armies of five kings because he believed the Lord's promise, and he saw God fight for him. In that spirit, he prayed a great prayer. May we be emboldened to pray great prayers when we see the Lord following through in our lives!

. . . . . . . . . . . . . . . . . . . . . . . . . . . . . . . . . . . . . . . . .

*God, fight for me! I believe in victory over my troubles and*
*my enemies. Their words and deeds pierce me like arrows,*
*but with Your great love You protect me. Amen.*

# DAY 33
# HE WILL GIVE YOU THE WORDS

*"Alas, Sovereign Lord," I said, "I do not know how to speak; I am too young." But the Lord said to me, "Do not say, 'I am too young.' You must go to everyone I send you to and say whatever I command you."*

JEREMIAH 1:6–7 NIV

Marianne was asked to give the message for an upcoming Sunday worship service when the pastor would be on a retreat. At first, she hesitated, then nicely said, "No." She remembered mentioning that she wasn't trained in the ministry and really didn't believe she had enough public speaking experience. Somehow, the lay leader didn't hear her. He just said, "Well, I believe you'll have a worthy message."

That evening, as Marianne considered her predicament, she took it to the Lord in prayer. She repeated her reasons for not being capable of preparing and giving the requested sermon. Her devotional reading the following morning was about how God told a young Jeremiah that he would one day be a prophet to nations. Could this be the answer to her prayer? Like Jeremiah responding that he was too young, Marianne had responded by saying she lacked training and experience. Marianne knew that, like Jeremiah, if she trusted the Lord, He would give her the message she needed to deliver.

* * *

*God, I trust You to show me the words You need me to share and with whom. As I go through each day, I want to obey Your will and speak as You direct. Amen.*

# DAY 34

## A DAILY JOLT FOR THE SPIRIT

*In all your ways submit to him, and he will make your paths straight.*
PROVERBS 3:6 NIV

Have you ever been caught in a rut for so long that it started to feel like a hopeless abyss? That is just where the enemy of your soul wants you to be—unable to be effective in this hurting and needy world, unable to share the love of Christ, unable to reflect His glorious light.

So, how does one emerge from those endless furrows that represent the monotone, monochrome grind of the everyday—the looking down into the mire instead of gazing up into the splendor? Just like the vehicle stuck in the rut, sometimes we need a jolt to pull us out. Prayer is that daily jolt for our spirit. Prayer is what gets us back on track, headed where we need to go.

If we submit to God in prayer, He will guide us on this earthly road. He will help us stay out of that dreaded rut and free of the daily abyss of hopelessness, so that we might rise and be all that Christ wants us to be in a world that needs His love.

That is a promise we can take to our knees every day.

. . . . . . . . . . . . . . . . . . . . . . . . . . . . . . . . . . . . . . . .

*Holy Spirit, don't ever let me lose hope. You are my protector, provider, and comforter. Even when I feel desperately alone and downtrodden, help me to remember that You are always there for me. Amen.*

# DAY 35
# PRAYERS OF CONFESSION

*"Come now, let us reason together, says the Lord: though your*
*sins are like scarlet, they shall be as white as snow; though*
*they are red like crimson, they shall become like wool."*
ISAIAH 1:18 RSV

God wanted to hear prayers of repentance, and He wanted that repentance to be followed by action. He commanded: "Cease to do evil, learn to do good" (vv. 16–17 RSV).

They were in the habit of living selfishly and trampling on others, but God promised that if they repented, though their sins were like scarlet, every stain would be washed away. The word *scarlet* means "double-dyed" and refers to dipping white garments in scarlet dye twice to make certain that it would not wash out. Yet God said He *would* wash every stain away.

This message is still true for us today: God can forgive the deepest sins and wash us clean, "as white as snow."

*I will confess my sins to You, God. I praise You for Your*
*forgiveness. How wonderful You are to forgive even my*
*worst sins and reward me with a clean heart. Amen.*

# DAY 36
## PRAISE TO BE RAISED

*My God, I cry out by day, but you do not answer, by night,*
*but I find no rest. . . . To you they cried out and were saved;*
*in you they trusted and were not put to shame.*

PSALM 22:2, 5 NIV

Life isn't easy. We've heard many platitudes meant to encourage us. Being a complainer is not attractive. You need to find the silver lining in every cloud. If life gives you lemons, make lemonade. Smile even when it hurts.

Most of us try to begin our day by thanking God for our blessings before we face our challenges. But when we feel despair, is it acceptable to complain or do we need to bury those emotions? The Bible recounts times when people cried out to the Lord, times when they voiced their complaints. In Psalm 22 we're told that Christ poured out His soul to His heavenly Father throughout His sufferings. If we follow Christ's example, we can take our complaints to God in prayer as long as we, like Christ, also acknowledge our love for and trust in God.

If we just complain to others, we won't solve our problems. If we praise God and trust Him to stand with us during our trials, He will raise us up to handle our problems. Maybe we need to replace those old platitudes with this one: complain and remain, or praise to be raised.

*Lord, thank You for listening to my complaints and saving me from my sins.*
*Even during my struggles, I will praise You as my God and Savior. Amen.*

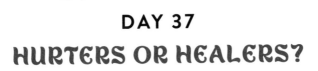

# DAY 37
# HURTERS OR HEALERS?

*"A new command I give you: Love one another. As I have loved you, so you must love one another. By this everyone will know that you are my disciples, if you love one another."*

JOHN 13:34–35 NIV

We have a choice each morning as we wake up to a new day. Will we be the kind of person who causes more hurt in the world, or will we be healers? Will we be a battering blow to someone's spirit instead of a blessing? Will we choose love when it's easier to hate? This choice is ours with every word we speak. Every action we take. Every thought that passes through our minds. For everything has an effect.

Everything.

The Lord's command is to love one another. How hard can that be? Pretty hard when it comes to loving the unlovable. To be honest, loving prickly folks—not you and me, of course—well, it's as easy as giving a porcupine a big bear hug. Not pleasant.

But God can make possible what appears impossible to man. Through prayer, the Lord can help us love those folks who appear unlovable.

So what will you choose to be when you get up in the morning to a new dawn—a hurter or a healer? The world has an overabundance of the former and a serious shortage of the latter!

. . . . . . . . . . . . . . . . . . . . . . . . . . . . . . . . . . . . . . . .

*God, give me the strength and patience to encounter the world with the abounding love of Christ. Help me to love as You love. Amen.*

# DAY 38
# THE HEALING PROCESS

*"I do believe; help me overcome my unbelief!"*
MARK 9:24 NIV

Healing was a significant part of Jesus' ministry. Throughout the four Gospels, we read about Jesus healing lepers, the blind, and those possessed with evil spirits.

Interestingly, Jesus didn't always choose to heal upon request (Matthew 13:58). So why did He heal this man's son, despite his doubt? Mark 9:24 may give us the answer. In one breath, the man confidently states his belief, and in the next, he honestly confesses his doubt, asking Jesus for help.

The father's contradictory response speaks for us all. Like him, we confidently profess our faith until tested, then we find ourselves slipping into doubt. In times like these, we must be honest about our faith, praying for God to strengthen it. Only then can God truly begin the healing process.

. . . . . . . . . . . . . . . . . . . . . . . . . . . . . . . . . . . . . . . . . . .

*Dear Lord, there are days when my faith is strong and others when I slip into doubt. Strengthen my faith! Destroy those seeds of doubt. Prevent them from growing within me. Amen.*

# DAY 39

# THE SEASON OF SINGING

*See! The winter is past; the rains are over and gone. Flowers appear on the earth; the season of singing has come, the cooing of doves is heard in our land.*
SONG OF SONGS 2:11–12 NIV

Is your life caught up in a cold winter that never seems to end? Then snuggle up in a warm blanket of truth.

God may allow you to stay in that winter season for now, but He will never leave your side. He will stay with you and bring you all that you need. He'll send the comforting presence of the Holy Spirit. He provides you with His mighty Word to heat and stir your soul. He offers you the safe and sheltering knowledge of eternal life through Christ. Under the lamp of these truths, we can sing in our hearts, knowing spring is near.

In time, the cold will go. The ice will thaw. The rain will cease, and the sun will burst boldly through the clouds in rays of pure gold. The earth will turn a lush green, and flowers will spring up in a profusion of color. Even the gentle cooing of doves will be heard all through the land. What beauty. What hope. What joy.

In times of winter, let us pray and seek His face and know too that the season of singing will indeed come again.

· · · · · · · · · · · · · · · · · · · · · · · · · · · · · · · · · · · · · ·

*God, give me joy and patience in the long winters of life. Remind me of Your steadfast presence, and may Your Word strengthen and comfort me. Amen.*

# DAY 40
# HEAVIER THAN I CAN CARRY

*"For my yoke is easy and my burden is light."*
MATTHEW 11:30 NIV

Kids are so honest. Don't you love their direct, unguarded approach to life? It's refreshing to see, since as we grow up, we tend to become more closed off and less open and vulnerable with other people, with God, and with ourselves.

For instance, if a child is walking alongside her dad at the beach, and she is trying to carry a full bucket of wet sand, most likely she will turn to her father easily, happily, and expectantly to say, "Daddy, can you carry this? It's too heavy for me."

That is how our Father in heaven would like us to come to Him in prayer. We weren't created to carry the heavy burdens of this world. We were made for better things, for loftier things—for joy and peace and love and laughter. For harmony.

So, when we are burdened in this life, let us take on the guileless honesty of a child. Let us turn to Him and, like the little girl, say to God, "Daddy, this is too heavy. Can You carry this for me?" Then we can let it go, whatever *it* is, into His hands—easily, happily, and expectantly.

* * * * * * * * * * * * * * * * * * * * * * * * * * * * * * * * * * * * * * * * * *

*Father, please take away my heavy burdens. Just as a child trusts her earthly father, help me to trust You with every aspect of my life. I give it all to You. Amen.*

# DAY 41
# THE VERY BEST

*"But if you remain in me and my words remain in you,*
*you may ask for anything you want, and it will be granted!"*
JOHN 15:7 NLT

Wow! Really? Is that true?

As silly as this may sound, there are some who assume that they have license to treat God as a concierge of some kind, who is standing by to rush to fulfill their every request.

As we present our requests to God, we need to realize that He knows what is best for us and that we should never demand "our way." We must not forget the first part of John 15:7 that says, "If you remain in me and my words remain in you." This should clearly tell us that our first desire needs to be that God's will is done.

Since God only wants to give us the very best, and He knows how to make that happen, why would we pray for anything else?

· · · · · · · · · · · · · · · · · · · · · · · · · · · · · · · · · · · · · · ·

*Father, I say, "Thy will be done!" You know best. I want*
*what You want for me, even if it's not what I ask for. Amen.*

# DAY 42
# HE WILL FILL YOU UP

*"I am the LORD your God, who brought you up out of
Egypt. Open wide your mouth and I will fill it."*
PSALM 81:10 NIV

Beth didn't understand why her best friend, Nicole, got up each Sunday for Bible study and church. As an adult, Beth felt free to make her choice to skip the organized religion thing.

Life was good. Beth and Nicole had jobs at the same bank. Beth's car was almost paid for, and she had just purchased her first home. Then came the announcement that their bank had been bought by a larger one with a branch down the street. Beth and Nicole would lose their jobs when their location closed.

Beth railed to Nicole about how unfair it was that they were being eliminated. She feared she might lose her house. Nicole let Beth vent her financial worries until she started to blame God.

Nicole told Beth that God would never forsake them. He wanted to help them with their problems and fill their souls with His blessings. Nicole encouraged Beth to attend church with her on Sunday and open herself to the Lord's blessings.

The following day, Beth said, "Nicole, I've been so foolish. I thought I could handle things without attending church. I want what you have. I want to feel the peace that comes from knowing my happiness is found in my relationship with God and not in my earthly possessions."

- - - - - - - - - - - - - - - - - - - - - - - - - - - - - - - - - -

*Lord, thank You for knowing what blessings I truly need. Help me
to hunger for You more than I hunger for earthly things. Amen.*

# DAY 43
# GOT PRAYER?

*The Lord is near to all who call on him, to all who call on him in truth.*
PSALM 145:18 NIV

Prayer is communicating with God. Wow, really? You mean, we can connect with the Creator of the universe like He's our best friend, only better? Yes, that's it. Sounds unbelievable and more than a little audacious, doesn't it? Yet it's what God desires of us. A sweet and holy rapport. A relationship. Communion.

Still hard to grasp? Perhaps the concept seems so inconceivably wonderful and so simplistic that man feels a need to add to the process, give it his own style, and do it his own way. Perhaps even conjure up his own gods. Yet man cannot change what God has ordained. It would be like filling our car's gas tank with a fuel mixture from miscellaneous liquids we found in the garage, which would, of course, ruin the car for any good use.

Maybe it's easier to explain what biblical prayer is not: Prayer is not meditation. Prayer is not happy thoughts or wishful thinking. Prayer is not sitting in a certain position and clearing one's mind. Prayer is not chanting, visualization, or communicating with a spirit guide.

Prayer is talking directly to God through Jesus Christ. It is indeed that simple. That intimate. That inconceivably wonderful!

Got prayer?

*Creator God, help me to grasp the beautiful simplicity of prayer. I want an unceasing, rich communion with You, my Lord and Savior. Amen.*

# DAY 44
# WHEN WORDS FAIL ME

*Before a word is on my tongue you, LORD, know it completely.*
PSALM 139:4 NIV

Sometimes Christians feel so overwhelmed by their needs or by the greatness of God that they simply can't pray. When the words won't come, God helps to create them. Paul says in Romans 8:26 (NLT), "And the Holy Spirit helps us in our weakness. For example, we don't know what God wants us to pray for. But the Holy Spirit prays for us with groanings that cannot be expressed in words."

God hears your prayers even before you pray them. When you don't know what to say and the words won't come, you can simply ask God to help you by praying on your behalf.

. . . . . . . . . . . . . . . . . . . . . . . . . . . . . . . . . . . . . . . . .

*Dear God, I'm grateful today that in my silence You still hear me. Amen.*

# DAY 45
# PLAYING IN THE MUD

*However, as it is written: "What no eye has seen, what no
ear has heard, and what no human mind has conceived"—
the things God has prepared for those who love him.*
1 CORINTHIANS 2:9 NIV

Did you ever make mud pies and cakes when you were little? Pretty fun stuff, eh? Interesting to think that all the time we were mixing and shaping and generally mucking around, we were envisioning something much grander. We had the hope that when we were finished baking our mud in the sun it might be somehow transformed into a spectacular three-tiered wedding cake. But it was only mud decorated with leaves and twigs.

As adults, we know that all we create can be beautiful, exquisite really, but it is still only a shadow of what's to come for those who live in Christ. We are still only children playing in the mud. . .but with the hope of glorious things to come.

When we pray, let it be with the eyes of heaven, knowing and believing full well what is to come. Someday the earthly vision, this promise of more, will no longer be a shadow or a dream. It will be real.

*Dear Jesus, as I live out my life on earth, help me to never forget my true,
eternal home in heaven. I was made for more than mud. You created me for
beauty, freedom, joy, and an intimate, unbroken fellowship with You. Amen.*

# DAY 46
# THE PRISONER'S PRAYER

*If you declare with your mouth, "Jesus is Lord," and believe in*
*your heart that God raised him from the dead, you will be saved.*
*For it is with your heart that you believe and are justified, and it*
*is with your mouth that you profess your faith and are saved.*
ROMANS 10:9–10 NIV

We are all prisoners on death row. Yet Christ, with His sacrifice on the cross, has thrown open the cell door for us. All we need to do is walk through. Take His hand as He walks us through the iron gates, the tower with armed guards, the concrete barriers, the barbed wire, and out into the beautiful blue sky of redemption.

Why do some people insist on staying in the confines of a prison cell when beyond the walls of sin is freedom? It comes down to one tormenting word. . .*pride*.

Pride keeps us paralyzed; it keeps us fooling ourselves. Pride allows us to accept the lies of Satan—that we are better off on our own, calling our own shots. How else can we convince ourselves that a dark and cold dungeon is better than the pure warm light that streams through the window?

Once again, Christ has already broken our chains. He's opened the prison door. All we need to do is walk through.

The prisoner's prayer of freedom is on our lips. It is written in our hearts by the Holy Spirit. Will we stay or step out into the warm rays of redemption?

. . . . . . . . . . . . . . . . . . . . . . . . . . . . . . . . . . . . . . . . . .

*Heavenly Father, I believe that Jesus died for my sins and that He is*
*Lord. Please forgive my rebellion, and come into my heart. Amen.*

# DAY 47
# ANSWER ME, GOD!

*Answer me when I call to you, my righteous God. Give me relief*
*from my distress; have mercy on me and hear my prayer.*
PSALM 4:1 NIV

No matter our maturity level, there will be times when we feel abandoned by God. There will be times when our faith wavers and our fortitude wanes. That's okay. It's normal.

But David didn't give up. He kept crying out to God, kept falling to his knees in worship, kept storming God's presence with his pleas. David knew God wouldn't hide His face for long, for he knew what we might sometimes forget: God is love. He loves us without condition and without limit. And He is never far from those He loves.

No matter how distant God may seem, we need to keep talking to Him. Keep praying. Keep pouring out our hearts. We can know, as David knew, that God will answer in His time.

*Dear Father, thank You for always hearing my prayers.*
*Help me to trust You even when You seem distant. Amen.*

# DAY 48

# EVEN MORE BEAUTIFUL

*The righteous cry out, and the LORD hears them; he delivers them*
*from all their troubles. The LORD is close to the brokenhearted and*
*saves those who are crushed in spirit. The righteous person may*
*have many troubles, but the LORD delivers him from them all.*
PSALM 34:17–19 NIV

There is an amazing Japanese art form in which an artist will take broken pottery and painstakingly glue it back together with a lacquer resin. This resin is mixed or dusted with powdered metals such as silver or gold. This creative technique will take what was once broken and unusable and transform it into something even more beautiful than it was before.

God Almighty, the Master Craftsman, can do that very thing for each of us if we ask Him. When we cry out to God, when we trust Him, He will take our shattered lives and remake them into works of genius. God is a master of redemption as well as creation, and because of His love for us, He wants to not only make us new but make us even more exquisite than we ever imagined. He wants to give us daily purpose and soul beauty as well as eternal hope.

That kind of redemption, that kind of miraculous re-creation is ours, and it's only a prayer away.

. . . . . . . . . . . . . . . . . . . . . . . . . . . . . . . . . . . . . . . . .

*Father, thank You for the boundless power of Your redemption. Re-create,*
*restore, refresh, and redeem me from the clutches of death and sin. Amen.*

# DAY 49
# LISTEN AND FOLLOW

*Know that the LORD is God. It is he who made us, and we
are his; we are his people, the sheep of his pasture.*
PSALM 100:3 NIV

Sheep follow their shepherd and trust in him for provision. Submissive to their masters, they quietly graze the hillsides, counting on the shepherd to know what is best. What a wonderfully relaxing word picture: relying on God's guidance and timing, following His lead.

It is a simple prayer to ask Him to help us give up control, yet it is not a simple task. In obedience to His Word, we can bow our heads and ask for the Holy Spirit's direction and take our hands from the steering wheel. Then wait. Quietly on our hillsides, hearts "yielded and still." We wait for the still, small voice. This day, resolve to listen and follow.

• • • • • • • • • • • • • • • • • • • • • • • • • • • • • • • • • • • • • • •

*Lord, we humbly bow before You and ask for Your divine
guidance. Help us to follow Your plan with yielded hearts,
ever ready to give up control to You. Amen.*

# DAY 50

# DO YOU BELIEVE IN MIRACLES?

*Now while he was in Jerusalem at the Passover Festival, many people saw the signs he was performing and believed in his name.*
JOHN 2:23 NIV

Jesus asks us to believe in miracles. Do you?

Sometimes when we pray, we go away believing nothing will happen. Maybe our heart prayer should be as the boy's father in the Bible who exclaimed, "Lord, I believe. Help my unbelief!"

God does answer every prayer. It just may not fit our agenda. The answer might come as a yes, a no, or a wait. When miracles do come, it is easy to forget, as the Israelites did even though they witnessed miracle after miracle after miracle. Still, they doubted.

That is the nature of man.

So, let us keep a prayer journal and write down the answers to our prayers, the miracles we experience. They do happen. The journal will be a reminder that God is listening. That God does care about our comings and goings. That He is still all-powerful and able to perform signs and wonders. When the miracles do come, write them down. Praise Him for them. Tell others. From time to time, we should go back and read the journal, see the long list of His tender mercies, so that we might be encouraged.

What miracle are you praying for today?

. . . . . . . . . . . . . . . . . . . . . . . . . . . . . . . . . . . . . . . . . .

*Lord, don't let me forget the countless prayers You have answered. Don't let me doubt the power of prayer. Amen.*

# DAY 51
# CALL ON ME

*"Call on me in the day of trouble; I will deliver you, and you will honor me."*
PSALM 50:15 NIV

When God says He wants us to call on Him, He means it. He must lean closer, bending His ear, waiting, longing for the sound of His name coming from our lips. He stands ready to deliver us from our troubles or at least to carry us through them safely.

While He doesn't always choose to fix things with a snap of His fingers, we can be assured that He will see us through to the other side of our troubles by a smoother path than we'd travel without Him. He's waiting to help us. All we have to do is call.

. . . . . . . . . . . . . . . . . . . . . . . . . . . . . . . . . . . . . .

*Dear Father, I'm so glad I can call on You*
*anytime with any kind of trouble. Amen.*

# DAY 52
# WHO HOLDS THE TRUTH?

*And no wonder, for Satan himself masquerades as an angel of light.*
2 Corinthians 11:14 niv

Everybody is selling some kind of spiritual truth. Even if a person doesn't believe in God, that belief system is still a creed to live by—a conviction that requires faith.

There are many kinds of religions and cults to choose from in the marketplace of ideas, and all of them claim to carry the light. But remember, this is a supernatural world, and Satan, the enemy of your soul, would love nothing better than to whisper all manner of lies into your spirit and so blind and dazzle you. It becomes harder to recognize the truth and light when it does come.

How can we be safe in a world full of people who shout their spiritual wares at every corner like callers at a carnival arcade? Who masquerade as light bearers? We can attend a Bible-believing church. We can read God's Word so that we can recognize false prophets. We can pray for discernment, that we might know when someone comes to us with "tweaks" on the never-changing Gospel of Christ, that is, alterations in God's truth that might appease sinful man but do not honor a righteous God.

God has given us free will. What is our prayerful choice?

. . . . . . . . . . . . . . . . . . . . . . . . . . . . . . . . . . . . . . .

*Lord, help me to stand strong in Your truth and to not
be enticed by the popular, fickle views of man. I want
to stay within the light of Your Word. Amen.*

# DAY 53
# PRAY PERSISTENTLY

*Rejoice always, pray continually, give thanks in all circumstances; for this is God's will for you in Christ Jesus.*
1 Thessalonians 5:16–18 niv

The Gospel of Luke tells about a widow who had an ongoing dispute with an enemy. The woman was stubborn and determined to win, and she refused to give up her dispute until a judge ruled in her favor. Many times, she went to the judge demanding, "Give me justice!"

Jesus used this story to teach His followers about persistent prayer. He said, "Learn a lesson from this unjust judge. Even he rendered a just decision in the end. So don't you think God will surely give justice to his chosen people who cry out to him day and night?" (Luke 18:6–7 nlt).

When Christians pray, it shows not only their faith in God but also their trust in His faithfulness toward them. In His time, the Lord will come and bring justice to His people.

. . . . . . . . . . . . . . . . . . . . . . . . . . . . . . . . . . . . . . .

*Dear God, help me to remain faithful and not grow weary in prayer. Amen.*

# DAY 54
# TOO EASY

*Isaac prayed to the LORD on behalf of his wife, because she was childless.*
GENESIS 25:21 NIV

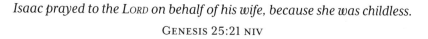

I know several families right now who are making the same request Isaac made. "God, please, please give us a child." It's the kind of prayer that can be prayed for weeks, months, and years on end or the kind that comes all at once, rushing in like some desperate wind.

For Isaac, it all seemed so simple. He prayed. God answered. His wife became pregnant with not just one baby but two! So, what are we to tell all the people who are still waiting for their answer? What are we to tell the ones who never get a baby of their own? Have they just not tried hard enough? Perhaps they didn't say the right words, or maybe God just doesn't think they would be fit parents.

Or maybe it's just not that easy. Some people pray and seem to get the answers they want. Others seem to get handed a harder pill to swallow. I don't think we can know all the plans God has for us.

What we can know is that God is in control, that He hears us, and that He loves us. And the best thing we can do for someone praying for a child is not to try to come up with some explanation for why their prayer has or hasn't been answered. The best thing is just to keep praying with them.

. . . . . . . . . . . . . . . . . . . . . . . . . . . . . . . . . . . . . .

*Lord, help me to remember that Your answers aren't always easy ones. Amen.*

# DAY 55
# PRAY INSTEAD OF PLOTTING

*"Pray that the Lord your God will show us what to do and where to go."*
JEREMIAH 42:3 NLT

However bleak your situation seems, God hasn't forgotten you. Philippians 4:6–7 (NLT) says, "Don't worry about anything; instead, pray about everything. Tell God what you need, and thank him for all he has done. Then you will experience God's peace, which exceeds anything we can understand. His peace will guard your hearts and minds as you live in Christ Jesus."

Jeremiah 42:3 echoes this statement. It urges believers to pray for guidance instead of setting out with a preconceived notion of how the day (or month or decade) will turn out.

When you begin to worry that you don't have what it takes to meet life's demands, remember that you don't have to—because God does.

* * * * * * * * * * * * * * * * * * * * * * * * * * * * * * * * * * *

*Jesus, thank You for Your presence and the peace You so freely give.*
*Help me to pray before I worry, categorize, or strategize. Amen.*

# DAY 56
# PRAY FROM YOUR HEART

*My heart is not proud, LORD, my eyes are not haughty; I do not*
*concern myself with great matters or things too wonderful for*
*me. But I have calmed and quieted myself, I am like a weaned*
*child with its mother; like a weaned child I am content.*
PSALM 131:1–2 NIV

Josephine was busy. Between her job, family, and church activities, she barely found time for herself. She did feel good that, after six weeks, she was still meeting her New Year's resolution to read her daily devotional. She wasn't as pleased with her goal of quieting herself for her daily prayer time. She talked with the Lord each day, but she hadn't found quality quiet time for prayer and reflection. Yes, she was quiet during her hurried prayers at bedtime, but she was so tired by the end of the day that she didn't think of that as quality time.

Josephine loved the image of Jesus praying in the garden surrounded only by the beauty of nature. Honestly, though, sitting quietly made her feel antsy. She was the kind of person who had to be busy. Her method of enjoying nature was taking a thirty-minute brisk walk.

Josephine decided to leave her headphones at home and try praying during her daily walk. She was amazed at the satisfaction she derived from sharing this time with the Lord. Brisk walking raised Josephine's heart rate, but it also lowered her defenses and opened her heart for personal reflection.

*Lord, I want to share my heart with You when I pray.*
*Help me find the quiet time that will content my soul. Amen.*

# DAY 57
# GRABBER HOGS

*For although they knew God, they neither glorified him as God nor gave thanks to him, but their thinking became futile and their foolish hearts were darkened.*
ROMANS 1:21 NIV

So, what is a grabber hog anyway? Some people would say it's a lifestyle—an insatiable appetite for more of everything. The problem is the more we get, the more we want. Sometimes we treat God like we're calling up room service at a hotel. While we're still eating, we're already planning the next feast. While we pay off one credit card, we're already window shopping for more dainty desires. And waiting? Forget it. We want what we want when we want it. After all, the world says we can have it all. Right?

The Bible clearly tells us that we can make our requests known to God. He cares very much for our needs. And yet, there is more to prayer than the material world and what we want right now. There is thanksgiving, praise, repentance, praying for the needs of others, listening to that still, small voice for knowledge and guidance, for peace and for strength for the day. And there is tender communion.

Ask Him for a change in your heart's desires—that they will be aligned with His—and the need to have it all will be replaced with something more lasting, more treasured. Doesn't the word *contentment* have a sweeter feel to it than the world's "grabber hog" philosophy?

• • • • • • • • • • • • • • • • • • • • • • • • • • • • • • • • • • • • • • •

*Father, forgive me for neglecting to thank You for all that You've given me. Give me a spirit of contentment, that I might praise and thank You in all circumstances. Amen.*

# DAY 58
# BIG EARS

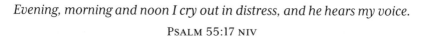

*Evening, morning and noon I cry out in distress, and he hears my voice.*
PSALM 55:17 NIV

A child once was asked to draw a picture of God. She drew an old man with a long white beard, striking blue eyes, and humongous ears. When asked why God's ears were so large, the girl replied, "God listens to everyone all the time around the whole world. That takes big ears!"

Aren't you glad God has big ears? That He is able to listen to us all the time, no matter where we go or what time of day it is?

David wrote in Psalm 55 of a time of tremendous personal stress. "I am distraught" and "my heart is in anguish within me," he said (vv. 2 and 4). Why was he in such trouble? He reveals the answer in verses 12–13: "If an enemy were insulting me, I could endure it. . . . But it is you, a man like myself, my companion, my close friend."

Betrayed! Is there any kind of trouble that causes more worry and heartache? Betrayal gnaws at us day and night—there is no end to the wondering why and the self-doubt.

Thank goodness, God has big ears. We can take our heaviest burdens to Him, and He will hear us. Only He can silence the voices of doubt and despair in our heads.

"As for me, I call to God, and the Lord saves me" (55:16). Yes, David. Us too.

. . . . . . . . . . . . . . . . . . . . . . . . . . . . . . . . . . . . . . . . . .

*Lord, thank You for Your big ears! Amen.*

# DAY 59
# OH, WHEN SPRING COMES

*Therefore, if anyone is in Christ, the new creation*
*has come: The old has gone, the new is here!*
2 Corinthians 5:17 niv

Oh, when spring comes—the earth celebrates with newness. We see green sprouting up everywhere in every shade imaginable. Those budding leaves almost seem to have an illumination all their own. The melting snow floods the brooks, and the water tumbles down the mountains, spraying rainbows across the canyons. Spring, ahh, the flowers are peeking out their little heads, the bunnies are hopping about, the sun is warm, the breeze is silk, and the birds are nesting and singing their little hearts out. What could be more refreshing, inviting, and wonderful?

When spring comes, we think of the words *flourish, growth, expectations, possibilities, hope, newness,* and *promise.* That is the way with Christ. He brings those qualities to us when we become His, when we walk with Him, when we come to know Him through fellowship and His Word. We become new like spring. The old is gone, and the new is here.

Talk to God today, and let the newness of spring into your heart, into your life.

* * * * * * * * * * * * * * * * * * * * * * * * * * * * * * * * * * * *

*Lord, thank You for loving me and for washing me of my sins. Help me*
*to live as a new creation, that I might trust in Your will, have hope in*
*Your Word, and treat others as I would like to be treated. Amen.*

# DAY 60
# WHEN GOD'S PEOPLE PRAY

*Pray for the peace of Jerusalem: "May those who love you be secure."*
PSALM 122:6 NIV

God, in all His power, has invited us to come alongside Him. He's asked us to join Him in His work by praying for each other.

For centuries, God's people have been treated unfairly and unjustly. Yet we've survived when other groups haven't. The reason we've survived when so many have sought to silence us is because we have something our enemies don't have. We have the power of God behind us.

When we pray, we call upon every resource available to us as the children of God. We call upon His strength, His compassion, His ferocity, His mercy, His love, and His justice. We can extend God's reach to the other side of our town or the other side of the world, all because we pray.

. . . . . . . . . . . . . . . . . . . . . . . . . . . . . . . . . . . . . . . . . .

*Dear Father, thank You for letting me join You in Your work. Please*
*bless the people who love You wherever they are in this world.*
*Allow them to prosper according to their love for You. Amen.*

# DAY 61
# IN ALL CIRCUMSTANCES

*Rejoice always, pray continually, give thanks in all circumstances; for this is God's will for you in Christ Jesus.*
1 Thessalonians 5:16–18 niv

To-Do List: Go to grocery, pay bills, see about plumber, take kids to practice, pick up kids from practice, go to the dentist, cancel appointment, text friend, pray, make dinner, put laundry in washer, walk dog, go to bed.

Is prayer even on your to-do list? More often than not, we all forget to set aside specific time for prayer. Perhaps it gets put off until there's quiet in the house, until we are not so tired, until our work is done, until. . .

It is good to remember that we don't even have to set aside a certain special time. We don't have to sit in a prayer chair or wear a prayer robe. Our God is always there for us. We can talk to Him anytime. Indeed, we should.

Let's go back to that to-do list—how might your day go with prayer as your inner soundtrack? *God, thank You that I have so many choices of foods to eat. Help me feed those who are hungry. Thank You for the income we have. Thank You for the skills and talents of others. Thank You for healthy kids. . .and* on and on and on.

It's good to have special times set aside for rest and reflection. But it's also good to remember you don't have to wait until then.

. . . . . . . . . . . . . . . . . . . . . . . . . . . . . . . . . . . . . . . . . . .

*Lord, thank You for always being there for me. Amen.*

# DAY 62

# ARROW PRAYERS

*God knows how often I pray for you. Day and night*
*I bring you and your needs in prayer to God.*
ROMANS 1:9 NLT

Our prayers are often lost in the obscurity of brevity. We love fast food and instant success. All the while we struggle to take the time to utter a few extra syllables to God. We shoot "arrow" prayers while expecting God's response ASAP. We expect the Lord, who knows all, to interpret our every need.

Although arrow prayers are sometimes needed, God asks us to pray *specifically* and often for the person or problem just as Paul did. God made us to fellowship with Him. That includes open communication void of brevity mania!

. . . . . . . . . . . . . . . . . . . . . . . . . . . . . . . . . . . . . . . . . .

*Lord, forgive me for my abbreviated prayers, void of substance*
*and heart. Teach me to pray in specifics and less in generalities as*
*I openly pour out my innermost needs and desires to You. Amen.*

# DAY 63
# LISTEN FOR HIS WHISPER

*After the earthquake came a fire, but the LORD was not
in the fire. And after the fire came a gentle whisper.*
1 KINGS 19:12 NIV

In 1996 at the Brookfield Zoo, a three-year-old boy climbed a wall and fell eighteen feet into the gorilla enclosure. Sounds of panic came from spectators. Screams escalated as Binti Jua, an eight-year-old female gorilla, walked to the boy. Spectators reported feeling panic as they feared the gorilla would maul the child.

Instead, Binti Jua carefully picked the boy up and carried him to the zookeeper's gate. She appeared to console him as she stayed by his side, offering protection from other gorillas. Zoo personnel were able to safely retrieve the boy, who made a full recovery.

Often when tragedy occurs, people ask, "Where was God? How could He allow this to happen?" When a wild animal like Binti Jua displays compassion for an injured child, it's easy to see where God was in the incident. He didn't make the boy climb the wall or prevent his fall. God was not in the spectators' screams of horror. But after the tragic event came God's gentle whisper. He guided the safe rescue of the boy using one of His creatures, a gorilla.

When the storms of our lives occur, don't ask God how He could have let it happen. Instead, praise Him for the ways His gentle whisper provides us with His aid.

* * * * * * * * * * * * * * * * * * * * * * * * * * * * * * * * * * * * *

*Lord, thank You for being with me when I face tragic events in my life.
I appreciate the gentle whisper of Your support after each storm. Amen.*

# DAY 64
# THE MOUSE IN THE MAZE

*Give thanks to the LORD, for he is good; his love endures forever.*
1 CHRONICLES 16:34 NIV

Have you ever felt like a mouse trapped in a maze? You go around in circles, and you can't find your way out? Perhaps you have a financial situation that keeps coming back like an unwelcome guest. Maybe you're estranged from your family with no hope of reconciliation. Perhaps the doctor gave you test results that were an ugly surprise. Maybe your boss says that if you don't work harder and faster, you'll lose your job.

Do the days seem endless, and do the nights seem riddled with bad dreams—that is, if you ever get to sleep at all?

What a place to be. There is no one exempt from trials in this fallen world—these life moments that make you feel stuck and more than a little sick at heart. If you do find yourself trapped, and there is no place else to go but to your knees, and there's nowhere else to be but at the mercy of God, well, it's a mighty good place to find yourself. The Lord will never fail.

Seek Him now, whether you're on the mountaintop or you feel trapped in the deepest, darkest maze.

God is good. His love and His mercy endure forever.

Count on it.

* * * * * * * * * * * * * * * * * * * * * * * * * * * * * * * * * * * * * * * *

*Father God, I surrender to Your care and Your will. You are my mighty redeemer, my stronghold and comforter. Oh, how I need You. Amen.*

# DAY 65
# ALL OF THE ABOVE

*For the LORD gives wisdom; from his mouth*
*come knowledge and understanding.*
PROVERBS 2:6 NIV

Every day is full of so many decisions—from the time we wake up till the time our eyelids drop heavily at night, we are faced with decisions both small and significant. *What should I wear? What should I have for breakfast? What am I going to do today? What am I doing with my life?* It's easy to get overwhelmed, even before your Wheaties have a chance to get soggy.

It's also easy to fall into the trap of thinking that if we simply pray about an issue, God will give us the answer—and in fairly short order. Because God knows we need all the answers we need when we need them, and not a moment later. Right?

It seems that often when we want an answer, the only thing that will do is the answer we want. Nothing less. Yet God, our generous Father, has something better in mind. We want a solution; He wants to give us the formula. We want a simple yes or no; He wants to give us time to see if we even asked the right question. We want A, B, C, or D; He wants to give us all of the above.

* * * * * * * * * * * * * * * * * * * * * * * * * * * * * * * * * * * * * * * * * *

*Thank You, Lord, that Your ways are higher and wiser and*
*better than mine. Help me to be patient when I lack wisdom*
*and to see Your knowledge and understanding. Amen.*

# DAY 66
# KEEP TALKING

*The Lord is near to all who call on him, to all who call on him in truth.*
PSALM 145:18 NIV

When we call on God, no matter our circumstances, we become close to Him. He sees our hearts, He has compassion on us, and He longs to pull us into His arms and hold us there. When we call on Him, when we spend time talking to Him and telling Him what's on our minds, we strengthen our relationship with Him.

We get *close* to Him.

When we feel far from God, sometimes the last thing we want to do is talk to Him. But it is through honest, heartfelt conversation, however one-sided it may seem to us, that we draw into God's presence. When we feel far from God, we need to keep talking. He's there.

*Dear Father, thank You for Your promise to listen to me.*
*I love You, I need You, and I want to be close to You. Amen.*

# DAY 67
# A FRIEND LIKE NO OTHER

*"Before they call I will answer; while they are still speaking I will hear."*
ISAIAH 65:24 NIV

Just as honey makes the medicine taste better, so do good friends make this sometimes bitter life go down more easily. If you've known what it's like to be friendless, it can be as lonely as a howling wind blowing across a desert. No one to understand you, to listen and *hear* you, to share your life with—especially in those special moments that cry out to be experienced with someone else and not just by yourself.

If you find yourself friendless, know that Jesus is a friend—the very best kind. He will not abandon you when times get tough. He is a wise, listening friend who will tell you not merely what you want to hear but what you need to hear. A friend who will help you carry your burdens, rejoice with you, laugh with you, weep with you, and love you always. He is a friend who says, "Before you call, I will answer; while you are still speaking, I will hear." Now isn't that the kind of wonderful fellowship our lonely hearts have searched for?

The old hymn "What a Friend We Have in Jesus" says it so beautifully.

> *What a friend we have in Jesus,*
> *All our sins and griefs to bear!*
> *What a privilege to carry*
> *Everything to God in prayer!*
> *Oh, what peace we often forfeit,*
> *Oh, what needless pain we bear,*
> *All because we do not carry*
> *Everything to God in prayer!*

*Jesus, thank You for hearing me and for calling me Your friend. Amen.*

# DAY 68
# SOLITARY PRAYER

*Come near to God and he will come near to you.*
JAMES 4:8 NIV

Do you have a prayer closet?

Jesus warned against people praying in public with the intent to show others how pious they are. Instead, He advocated solitude. Jesus often went off by Himself to draw near to His Father and pray, and that is what He suggested in the passage from Matthew.

A secret room isn't necessary—rather a quiet place where one can be alone with God. Maybe your quiet place is your garden or the beach. It might be in the quiet of your own home when your husband and children are away. Wherever it is, enjoy some time alone with God. Draw near to Him in prayer, and He will draw near to you.

. . . . . . . . . . . . . . . . . . . . . . . . . . . . . . . . . . . . . . . . . .

*Dear God, when we meet in the quiet place,*
*allow me to breathe in Your presence. Amen.*

# DAY 69

# PRAYER OF COMPLAINT

*"What have I done to displease you that you*
*put the burden of all these people on me?"*
NUMBERS 11:11 NIV

Have you ever felt the weight of the responsibility of guiding, teaching, leading, and encouraging others? This point in Moses' story is just one of many when he became frustrated with those complaining Israelites. He must have longed for his days as a shepherd, when he could just give the animals a poke or two with his staff to get them to go in the right direction. This Israelite flock was a different story—disobedient, fickle, petty, and selfish. Basically, a normal group of human beings.

Moses knew what to do. He did what he often did when feeling overwhelmed—he talked to God. No, his prayer wasn't pretty—it wasn't full of praise and honor. One might say he was even a little snarky—"Did I conceive all these people? Did I give them birth?" (v. 12).

Chances are you've voiced your own prayer of complaint a time or two. And you know what? God didn't crush you. God knows our hearts. He knew Moses' heart. Before Moses even began his rant, God saw his need and heard his plea. So the Lord gave Moses the answer he needed—friends. "They will share the burden of the people with you so that you will not have to carry it alone" (v. 17).

. . . . . . . . . . . . . . . . . . . . . . . . . . . . . . . . . . . . . . . . .

*Lord, help me remember to call on You first when I'm feeling*
*overwhelmed. Thank You for being my friend. Amen.*

# DAY 70
## WHEN YOU CAN'T PRAY

*And the Holy Spirit helps us in our weakness. For example, we don't
know what God wants us to pray for. But the Holy Spirit prays
for us with groanings that cannot be expressed in words. And the
Father who knows all hearts knows what the Spirit is saying, for
the Spirit pleads for us believers in harmony with God's own will.*
ROMANS 8:26–27 NLT

Sometimes we literally cannot pray. The Holy Spirit takes over on such
occasions. Go before God; enter His presence in a quiet spot where there
will not be interruptions. And just be still before the Lord. When your heart is
broken, the Holy Spirit will intercede for you. When you have lost someone or
something precious, the Holy Spirit will go before the Father on your behalf.
When you are weak, the Comforter will ask the Father to strengthen you.
When you are confused and anxious, the Counselor will seek God's best for
you. You are not alone. Christ sent a Comforter, a Counselor, the Holy Ghost,
the Spirit of Truth. When you don't know what to pray, the Bible promises
that the Spirit has you covered.

*Father, please hear the groaning of the Holy Spirit who
intercedes on my behalf before Your throne. Amen.*

# DAY 71
# ALL THE PRETTY PEBBLES

*"Whoever tries to keep their life will lose it,*
*and whoever loses their life will preserve it."*
LUKE 17:33 NIV

Have you ever strolled along a stream, picking up pretty pebbles? The stones can be like finding treasures, and some of them sparkle like precious gems. Maybe you tend to gather so many that they start to spill from your hands, or you grasp them so tightly they make your fingers ache, or they weigh so heavily in your pockets that they become a burden instead of a blessing.

Isn't that just like our lives when we gather more than we can use and we cling too tightly to all that doesn't truly belong to us? Like our careers, our houses, our possessions, our families, our very lives. All belongs to God and all is under His authority, but that concept is hard for us to grasp, let alone embrace. In fact, it's at the heart of why mankind fell from grace. Humans want to own, control, and choose their own way.

God says we should not grasp too tightly to life or anything in it. It seems like such a paradox—that to lose is to gain. Yet it is the only way to live.

When we finally empty our pockets of all those pretty pebbles and release them to God's care, we will find a lighter way to travel life's road.

Pray for that kind of walk with the Lord, that kind of freedom.

. . . . . . . . . . . . . . . . . . . . . . . . . . . . . . . . . . . . . . . . . . . . . . .

*Holy Spirit, enable me to give You control,*
*and help me to live in freedom. Amen.*

# DAY 72
# JUST IN TIME

*Therefore let us [with privilege] approach the throne of grace [that is, the throne of God's gracious favor] with confidence and without fear, so that we may receive mercy [for our failures] and find [His amazing] grace to help in time of need [an appropriate blessing, coming just at the right moment].*

HEBREWS 4:16 AMP

As believers, our lives become exciting when we wait on God to direct our paths, because He knows what is best for us at any given moment. His plans and agenda are never wrong.

Once we fully realize He knows best and turn our lives over to the Spirit for direction, we can allow God to be in charge of our calendar; His timing is what is paramount.

When chomping at the bit for a job offer or for a proposal, His timing might seem slow. "Hurry up, God!" we groan. But when we learn to patiently wait on His promises, we will see the plans He has for us are more than we dared hope—or dream. God promises to answer us; and it never fails to be just in time.

. . . . . . . . . . . . . . . . . . . . . . . . . . . . . . . . . . . . . . . . .

*Lord, I want Your perfect will in my life.*
*Help me learn to wait on You. Amen.*

# DAY 73
# THE BEGGAR KING

*"Hear the supplication of your servant."*
1 Kings 8:30 niv

Solomon was a wise king. He had all the power of Israel in his hands. He built a magnificent temple, which he was chosen by God to build. He decided hard cases for his people and had riches that were the envy of the world.

Yet in his prayer to God, he sounded like a beggar.

*Supplication* is not a word that gets used much these days. It comes from a Latin root that means to plead humbly or beg. It's not the kind of action you would expect from a powerful monarch. Yet the Bible is full of unlikely people doing unexpected things.

Over and over in his prayer, Solomon humbled himself and asked for God to hear, to act, and to forgive. He didn't place himself above God or ask for things he did not need. He didn't highlight his own achievements or the greatness of his people. Rather, he focused heavily on their potential downfalls and their sin.

Standing before the "vast assembly" of Israel, he showed his people exactly who was in charge, who was taking care of them, and who they should count on. Not him. Not Solomon the king. But the Lord, the God of Israel. For "the Lord is God and. . .there is no other" (v. 60).

. . . . . . . . . . . . . . . . . . . . . . . . . . . . . . . . . . . . . . . . . . . . .

*God, there is no one like You. Help me to show others that anything good in my life comes from You and nowhere else. Amen.*

# DAY 74
# WHO GOD HEARS

*The Lord is far from the wicked, but he hears the prayers of the righteous.*
PROVERBS 15:29 NLT

When the righteous call God's name, He hears. Though none of us is righteous on our own, we can claim righteousness through Jesus Christ. He alone is righteous, and He covers us like a cloak. When we call on God, He sees the righteousness that covers us through Christ and recognizes us as His children. He leans over and listens carefully to our words because we belong to Him. He loves us.

Next time it seems like God isn't listening, perhaps we should examine our hearts. Have we pushed God away? Have we accepted the price His Son, Jesus Christ, paid on our behalf? If not, we can't claim righteousness. If we have, we can trust that He's never far away. He hears us.

*Dear Father, thank You for making me
righteous through Your Son, Jesus. Amen.*

# DAY 75
# NOTHING I DESIRE

*Whom have I in heaven but you? And earth has nothing I desire besides you.*
PSALM 73:25 NIV

There is no one like our God.

There is no king of heaven who waits for you except Him. There is no creator God who cares for you except Him. He alone made you and shaped you and caused you to grow. There is nothing on earth to desire that is like Him.

There is no one who can take your requests, answer your questions, or wipe away your sadness like God.

So when you look for fulfillment and completeness, for answers and forgiveness, you must make sure you are looking to God first and not get confused by other options. You must not mistake sources of good gifts on earth for the one great Source who made every good gift. You must be careful to reach out, not to just any spiritual power but to the Lord's all-powerful hands.

There are many voices out there in the world, begging for your attention. There are many ways to get deceived. To be clear-minded and alert and filter out all the different messages, it's likely you'll need some help.

God is the strength of your heart. God is the strength of your mind and soul and body too. Ask Him to guide you, and He will. Bring your desires to Him, and He will make you complete.

*Dear God, there is no one like You! I love You! Amen.*

# DAY 76
# THE GIFT OF PRAYER

*First of all, then, I urge that petitions (specific requests), prayers,*
*intercessions (prayers for others) and thanksgivings be offered*
*on behalf of all people. . . . This [kind of praying] is good and*
*acceptable and pleasing in the sight of God our Savior.*

1 Timothy 2:1, 3 amp

Perhaps the absolute greatest gift one person can give to another doesn't come in a box. It can't be wrapped or presented formally, but instead it is the words spoken to God for someone—the gift of prayer.

When we pray for others, we ask God to intervene and to make Himself known to them. We can pray for God's plan and purpose in their lives. We can ask God to bless them or protect them. You can share with them that you are praying for them or do it privately without their knowledge. Who would God have you give the gift of prayer to today?

. . . . . . . . . . . . . . . . . . . . . . . . . . . . . . . . . . . . . . . . . . . . . .

*Lord, thank You for bringing people to my heart and mind who need prayer.*
*Help me to pray the things that they need from You in their lives. Show me*
*how to give the gift of prayer to those You would have me pray for. Amen.*

# DAY 77
## LESS IS MORE

*"They devour widows' houses and for a show make lengthy prayers."*
MARK 12:40 NIV

When did quantity start being valued over quality? It probably goes back to ancient times. One guy starts collecting rocks. Another guy makes a bigger pile of rocks. And on it goes.

Greed is what makes people keep grabbing for more. . .that feeling of wanting what you cannot ever hope to get on your own. The feeling of being powerless and needing something—and lots of it—to fill the void.

The teachers of the law were afflicted with this disease. They had a measure of respect and power, but they wanted more. It was not enough for some of the people to acknowledge their greatness—they wanted everyone to do so. They must have known that the real power and honor and wisdom were nothing they could claim.

So they wore long robes and took long strides and sat at long tables and voiced long prayers—all to show that they deserved respect.

Just after Jesus comments about these teachers devouring widows' houses, we see Jesus sitting down, watching the crowds bringing their offerings. From the hands of the rich and powerful came large, showy quantities of coins. But a poor widow gave only a couple of pennies.

"Truly I tell you," Jesus said, "this poor widow has put more into the treasury than all the others" (v. 43). The lesson was clear.

* * * * * * * * * * * * * * * * * * * * * * * * * * * * * * * * * * * * * * * *

*Lord, please make me humble. Help me to use my words
and actions to point to You instead of myself. Amen.*

# DAY 78
# STAYING ON TRACK

*I have fought a good fight, I have finished my course, I have kept the faith.*
2 Timothy 4:7 kjv

Despite the pain and afflictions Paul suffered in his life, he kept his eyes on Jesus, using praise to commune with God.

Likewise, we can keep in constant communion with the Father. We are so blessed to have been given the Holy Spirit within to keep us in tune with His will. Through His guidance—that still, small voice—we can rest assured our priorities will stay focused on Jesus. As the author A. W. Tozer wrote, "Lord, guide me carefully on this uncharted sea. . .as I daily seek You in Your word. Then use me mightily as Your servant this year as I boldly proclaim Your word in leading others."

. . . . . . . . . . . . . . . . . . . . . . . . . . . . . . . . . . . . . . . . . . .

*Lord, no better words have been spoken*
*than to say I surrender to Your will. Amen.*

# DAY 79
# WATCH AND PRAY

*"Watch and pray so that you will not fall into temptation.*
*The spirit is willing, but the flesh is weak."*
MARK 14:38 NIV

Jesus told His disciples to watch and pray. It was a tense time. He knew what was coming and the kind of fallout that would be heading toward His followers after His death on the cross. He wanted them to be on guard. He wanted them to pray with Him.

Watch and pray. Those two little verbs can be so hard to accomplish sometimes, can't they?

Sometimes it's the watching that is the very thing that gets us into trouble. We watch what's going on around us instead of watching out for temptation. We're like children in a toy store, getting distracted with all the colorful delights that would be so easy to grab.

Sometimes it's the praying that is the problem. We just don't do it. We think about doing it. We put a time in our calendars to do it. We buy books about it and hear sermons about it. Every now and then in a group we might bow our heads and pretend to be listening. Yet none of that is actually doing the thing.

Watch and pray. The disciples found it hard to do even for an hour. Put yourself in their shoes. Do you think you would have done any better?

• • • • • • • • • • • • • • • • • • • • • • • • • • • • • • • • • • • • • • • •

*Dear God, help me to be disciplined so I can set my mind on You. Amen.*

# DAY 80
# SENDING GOD'S FAVOR

*You help us by your prayers. Then many will give thanks on our behalf*
*for the gracious favor granted us in answer to the prayers of many.*
2 Corinthians 1:11 niv

The power of prayer is better in a crisis than a casserole. It's better than being there, holding someone's hand, or doing their laundry. The power of prayer does more for a missionary on the other side of the world than a box of clothes or even a check.

Prayer brings peace. Prayer brings wisdom and clarity. Prayer is powerful.

Next time we offer to pray for someone, we can say it with the confidence that our prayers will be heard. They will be answered. And they will make a beautiful difference in the lives of those for whom we pray.

. . . . . . . . . . . . . . . . . . . . . . . . . . . . . . . . . . . . . . . . . . .

*Dear Father, thank You for hearing my prayers.*
*Thank You for showing favor to others at my request. Amen.*

# DAY 81
# GROCERY PRAYER LIST

*For from him and through him and for him are*
*all things. To him be the glory forever! Amen.*
ROMANS 11:36 NIV

God, thank You for the produce: for bananas and grapes, and carrots and cucumbers. Thank You even for brussels sprouts and for the lowly potato. Thank You for an abundance of crops and healthy foods. Thank You for the men and women that farm the land and take care of the orchards, for the ones who pilot the boats and planes and tractors and trains, for all the people involved in harvesting this food so shoppers can buy a fresh pineapple for ninety-nine cents on sale.

God, thank You for the people who care for the livestock that produce the meat we eat and for the fishermen who gather the bounty from the sea. Thank You for many hours of hard work that go into producing all the ingredients so cooks can create the perfect meat loaf.

Thank You for milk that nourishes little bones and teeth and helps everyone grow. Thank You for all the milk substitutes and that for every dietary need these days there is, somewhere, a product that will satisfy.

Thank You for the household goods in plentiful supply. Especially for toilet paper, Lord. Thank You for toilet paper. Enough said.

And thank You for convenience foods that make life a little easier, for doesn't everyone occasionally need to make dinner in just one minute and fifteen seconds?

* * * * * * * * * * * * * * * * * * * * * * * * * * * * * * * * * * * * * *

*For all these things, Lord, we thank You. Amen.*

# DAY 82
## AT ALL TIMES

*Pray in the Spirit at all times with all kinds of prayers.*
EPHESIANS 6:18 NCV

God wants to be included in our days. He wants to walk and talk with us each moment. Imagine if we traveled through the day with our children or our spouse, but we spoke to them only between 6:15 and 6:45 a.m.! Of course, we'd never do that to the people we care about. God doesn't want us to do that to Him either.

God wants to travel the journey with us. He's a wonderful Companion, offering wisdom and comfort for every aspect of our lives. But He can only do that if we let Him into our schedules every minute of every day.

• • • • • • • • • • • • • • • • • • • • • • • • • • • • • • • • • • • • • • • • • • • •

*Dear Father, thank You for always being there to listen.*
*Remind me to talk to You about everything all the time. Amen.*

# DAY 83
# IF AT FIRST YOU DON'T HEAR...

*The LORD came and stood there, calling as at the other times, "Samuel! Samuel!" Then Samuel said, "Speak, for your servant is listening."*
1 SAMUEL 3:10 NIV

Have you heard the anecdote about the man who wouldn't leave his home when asked to evacuate as a flood approached? When a van stopped for him, he said, "I'm a good Christian; God will take care of me." As the waters rose, the man went to a second-floor window. When a boat stopped for him, he again declined help. Eventually, he took refuge on the roof as the floodwater filled his home. A helicopter lowered a ladder to him, but he again refused to evacuate. He knew the Lord would save him. Unfortunately, the man drowned. In heaven he said to God, "I lived a Christian life; why didn't You save me?" God replied, "My son, I tried three times, but you refused My help."

Do we listen and respond when we hear something new or unfamiliar? Do we heed timely warnings of danger? Do we accept Christian help from others? If we at least try to listen for God and respond the best we know how to do, He will reach out to us more than once. Just as He did when He called to Samuel in the temple, God will keep trying to reach those who are listening for Him.

. . . . . . . . . . . . . . . . . . . . . . . . . . . . . . . . . . . . . . . . . . .

*Lord, thank You for patiently offering Your help to me.*
*Help me to listen and hear so that I might respond as I should. Amen.*

# DAY 84

## IF

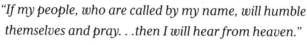

*"If my people, who are called by my name, will humble*
*themselves and pray. . .then I will hear from heaven."*
2 CHRONICLES 7:14 NIV

Did your mom ever give you one of those never-ending "if" clauses as an answer to a request to go somewhere or do something? "Well, if you get your room cleaned up and if your homework is done and if dinner is ready on time and if. . ." You might think she never wanted to take you to the park/mall/toy store/wherever at all!

God gave a list of "if" clauses in His message to Solomon. But He was hoping His people *could* get these "ifs" accomplished. He wanted His people to humble themselves—perhaps a good reminder right after the people had just finished proudly celebrating the establishment of the temple of the Lord.

He wanted His people to seek His face and turn from their wicked ways. It's difficult to look for God if you are met at every turn with yourself—your selfish longings and self-absorbed acts. You must start by seeking God through prayer, worship, and meditation on His Word.

God certainly wanted the people to pray. If they could submit to the Father in prayer, give up their wicked ways for a time to pray—if they could do all this, then God could hear them and forgive them and heal them.

God wants the same for you.

. . . . . . . . . . . . . . . . . . . . . . . . . . . . . . . . . . . . . . . . . . .

*Dear Lord, help me to be humble, prayerful, and ever seeking You. Amen.*

# DAY 85
# A WARNING

*Do not be arrogant, but tremble.*

ROMANS 11:20 NIV

In Romans 11, Paul delivers this rather stark warning. He has been talking about the Israelites and how they did not receive all the blessings they could have received because of their disobedience. He reminds the Gentiles to not feel as though they are superior simply because they have been granted salvation—a place of standing in the family of God. No, instead he encourages them to remember that they are just a branch of a very old and long-standing tree. Just as God has pruned the tree before, they are vulnerable to trimming as well. It is only through faith, which comes from God, that any people can belong to the Creator of all.

Can you think of any people today who act as though they own the market when it comes to true Christianity? That they are the real Christians, and others are just lame imitations? If you've lived long enough, you will know that just about every person who ever called on the name of the Lord has at one time or another made the mistake of thinking they were the only ones who knew how to pronounce that name just right.

Tremble at the almighty power of our great God, who gives and takes away and gives again out of His abundant grace. Let us strive to be so generous.

. . . . . . . . . . . . . . . . . . . . . . . . . . . . . . . . . . . . . . . . . . .

*Dear Lord, help me be more filled with faith than I am with criticism. Amen.*

# DAY 86
# ASK IN FAITH

*But when you ask God, you must believe and not doubt. Anyone who*
*doubts is like a wave in the sea, blown up and down by the wind.*
JAMES 1:6 NCV

What does it mean to ask God for something *in faith*? Does it mean we believe that He *can* grant our requests? That He *will* grant our requests? Exactly what is required to prove our faith?

There is no secret ingredient that makes all our longings come to fruition. The secret ingredient, if there were one, would be faith that God is who He says He is. It's faith that God is good and will use our circumstances to bring about His purpose and high calling in our lives and in the world.

When we don't get the answers we want from God, it's okay to feel disappointed. He understands. But we must never doubt His goodness or His motives. We must stand firm in our belief that God's love for us will never change.

. . . . . . . . . . . . . . . . . . . . . . . . . . . . . . . . . . . . . . . . . . . . .

*Dear Father, I know that You are good and that You love me. I know Your love for me will never change, even when my circumstances are hard. Help me cling to Your love, even when You don't give the answers I want. Amen.*

# HEAR GOD'S WORDS

*Naaman's servants went to him and said, "My father, if the prophet
had told you to do some great thing, would you not have done it?
How much more, then, when he tells you, 'Wash and be cleansed'!"*

2 KINGS 5:13 NIV

Janet was in awe when someone at church would report that the Lord had talked to them. Janet didn't think the Lord had ever "talked" directly to her.

She decided to privately ask how people knew the Lord had talked to them. Andrew told Janet he heard the Lord tell him this girlfriend would become his wife. How? When both his sister and his best friend told him, "She's the one," he just knew. Lucia said, "The Lord told me to attend this church." How? The third time her roommate invited her to attend, she just knew. Rose told Janet that the Lord told her she should relocate. How? One evening Rose told her daughter that she still hadn't decided where to move. Her daughter responded, "I think you have." After Rose repeated that she hadn't yet decided, her daughter repeated her opinion that Rose had. The following morning, Rose just knew the Lord had spoken to her.

As with the story of Naaman, we need to listen to those who care about us. God can use those who serve Him to deliver His messages. God may use a servant who appears to us as a family member or friend.

. . . . . . . . . . . . . . . . . . . . . . . . . . . . . . . . . . . . . . . . . .

*Lord, thank You for talking to me. Help me to know when
Your message is coming through one of Your servants. Amen.*

# DAY 88
# CANVAS

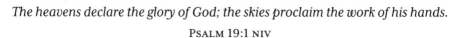

*The heavens declare the glory of God; the skies proclaim the work of his hands.*
PSALM 19:1 NIV

Next time you cannot think of what words to pray, pick a warm day and find a soft, grassy field. Lie down on the bed of green and watch clouds swim across the ocean on high. Study the shades of blue as they change from one end to the other. Look for where the sky meets the land on the horizon and wonder how far it must be to the ends of the world. Observe the birds winging their way high above you and imagine the delicate construction of their bones and feathers that allows them to transport themselves so easily for so far.

"The heavens declare the glory of God; the skies proclaim the work of his hands. Day after day they pour forth speech; night after night they reveal knowledge. They have no speech, they use no words; no sound is heard from them. Yet their voice goes out into all the earth, their words to the ends of the world" (vv. 1–4).

The heavens and skies declare God's glory like a painted canvas tells the ability of the artist. The canvas itself is not the art or skill. The skill of the painter is merely captured there for all to see.

When you have no words, be a canvas on which God's artistry can be revealed. The words will come later.

• • • • • • • • • • • • • • • • • • • • • • • • • • • • • • • • • • • • • • •

*Dear creator God, thank You for Your amazing creations. Amen.*

# DAY 89

# A CONVERSATION

*"Simon son of John, do you love me more than these?"*
JOHN 21:15 NIV

There's a beautiful recording of an example of prayer in John 21. It's a conversation that took place between Peter and Jesus, after Jesus had risen from the dead and had appeared to His disciples. Three times in the conversation, Jesus asks Peter about his love for Him, and three times He gives Peter a command to take care of, or feed, His sheep.

People often have similar conversations with God in prayer. God asks something of you, and you respond. He asks again, and you respond again. He asks again, and so on. If you're honest, you'll admit that there's probably a good reason you keep hearing the same question asked of you again and again.

Let's face it—Simon Peter isn't exactly pictured as the tender-loving type in the Bible accounts that include him. He's more of a go-getter, a doer of the Word, not a lover of the people. So it's not surprising to hear Jesus pressing him on the subject that was likely to be a point of weakness for him.

What is Jesus pressing you about? What question have you heard God asking you over and over again? What has your response been? Better yet, what will it be?

. . . . . . . . . . . . . . . . . . . . . . . . . . . . . . . . . . . . . . . . .

*Dear Father in heaven, thank You for our conversations.*
*Help me to constantly listen for what You have to say to me. Amen.*

# DAY 90
# POWERFUL PRAYING

*Therefore confess your sins to each other and pray for each other so that you may be healed. The prayer of a righteous person is powerful and effective.*
JAMES 5:16 NIV

When we have God's approval, when we live with integrity and faith, He listens to us. But when we consistently make poor choices and disregard God's guidance, He may not take our prayers as seriously.

Oh, He will never take His love from us, no matter what. And He will always listen when we ask for help out of our sin. But if we want our prayers to hold extra power, we need to live righteously. When we have God's approval on our lives, we can also know we have God's ear about all sorts of things. When we walk in God's will, we have access to God's power.

. . . . . . . . . . . . . . . . . . . . . . . . . . . . . . . . . . . . . . . . . .

*Dear Father, I want my prayers to be powerful and effective.*
*Help me to live in a way that pleases You. Amen.*

# DAY 91
## OBEY WITHOUT DELAY

*I will hasten and not delay to obey your commands.*
PSALM 119:60 NIV

Belinda felt compelled to personally deliver the shawl her church was praying over. The hand-crocheted shawl was intended for her friend Cheryl, who was now in hospice care near her family over one thousand miles away. After worship, Belinda asked the pastor if there was a plan for getting the shawl to Cheryl. When she learned there wasn't a plan, Belinda knew what she needed to do. Amazingly, there was a reasonably priced round-trip flight available that very day.

By making the impromptu trip and taking the shawl, Belinda was able to personally share the love and prayers of their church with her dear friend Cheryl and her family. Soon after Belinda returned home, she received a call from Cheryl's husband. He told her that Cheryl had gone home to be with the Lord, wrapped securely in the prayer shawl. When she heard the peace in his voice, Belinda understood why the Lord had needed her to immediately make the trip to Cheryl's bedside.

Often, we rationalize why we can't do something we feel called to do. We tell ourselves we don't have enough time, money, or skill. As Christians, we need to use our talents to determine how to accomplish the tasks our Lord asks us to accept. We need to be prompt "can do" Christians, like Belinda.

. . . . . . . . . . . . . . . . . . . . . . . . . . . . . . . . . . . . . . . . . .

*Lord, thank You for using me to meet the needs of others.*
*Help me listen for Your commands and for the urgency needed. Amen.*

# DAY 92
# THE HARD PRAYERS

*"Will not the Judge of all the earth do right?"*
GENESIS 18:25 NIV

What makes a question dangerous?

Some questions are dangerous because of the responses they require. "Do you love me?" Whatever reply is made to that question could change a person's life.

Some questions are dangerous because of what they might imply about the one who asks. "Do you love me?" could be met with "Why would you have to ask that?"

But you don't ever have to be afraid to ask a question of God. Some people go their whole lives, it seems, without ever asking God those pesky questions that have been a stumbling block to them for ages. It's easy to see why. It's frightening to face the King of kings with hard questions.

Yet God's been answering hard questions for centuries. Abraham wondered if a just God would kill both righteous and wicked together in order to destroy sinful cities. It was not just a question—it was a challenge: Are You truly a just Judge, God? Who are You, anyway?

It's just a guess, but probably most of the hard questions people are afraid to bring up in prayer would fall into the categories of wanting to define who God is and why He does what He does. Is there anyone better to ask those questions of than God Himself?

. . . . . . . . . . . . . . . . . . . . . . . . . . . . . . . . . . . . . . . . .

*Dear God, give me courage to ask You anything. Amen.*

# DAY 93
# WITHOUT PUNISHMENT

*The punishment that brought us peace was*
*on him, and by his wounds we are healed.*
ISAIAH 53:5 NIV

If you are a caregiver to children, you will have witnessed the relief that punishment can bring. A child does a bad thing. That child tries to cover up aforementioned bad thing. The child becomes increasingly miserable and/or mired in more trouble as the deceit rises to ridiculous proportions. Finally, the child is punished, and after the required amount of sobbing, yelling, or complaining has been achieved, the child goes and plays in peace. All is right with the world. . .for now.

In each of us is a built-in, God-created desire for justice. We want good to win over evil. We want wrongs to be made right. We want no bad guy to go free even, as it turns out, if that bad guy happens to be us.

When we pray and ask for peace, it would be good to remember we are asking the One who created peace—the only One through whom our peace can ultimately come. Only Jesus can give us that. It is by His wounds we are healed, no one else's. His wounds are our punishment—a punishment we would not have been able to bear. God loves us so; He wanted us to be able not just to survive but to live eternally.

. . . . . . . . . . . . . . . . . . . . . . . . . . . . . . . . . . . . . . . . . . . . . . . . . .

*Dear Jesus, thank You for taking on what we could not.*
*Please help us to live to understand Your peace. Amen.*

# DAY 94
# A GOOD MORSEL

*Taste and see that the L*ORD* is good; blessed is the one who takes refuge in him.*
P*SALM* 34:8 NIV

The world gives the idea to nonbelievers that God isn't worth a taste. The world emphasizes a self-focus, while the Lord says put others before self and God before all. In reality, walking and talking with God is the best thing you can do for yourself. As you walk with God, learning to pray and lean on Him and operate in His will, you are storing up treasures for yourself in heaven. In the world, you are demonstrating the love of Christ and being an influence to get others to taste of the Lord.

Like so many foods that are good for us, all it requires is that first taste, a tiny morsel, which whets the appetite for more of Him. Then you can be open to all the goodness, all the fullness of the Lord.

. . . . . . . . . . . . . . . . . . . . . . . . . . . . . . . . . . . . . . . . . . . .

*Lord, fill my cup to overflowing with Your love so that it pours*
*out of me in a way that makes others want what I have. Amen.*

# DAY 95
# PEACEMAKING

*Therefore I want the men everywhere to pray,*
*lifting up holy hands without anger or disputing.*
1 TIMOTHY 2:8 NIV

There were lots of conflicting opinions about how things ought to be done. What kinds of ceremonies to perform and when, who should be in charge, what scripture calls for, what Jesus would have said or done—there were plenty of things to argue about.

Does this sound like any church you know?

The early church, just like churches today, was made up of people. Anytime you have human beings coming together over something as significant as the act of worshipping God, it's going to be a little messy. People at times have strong emotions, firmly held beliefs, and loud opinions—often all at once!— about their church.

Paul had told Timothy to stay at Ephesus for a reason. False teachers were sowing seeds of discord among the Christians there, promoting "controversial speculations rather than advancing God's work" (1 Timothy 1:4). Paul advised his friend to "fight the battle well" (v. 18), which gives us another clue as to the state of the Ephesian church at the time. Peace did not reign.

Prayer can be a peacemaker. If you can get two adversaries to stand and pray together, at the very least their hands will be stilled long enough not to come to blows. What's the mood of your church? Is there anyone that you need to stand in prayer with and come to peace?

. . . . . . . . . . . . . . . . . . . . . . . . . . . . . . . . . . . . . . .

*Dear God, help me be a peacemaker. Amen.*

# DAY 96
# OUR PRAYER CALLING

*Then she [Anna] lived as a widow to the age of
eighty-four. She never left the Temple but stayed there
day and night, worshiping God with fasting and prayer.*
LUKE 2:37 NLT

Have you ever felt useless to the kingdom of God? Do you think you have little to offer so you offer little? Consider the eighty-four-year-old widow, Anna. She stayed at the temple worshipping God through prayer and fasting. That was her calling, and she was committed to prayer until the Lord ushered her home.

We need not pray and fast like this dedicated woman did. (In fact, for health reasons, fasting is not always an option.) Yet we are all called to pray. We can pray right where we are, regardless of our age, circumstances, or surroundings. Like Anna, it's our calling.

. . . . . . . . . . . . . . . . . . . . . . . . . . . . . . . . . . . . . . . . . .

*Lord, please remind me of the calling of prayer
on my life, despite my circumstances. Amen.*

# DAY 97
# BE QUIET

*"In repentance and rest is your salvation,*
*in quietness and trust is your strength."*
ISAIAH 30:15 NIV

This verse sounds lovely. . .until you go on: "But you would have none of it."

These are the words Isaiah relayed to God's "obstinate children." They could just as easily be directed to any of us today. The words of the Lord speak of people who "carry out plans that are not [His]" and heap "sin upon sin" (v. 1). They are "children unwilling to listen to the Lord's instruction" (v. 9), who ask their prophets instead to "tell us pleasant things" (v. 10).

How easy it is to fall into the bad habit of relying on our own way! There are hundreds, maybe thousands, of books each year published with the sole purpose of helping us to help ourselves. They teach us to distract ourselves with compliments and inspirational fluff. God compares this kind of living to the creation of a wall that is cracked and bulging, not able to stand up under its own weight, so it collapses. Yet it doesn't just fall down. It crumbles into such a worthless heap that not even a bit of it is functional (vv. 12–14).

So, how do you fight this result? God gives us the answer. Through repentance and rest, quietness and trust. You won't find a better way to develop those qualities than through daily prayer.

* * * * * * * * * * * * * * * * * * * * * * * * * * * * * * * * * * * * * * * * *

*Dear Lord, help me to trust You and to want to see through Your eyes. Amen.*

# DAY 98
# HAND HOLDERS

*As long as Moses held up his hands, the Israelites were winning,*
*but whenever he lowered his hands, the Amalekites were winning.*
*When Moses' hands grew tired, they took a stone and put it under*
*him and he sat on it. Aaron and Hur held his hands up—one on*
*one side, one on the other—so that his hands remained steady till*
*sunset. So Joshua overcame the Amalekite army with the sword.*
EXODUS 17:11–13 NIV

How do you view your pastor? Do you see him as the cheerleader of your congregation, trying to motivate them to be better Christ-followers? Perhaps the teacher? Maybe even the ultimate decision-maker? The truth is some pastors feel that they are expected to be all things to all people and to do it with perfection.

Our verse today shows that Moses was an ordinary (but called) person trying to do a huge job by himself. No one could be expected to hold his hands up for the duration of a battle. He needed help. One way we can help our pastors in the work they have been given is by the power of consistent prayer for them personally, for their families, and for their ministry.

*Father, our pastors are precious to us. Yet, we know they have been*
*given big assignments with sometimes unrealistic expectations.*
*Remind us to keep our pastors, their families, and their ministry in*
*prayer. It is one way we can hold their hands high to You. Amen.*

# DAY 99

# THE PRAYER OF SPECULATION

*A gossip betrays a confidence, but a trustworthy person keeps a secret.*
PROVERBS 11:13 NIV

In some circles, the prayer line is known as the gossip train. Instead of being an act of love and care for our neighbors in trouble, the sharing of prayer concerns can become a time to talk freely about the private issues of friends and acquaintances, inserting judgments and drawing (most likely erroneous) conclusions along the way.

When does that line get crossed? There are several points of weakness in this fence, but here are a few. Anytime someone has shared a problem with you in confidence, whether that security is spelled out or implied, the sharing of that prayer stops with you and God. Unless you have been given permission to ask others to pray on the issue, word of it should go no further. Period.

If someone does ask you to deliver a request for prayer to others, do so as requested. But only as requested. Don't insert your own opinions or speculations. Don't drop hints or let your tone imply meaning that is not yours to give. Stick to the facts.

Being asked to lift someone's personal burdens up before our Father is a privilege. It was the duty of the priests of ancient times to do this for the people in the holy dwelling of God. Do not take this duty lightly. Be a trustworthy prayer partner.

. . . . . . . . . . . . . . . . . . . . . . . . . . . . . . . . . . . . . . .

*Dear God, guard my lips from slips that could hurt others. Amen.*

## DAY 100

# GOD'S GOOD AND PERFECT WILL

*For this reason, since the day we heard about you, we have not stopped praying for you. We continually ask God to fill you with the knowledge of his will through all the wisdom and understanding that the Spirit gives.*

COLOSSIANS 1:9 NIV

The apostle Paul reminded the Colossians that he was continuously praying for them to be filled with the knowledge of God's will. Christians have received the Holy Spirit as their Counselor and Guide. Those who do not have a personal relationship with Christ are lacking the Spirit, and thus, they are not able to discern God's will for their lives. Always take advantage of the wonderful gift that you have been given. If you have accepted Christ as your Savior, you also have the Spirit. One of the greatest things about the Holy Spirit is that He helps us to distinguish God's call on our life from the other voices of the world. Pray that God will reveal His good and perfect will for your life.

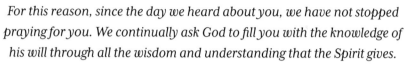

*God, help me to draw upon the wonderful resources that I have as a Christian. Help me, through the power of the Holy Spirit, to know Your will. Amen.*

# DAY 101
# GRACE

*When you have eaten and are satisfied, praise the LORD*
*your God for the good land he has given you.*
DEUTERONOMY 8:10 NIV

Repetition can be a very good thing. For those of us who are growing older, it can be the only way of hanging on to our memory of names, places, dates, our own birthday, and so on. Some people place a picture of a special person or event in a place where it can be seen every day, and every day the picture serves as a reminder to be thankful for that person or opportunity.

How many times do you eat in a day? Three, maybe more? Do you pray each time before you eat? Maybe we should wait, as Deuteronomy 8 suggests, and pray afterward, thanking God for the good He has given to us.

Perhaps you aren't in the habit of praying at all with meals. However, there is definitely a reason for it. Moses points it out here in the following verses: "Be careful that you do not forget the LORD your God. . . . Otherwise, when you eat and are satisfied. . .then your heart will become proud and you will forget the LORD your God" (vv. 11–12, 14).

So use your mealtimes as reminders, as a picture of all the good opportunities God has given you. Eat, and remember. Drink, and remember. Be satisfied, and remember. Pray, and remember.

. . . . . . . . . . . . . . . . . . . . . . . . . . . . . . . . . . . . . . . . .

*Dear Lord, thank You for this food and for the people*
*who made it. Thank You for everything. Amen.*

# DAY 102
# PRAYER TOUCHES GOD

*He [Cornelius] was a devout, God-fearing man. . . .*
*He gave generously to the poor and prayed regularly to God.*
ACTS 10:2 NLT

In the book of Acts, a centurion named Cornelius received a vision from God. Though a Gentile, this man loved God, praying and fasting regularly. While he prayed, an angel of the Lord told Cornelius that God heard and honored his prayers. Accordingly, God instructed the centurion to go talk to Peter, God's servant.

Jesus takes note of a praying, giving heart like Cornelius had. Denominations mean little, while a contrite, teachable spirit touches God. Cornelius was a good, God-fearing man who needed to hear about salvation through Christ. So God honored his prayers and led him to the preacher—while teaching the preacher a thing or two at the same time.

Have you hesitated to share your faith with someone you think unseemly or beyond your realm of comfort? Begin now. Look what happened when Peter did.

* * * * * * * * * * * * * * * * * * * * * * * * * * * * * * * * * *

*Father, forgive me for my self-righteousness. Open the way for me to witness to whomever You have prepared to hear the Gospel. Amen.*

# DAY 103
# ASKING FOR IT

*For what children are not disciplined by their father?*
HEBREWS 12:7 NIV

It is a rare child indeed who loves discipline. There's something about the human will that balks at being told what to do. It does not matter who you are or how you were raised—this fact is true for everyone. Even very small children will often learn *no* as one of their first words.

Though not all earthly fathers deliver helpful instruction, we have no reason whatsoever to doubt that our heavenly Father's guidance will be "for our good, in order that we may share in his holiness" (v. 10). It may be hard. It may be annoying. It most certainly will not fit into our own plans. It may involve dealing with people we don't like or going places that make us uncomfortable. It may mean speaking out or shutting up. It will take a lot of listening. It will take a lot of work.

However painful it is at the time, we have to know it will be worth it. Our perfect Father has nothing but our good in mind. His view of that good is far purer and higher and deeper than what we could imagine.

So go ahead. Take the chance. Ask in prayer for God to discipline you. It's going to come someday anyway. You might as well get started!

• • • • • • • • • • • • • • • • • • • • • • • • • • • • • • • • • • • • •

*Dear Father, train me in Your ways. Amen.*

# DAY 104
# LISTENING CLOSELY

*I will listen to what God the Lord says.*
PSALM 85:8 NIV

In today's hurried world, with all the surrounding noise, it's easy to ignore the still, small voice nudging us in the right direction. We fire off requests, expect microwave-instant answers, and get aggravated when nothing happens. Our human nature demands a response. How will we know what to do/think/say if we do not listen? As the worship song "Speak to My Heart" so beautifully puts, when we are "yielded and still" then He can "speak to my heart."

Listening is a learned art, too often forgotten in the busyness of a day. The alarm clock buzzes; we hit the floor running, toss out a prayer, maybe sing a song of praise, grab our car keys, and are out the door. If only we'd slow down and let the heavenly Father's words sink into our spirits, what a difference we might see in our prayer life. This day, stop. Listen. See what God has in store for you.

· · · · · · · · · · · · · · · · · · · · · · · · · · · · · · · · · · · · · · · ·

*Lord, how I want to surrender and seek Thy will.*
*Please still my spirit and speak to me. Amen.*

# DAY 105
# THE UNBELIEVER'S PRAYER

*The boy's father exclaimed, "I do believe; help me overcome my unbelief!"*
MARK 9:24 NIV

This prayer could be called "the Parents' Prayer." Is this not the cry of every mother and father? Perhaps especially so for those who have children suffering with chronic illness, mental illness, addiction, school struggles, or spiritual battles.

Let's be honest, none of us would want to deal with this father's struggle for more than an hour let alone years. It was bad enough that his son had an unexplained condition that didn't allow him to speak. Every parent knows the frustration of trying to figure out what a pre-speech toddler wants or doesn't want—generally while he's in the middle of a piercing scream that could wake the dead. Yet here is a child who periodically throws himself into harm's way—"into fire or water to kill him" (v. 22). We can guess who has been there every time to save his boy from being burned or drowned.

This father believes there is a cure, an answer. Why else would he come to see Jesus? At the same time, this man is tired. He has been disappointed so many times. It is not hard at all to understand his cry for help. Anne Brontë echoed this feeling in her poem "The Doubter's Prayer":

> *Without some glimmering in my heart,*
> *I could not raise this fervent prayer;*
> *But, oh! a stronger light impart,*
> *And in Thy mercy fix it there.*

* * * * * * * * * * * * * * * * * * * * * * * * * * * * * * * * * * * * * * * * * * *

*Dear Lord, help me believe more. Amen.*

# DAY 106

# A DECLARATION OF DEPENDENCE

*"Sacrifice thank offerings to God, fulfill your vows to the Most High, and call on me in the day of trouble; I will deliver you, and you will honor me."*
PSALM 50:14–15 NIV

Most of us value our relationships, whether they are family, friends, or coworkers. We like being in relationships with those who offer love, commitment, and trust because we feel valued. Perhaps not so ironically, today's verse reveals that God wants the same things from us. He wants thankful, trusting, and faithful children, people whom He can delight in and who can delight in Him.

As our heavenly Father, He wants to help us, especially in times of trouble. That dependency on Him recognizes that everything we have comes from Him. The practical way to depend on Him comes through an honest, consistent lifestyle of prayer, where we offer ourselves and our needs. Through prayer, we draw near to Him and get to know Him better. In doing that, we'll become the thankful, trusting, and faithful children He desires.

*Gracious and generous Father, thank You for loving me so much that You are interested in every facet of my life. I commit to bring everything to You in prayer and acknowledge that I am dependent on You for my provision and safety. I pray for the continued outpouring of Your Spirit in me so I can ask for continued blessings for myself as well as others. I love You, Lord. Amen.*

# DAY 107
# SHAME

*To you they cried out and were saved; in you*
*they trusted and were not put to shame.*
PSALM 22:5 NIV

*Shameless* is one of those funny English words that mean the opposite of what they sound like. A shameless person is not, as it would seem, a person who has no reason to be shamed. Quite the contrary. A shameless person is one who has lived such a dishonorable life that she doesn't even have the ability to feel shame anymore.

The closer you are to God, the more likely you are to feel shame when you do wrong things. It is an honor to be a child of God and to have an intimate relationship with Him. Anything that hurts that relationship, especially because of your own doing, will make you feel the marring of that honor. And the more you desire God and spend time with Him, the more sensitive you will become to those little parts of your life that don't align with His will.

In some societies, shame and honor are equal to weakness and strength. In God's kingdom, we are made strong through our weakness. When we come to Him, cry out to Him, pray to Him, and submit to Him, we are saved. By humbling ourselves before Him and trusting in Him, we will not be put to shame but receive His honor instead.

* * * * * * * * * * * * * * * * * * * * * * * * * * * * * * * * * * * * * * * * * *

*Dear Lord, help me to be an honorable child of Your kingdom. Amen.*

# DAY 108
## HE CARES FOR YOU

*"You have seen what I did to the Egyptians, and how I
carried you on eagles' wings, and brought you to Myself."*
EXODUS 19:4 AMP

Often, we feel deserted, as though God doesn't hear our prayers. And we wait. When Moses led the children of Israel out of Egypt toward the Promised Land, God directed him to go the distant way, lest the people turn back quickly when things became difficult. The people placed their hope in an almighty God and followed His lead. When they thirsted, God gave water. When they hungered, He sent manna. No need was unmet.

If God can do this for so many, you can rest assured that He will care for you. He knows your needs before you even ask. Place your hope and trust in Him. He is able. He's proven Himself over and over. Read the scriptures and pray to the One who loves you. His care is infinite. . .and He will never disappoint you.

. . . . . . . . . . . . . . . . . . . . . . . . . . . . . . . . . . . . . . . . . . . . .

*Heavenly Father, I know You love me and
hear me. I bless Your holy name. Amen.*

# DAY 109
# EXPOSED

*He will bring to light what is hidden in darkness*
*and will expose the motives of the heart.*
1 CORINTHIANS 4:5 NIV

Have you ever replaced light bulbs in a room? Listen to the voice of experience: Don't do this while company is over. Suddenly, every dust bunny, every finger smudge, every piece of lint is exposed for all the world to see. No, it's better to do this well before your visitors arrive so you have time to do something about it. Or just take the light bulbs out again, light some candles, and call it mood lighting. Who cares if it's only four in the afternoon?

When would you like your secrets brought to light? In what setting would you like the motives of your heart laid bare? Why not ask God to reveal truth to you in the quiet and privacy of your own conversations with Him?

When you pray, ask God to bring to light the sins you have forgotten that day. Ask Him to point out things that you haven't even realized you are struggling with. Paul said, "My conscience is clear, but that does not make me innocent" (v. 4). Just because you think you are on the right path doesn't mean you've never taken a wrong step. Ask God to turn on the lights and reveal the weak points in your faith.

But then, don't be surprised if what you see is a messy room!

. . . . . . . . . . . . . . . . . . . . . . . . . . . . . . . . . . . . . . . . . . . .

*Dear Lord, shine Your light on my heart so*
*I can be a better witness for You. Amen.*

# DAY 110
# EARNEST PRAYER

*"[If] My people, who are called by My Name, humble themselves, and pray and*
*seek (crave, require as a necessity) My face and turn from their wicked ways,*
*then I will hear [them] from heaven, and forgive their sin and heal their land."*

2 CHRONICLES 7:14 AMP

The Amplified Bible specifies how believers are to humble themselves and pray. We are to seek (crave, require as a necessity) God's face.

We should *seek* God relentlessly.

*Crave.* Our desire for God's presence in our lives ought to be strong and irresistible.

*Necessity.* Our hearts need God for survival. He is our one and only true necessity.

When you pray, call out to God with your whole heart. Prayer must be more than an afterthought to close each day, as eyelids grow heavy and sleep wins the battle. Seek God. Crave and require His face. Turn toward Him. He stands ready to hear, to forgive, and to heal.

. . . . . . . . . . . . . . . . . . . . . . . . . . . . . . . . . . . . . . . . . .

*Lord, be my greatest desire, my craving, my all. Amen.*

# DAY 111
# CALM

*"Teacher, don't you care if we drown?"*
Mark 4:38 niv

The clouds rolled in, gray and heavy. The rain gradually gained speed and density. The formerly calm sea began churning. A large wave broke over the boat, flooding it and drenching everyone inside. The anxiety that had been growing on board reached a high point. Some of the men were fishermen; they were accustomed to stormy seas. But this storm was different. It had come on so suddenly and was so strong! The mysterious abyss seemed determined to either suck them in or burst them apart.

Men ran this way and that, trying to find ways to hold on, tying themselves to the boat, to each other, to anything they could grasp. People shouted directions to one another, trying to be helpful. Someone took a head count—making sure all the passengers were there. But one was missing. Where was Jesus?

They spotted Him sleeping in the stern. Sleeping! In this squall? How could He? Why wasn't He helping them? Why wasn't He doing something? Didn't He care?

Have you ever asked God these questions in the middle of a personal storm?

The disciples found out that not only did Jesus care, but He had the ability to calm *their* cares all at once. "Quiet! Be still!"

He said it to the wind and the waves. He says it to us. Be still and know who is in the boat with us.

· · · · · · · · · · · · · · · · · · · · · · · · · · · · · · · · · · · · · · · · · · ·

*Dear God, help me to feel Your presence, and calm my fears. Amen.*

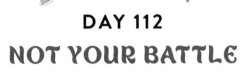

# DAY 112
# NOT YOUR BATTLE

*"All those gathered here will know that it is not by sword or spear that the Lord saves; for the battle is the Lord's, and he will give all of you into our hands."*

1 Samuel 17:47 niv

Have you ever been involved in a really ugly fight? Harsh words are hurled on both sides, personal attacks are launched, people pick sides, and soon it seems your whole world is at war.

But that battle that you are fighting? It isn't yours. So lay down your weapons and squelch the fires of vengeance. Pack up your warhorses and get down on your knees instead.

David was in an ugly fight. Goliath was not exactly a humble opponent. He was big and loud and mean and scary. The Israelites were not showing themselves to be especially brave at the time. So David, the shepherd, stepped into the middle of this mess armed not with swords and catapults and spears, and not even with a sling and a stone. No, David was armed with the strength and power and might of the living God.

You are too. Perhaps you haven't seen God rescue you from the paw of a lion or bear, as David had. Yet you can be confident that God is more than able to get you through whatever challenge you are facing. Spend some time with Him. Ask Him to help you. Place your battle in His capable hands.

. . . . . . . . . . . . . . . . . . . . . . . . . . . . . . . . . . . . . . . . . .

*Dear Lord, please let me lean on You. Amen.*

# DAY 113

# PRAYING FOR ALL PEOPLE

*I urge, then, first of all, that petitions, prayers, intercession and thanksgiving be made for all people—for kings and all those in authority, that we may live peaceful and quiet lives in all godliness and holiness. This is good, and pleases God our Savior, who wants all people to be saved and to come to a knowledge of the truth.*

1 TIMOTHY 2:1–4 NIV

Whether we like the person who is in office or not, God commands us to pray for those He placed in authority over us. In ancient times, this could have meant praying for those who hated Christians and were possibly plotting harm to them. Even today, as issues concerning Christ-followers emerge, we are called to pray for all people, including those with whom we don't see eye to eye politically. Today's verses remind us that to do so is good and pleasing to the Lord.

. . . . . . . . . . . . . . . . . . . . . . . . . . . . . . . . . . . . . . . . . . . . .

*Gracious Lord, thank You for the admonition to pray for all people, including those with whom we disagree. All people are precious to You, Lord. Please help me put my own feelings aside and be obedient in praying for all those in authority. Amen.*

# DAY 114
## ON THE MAT

*He is always wrestling in prayer for you, that you may stand*
*firm in all the will of God, mature and fully assured.*
COLOSSIANS 4:12 NIV

Praying for someone takes a lot of endurance. To follow a person through their ups and downs, successes and failures can be emotionally exhausting, especially if you love that person very much. Thinking about them, asking God to guide them, hoping for them—it can all feel like a mental wrestling match.

But who are you wrestling with? Not the person at the center of your prayers—they might not even be aware of your efforts. Not God. This is no Jacob vs. the angel story (see Genesis 32 for that account).

No, you are wrestling with yourself. With your own thoughts and worries about the person and how to ask God for help. Sometimes you might be wrestling with frustration at your inability to fix everything (because some things just won't be fixed that way). You might be wrestling with perseverance and patience in your prayers—struggling to hold on to hope for a person's life when it seems there's only a slim chance for things to get better. You might struggle to find the right requests to make on their behalf. You might fight with yourself to push down negative feelings such as bitterness, anger, and despair.

Engaging in the care and prayer for others can be a workout. But it's totally worth it.

. . . . . . . . . . . . . . . . . . . . . . . . . . . . . . . . . . . . . . . . . . .

*Dear Lord, help me to persevere in my prayers for others. Amen.*

# DAY 115

# PUBLIC PRAYER

*So I bow in prayer before the Father from whom every
family in heaven and on earth gets its true name.*
EPHESIANS 3:14–15 NCV

A heartfelt prayer offered in public glorifies God and allows others to feel His presence; however, the scriptures include a warning about public prayer. Matthew 6:5 advises people not to act like the hypocrites who want to be seen and heard praying just to show how pious and religious they are. Public prayer must be sincere and directed toward God and not toward others.

Every day, Christians gather together, bow their heads, and pray publicly in churches, at prayer groups, at funeral and memorial services, in restaurants before meals, and even around school flagpoles. They pray sincerely, sometimes silently and sometimes aloud, setting aside the world and entering God's presence.

Are you shy about praying in public? Don't be. Step out in faith, bow your head, and pray like God is the only One watching.

. . . . . . . . . . . . . . . . . . . . . . . . . . . . . . . . . . . . . . . . . . . .

*Heavenly Father, I am not ashamed to bow my head
and be in Your presence wherever I go. Amen.*

# DAY 116
# PILLOW TALK

*In peace I will lie down and sleep, for you alone, Lord, make me dwell in safety.*
PSALM 4:8 NIV

It's happened to the best of us. You wait until the house is all quiet to spend some time with the Lord. You grab your Bible, and you get your notebook. Your pen is poised over the page as you wait on the Lord. You open your mouth a little as you begin your prayer. You breathe deeply and relax as you list the ways you are grateful that day for God's help and blessings.

Your Bible slips a little down your comforter. Your notebook pages crumple. Your pen rolls to the floor. Your mouth opens broadly as the snoring begins. You breathe deeply in heavenly sleep as you dream about God's blessings. . . or something like that.

A mind stilled in prayer can easily become a mind stilled by sleep. That's okay. At least some of the time. You wouldn't want your prayer time to end up being nap time every day. Yet one of the benefits of a relationship with the Maker of heaven and earth is the peace that comes from nowhere else. It's better than any super, high-tech mattress or the latest ultra-essential oil.

In the peace that comes with prayer, you can lie down and sleep, knowing God is watching over you.

. . . . . . . . . . . . . . . . . . . . . . . . . . . . . . . . . . . . . . . . . . .

*You alone, Lord, make me dwell in safety. Amen.*

# DAY 117
# CALL UNTO ME

*Look to the LORD and his strength; seek his face always.*
PSALM 105:4 NIV

David, the psalmist, had no choice but to rely on the Lord as he fled his enemies. The lyrics of the psalms remind us he was no stranger to loss and fear. Yet he cried unto the Lord. His words in Psalm 105 encourage us to remember what He has done before. Paul sat in the pits, literally, and sang songs of praise. While we might not be in dire straits like those men, we certainly have problems, and we can read scripture to see how the Lord has worked to have confidence that He is near.

Let us work to seek His face always. Know the Lord cares about each detail of your life, and nothing is a secret or a surprise to Him. Reach for the best, and expect results. It might require a time of waiting, but His answers are always unsurpassed.

* * * * * * * * * * * * * * * * * * * * * * * * * * * * * * * * * * * * * * * * * *

*Almighty Father, thank You for loving me so well.*
*In times when I fear, help me fall into Your embrace. Amen.*

# DAY 118
# WHO IS ABLE?

*"Give your servant a discerning heart to govern your
people and to distinguish between right and wrong."*
1 KINGS 3:9 NIV

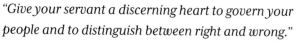

There's no doubt about it. If Solomon were to run for any high elected office today, he would win. He was wealthy. He was apparently not bad with wooing the ladies. Most of all, he was wise.

Wouldn't it be wonderful if every government official in our country today stopped what they were doing and just prayed this simple prayer of Solomon's? *Give me a discerning heart, God. Help me know the difference between what is right and what is wrong.* The earth might actually tremble if such an event happened.

Solomon's rhetorical question is apt today—"Who is able to govern this great people of yours?" (v.9). Indeed. Who? It's a complex job, clouded by power, control, and a thousand other schemes the devil lays to ensnare the participants.

While we would like to think that things are more black and white, figuring out what is right or wrong to do as a governing body is quite difficult. Making a ruling for one person in one situation might not be so hard. But making a law that has to last and cover a multitude of possibilities, known and unknown, can be extremely complicated.

Pray for your nation's leaders. And ask them to be praying too—for discerning hearts and wise choices.

*God, my King, pour out Your wisdom on the rulers of this nation. Amen.*

# DAY 119
# A PRAYER TO ARMS

*Finally, be strong in the Lord and in his mighty power.*
EPHESIANS 6:10 NIV

Dear God, help me to know my real enemy—not my annoying neighbor, or my demanding boss, or my fickle friend. Help me to recognize the powers of this dark world when they come at me, and help me not to waste my time fretting over little offenses that mean nothing. Help me to think bigger, to see broader, to know more of Your wisdom.

Help me to stand my ground.

God, make my tongue speak Your truth. Wrap Your Word around me tight like a belt—help it to hold all things together. Please mold for me a guard around my heart so that I can long to follow Your righteous path and not the desires of this world.

Make me ready, Lord, with answers to those who ask questions and wonder about You. Help me not be afraid to speak but to be confident in my replies because I know You are behind every word of the Gospel of peace.

Make me strong so I can bear Your shield of faith, repelling insecurities and fears and doubts that are the weapons of my enemy. God, You know the words and thoughts and actions that sting me the most. Please help me let Your peace and the certainty of You be a salve on my soul.

· · · · · · · · · · · · · · · · · · · · · · · · · · · · · · · · · · · · · · ·

*Fill my head and heart with Your Spirit so I can go out and
pierce others with the security of salvation in You. Amen.*

# DAY 120
# RENEW YOUR STRENGTH

*But those who wait for the L*ORD* [who expect, look for, and hope in*
*Him] will gain new strength and renew their power; they will lift up their*
*wings [and rise up close to God] like eagles [rising toward the sun];*
*they will run and not become weary, they will walk and not grow tired.*
ISAIAH 40:31 AMP

Andrew Murray was a South African writer, teacher, and Christian pastor in the late 1900s who captured the heart of prayer with these words about Jesus: "While others still slept, He went away to pray and to renew His strength in communion with His Father. He had need of this; otherwise He would not have been ready for the new day. The holy work of delivering souls demands constant renewal through fellowship with God."

Each day you give a part of yourself to that day—spiritually, emotionally, physically, financially, and socially. Within each of those areas of life, you need to refuel. Spiritually, the only way to recharge is a renewal that comes from God. Waiting for a fresh outpouring of His life-giving Spirit brings a newness and a fresh perspective on all the other areas of your life. Give your best each day by drawing on the strength of your heavenly Father.

. . . . . . . . . . . . . . . . . . . . . . . . . . . . . . . . . . . . . .

*Heavenly Father, Your Word and prayer are strength to my*
*soul. Renew me and pour Your life into me. Fill me with*
*Your power and give me courage for a new day. Amen.*

# DAY 121
# GIVING GOOD GIFTS

*"Which of you fathers, if your son asks for a fish, will give him a snake instead?"*
LUKE 11:11 NIV

It's probably not right to laugh at this scene, but can you imagine it? The little boy and his father are out on a campout, having some wonderful father-son bonding time together. They've been fishing all afternoon, and the father has gathered their load to prepare some fish to cook over the fire for dinner. The boy is eager to taste the fruit of his labors and asks, "Hey Dad, can you pass me one of those fish?" His father tosses him a plate—full of rattlesnake!

Okay, maybe it wouldn't be so funny. But Jesus was making a point here by presenting the ridiculous. The crowd He was talking to would have gotten the joke—no honorable father would give his son gifts that would hurt him. A father in those times might well have been judged by the blessings bestowed on his children. The more prosperous and at ease his children appeared to be, the more respected the father would be.

So if mere human fathers are able to figure out how to give their children good things for dinner (even if it's just peanut butter sandwiches!), how much more ought we to trust God our Father to give us what we need?

Ask your Father for what you need. He will provide everything you ask and much more.

. . . . . . . . . . . . . . . . . . . . . . . . . . . . . . . . . . . . . . . .

*Dear Father, fill me up with what I lack. Amen.*

# DAY 122
# FOCUSED PRAYER

*Pray in the Spirit at all times and on every occasion. Stay alert
and be persistent in your prayers for all believers everywhere.*
EPHESIANS 6:18 NLT

The Bible warns us to stay alert and to pray persistently. The key is to focus on Jesus even in the midst of the storm. If the captain of a ship or the pilot of a plane loses focus in the middle of a storm, it can be very dangerous for all involved. Our job as believers is to trust the Lord with the outcome and to remain deliberate and focused in our prayers.

The Bible does not say to pray when it is convenient or as a last resort. It does not say to pray just in case prayer might work or to add prayer to a list of other things we are trying. We are instructed in Ephesians to pray at *all* times and on *every* occasion. When you pray, pray in the Spirit. Pray for God's will to be done. Pray in the name of Jesus.

*Jesus, I set my eyes upon You, the Messiah,
my Savior, Redeemer, and Friend. Amen.*

# DAY 123
## MORNING ROUTINE

*In the morning, Lord, you hear my voice; in the morning*
*I lay my requests before you and wait expectantly.*
PSALM 5:3 NIV

Dog owners are often greeted by their companions in the morning, with eyes full of expectation. The request of the dog is quite clear—take me on a walk, please! It is certain that dogs are the most energetic waiters in the animal kingdom. Even a well-trained dog, while seemingly sitting patiently, has every muscle fiber in its body just straining to be released. Why is this? Because they are certain, with not a shadow of a doubt, that very soon indeed they will be allowed out. They will be let go. They will run.

Maybe you wait for the Lord's answers in the same way. But many of us do not. Do you ever lay requests before God morning after morning (or night after night), going through the routine, but not really believing God will come through?

Oh, to be like an expectant dog! Waiting for God's response to our prayers with eagerness and readiness to spring into whatever discipline or action God requires. Waiting with certainty, sure that our Father will answer soon. Waiting with utter trust in the Master because we know He has our best interests always in mind. Waiting expectantly.

. . . . . . . . . . . . . . . . . . . . . . . . . . . . . . . . . . . . . . . . . . . . . .

*Dear God, help me have confidence and faith to ask*
*You anything and to wait eagerly for the reply. Amen.*

# DAY 124
## THE RIGHT FOCUS

*Turning your ear to wisdom and applying your heart to understanding—
indeed, if you call out for insight and cry aloud for understanding, and if
you look for it as for silver and search for it as for hidden treasure, then
you will understand the fear of the Lord and find the knowledge of God.*
PROVERBS 2:2–5 NIV

Even when you're looking in the right direction, you can still miss something because your focus is slightly off. This can be the challenge in our relationship with God. We can ask God a question and be really intent on getting the answer, only to find that His response to us was there all along—just not the answer we expected or wanted.

Frustration and stress can keep us from clearly seeing the things that God puts before us. Time spent in prayer and meditation on God's Word can often wash away the dirt and grime of the day-to-day and provide a clear picture of God's intentions for our lives. Step outside the pressure and into His presence, and get the right focus for whatever you're facing today.

. . . . . . . . . . . . . . . . . . . . . . . . . . . . . . . . . . . . . . . . . .

*Lord, help me to avoid distractions and keep my eyes on You. Amen.*

# DAY 125
# ALL NATIONS

*"Who will not fear you, Lord, and bring glory to your name?"*
REVELATION 15:4 NIV

If you began right now praying for one nation on earth every day, it would probably take you the better part of a year to finish the job. Estimates vary, and the status of nations vary as wars continue to be fought and political conditions change, but there are somewhere around two hundred nations in this world. And if you count the different tribes living among those nations, the number grows even larger.

So many different people, so many different interests—can you imagine them all standing and giving glory to God? It seems impossible. But it also seems impossible that any people, no matter their background, could resist the awesome and majestic power of the almighty God.

Pray for the people living now in nations where Christ is not preached. Pray for them that they might hear the Gospel message in time to start living for Him. Pray for God's mercy and grace to be spread in cultures where fear and suffering still reign. Pray for whatever part you can have in delivering the message of love to those who are longing to hear it.

. . . . . . . . . . . . . . . . . . . . . . . . . . . . . . . . . . . . . . . . . .

*Dear Lord, let me help in whatever way I can to*
*spread Your love and hope to every nation. Amen.*

# DAY 126
# TEACH ME YOUR PATHS

*Show me your ways, Lord, teach me your paths. Guide me in your truth and*
*teach me, for you are God my Savior, and my hope is in you all day long.*
PSALM 25:4–5 NIV

Hebrews 4:12 tells us that the scriptures are living and active. Just think about that for a moment. God's Word is alive! As busy women, it can be difficult to find the time to open the Bible and meditate on the message—but it's *necessary* if you want God to teach you His path for your life.

Instead of giving up on finding time for Bible reading, get creative. Download a free Bible app on your phone. Have a daily scripture reading and devotion emailed to you from Heartlight.org. Jot down a few verses on a note card to memorize. There are many ways to get in the Word of God and be trained by it. Start today!

. . . . . . . . . . . . . . . . . . . . . . . . . . . . . . . . . . . . . . . . . . . . .

*Lord, I believe Your Word is living and active. I want to know Your will for my*
*life. Help me get in Your Word more and understand Your plan for me. Amen.*

# DAY 127
# SUCCESS

*Then he prayed, "Lord, God of my master Abraham, make me successful today, and show kindness to my master Abraham."*
GENESIS 24:12 NIV

How often do you pray for job success? Perhaps a promotion or a raise or some sort of recognition?

How often do you pray for God to show kindness to your boss?

Imagine if the CEO of a corporation sent his top executive out on a matchmaking mission for his own son! That would seem like a fairly trivial matter in today's business terms. Back in the age of Abraham, the family *was* the business. So Abraham sent his most important servant—the one in charge of everything he owned (which was a lot, in those days)—on this very important mission. This servant is the only one he could trust to do the significant and delicate negotiation required to obtain a good wife for his son, who would carry on the family business.

The servant knew the weight of his responsibility. He wanted to do well not just for himself but for his master and his master's family. So he prayed. He asked God to help select the right woman for Isaac. God did not let him down.

Next time you are handed an important mission, remember to ask the ultimate CEO for help. Ask to do well not just for yourself but for your boss and for the whole company. God will not let you down.

. . . . . . . . . . . . . . . . . . . . . . . . . . . . . . . . . . . . . . . . . .

*Dear God, thank You for good work and the will to do it. Amen.*

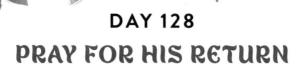

## DAY 128
# PRAY FOR HIS RETURN

*The end of all things is near. Therefore be alert
and of sober mind so that you may pray.*
1 PETER 4:7 NIV

Around AD 600, Jerusalem fell to the Babylonians. The Jews were exiled to Babylonia and held captive for seventy years. God told the prophet Jeremiah to tell His people to settle there and live normally. He said they should seek peace in the place in which they lived until He came back to get them (Jeremiah 29:4–7).

Today's Christians are similar to those Jews. They live normally in an evil world, seeking peace on earth while holding on to the promise of Jesus' return.

Paul wrote, "Brothers and sisters, whatever is true, whatever is noble, whatever is right, whatever is pure, whatever is lovely, whatever is admirable . . .think about such things. . . . And the God of peace will be with you" (Philippians 4:8–9 NIV).

May God's peace be with you today and every day until Jesus comes.

. . . . . . . . . . . . . . . . . . . . . . . . . . . . . . . . . . . . . . . . . . . .

*Lord, may Your kingdom come and the earth be filled with Your glory. Amen.*

# NOT STOPPED

*Since the day we heard about you, we have not stopped praying for you.*
COLOSSIANS 1:9 NIV

How do you feel when you learn that someone has been praying for you? *Grateful* is the word that springs to mind. What a gift to receive! To know that someone is remembering you and lifting your name up to God. It's one of the best things anyone could do for another person.

Scripture is not clear on who might be praying for us in heaven, though we know for certain Jesus intercedes for us. But it seems that if there's rejoicing in heaven when one sinner repents (Luke 15:10), then it's not unreasonable to think that quite a bit of praying is going on too.

Even now, someone in heaven might be lifting his voice and saying your name. Praying for you to be filled "with the knowledge of his will through all the wisdom and understanding that the Spirit gives, so that you may live a life worthy of the Lord and please him in every way" (Colossians 1:9–10 NIV). Someone might be praying for you to do good work, to learn well and acquire knowledge. Someone might be asking for God's power to make you strong and able to endure all things. Someone might be joyfully thanking our Father in heaven just because you were born and you are a member of God's family.

Someone somewhere is praying for you. Aren't you glad?

*Dear Lord, help me be faithful in my prayers for others. Amen.*

# DAY 130

# PRAY FOR CHRISTIAN HOUSEHOLDS

*When she speaks, her words are wise,*
*and she gives instructions with kindness.*
PROVERBS 31:26 NLT

In Christian households, children learn about God's love and faithfulness. Discipline is administered out of loving-kindness, not anger, and love is taught through the parents' example. It is a home in which Christlike wisdom is passed from generation to generation.

In Timothy's household (see 2 Timothy 1:5), he learned from his mother's and grandmother's faith; and according to Paul, those seeds of faith grew in young Timothy and led him to become a servant of the Lord.

Whether you are married or single, have children or not, you can plant seeds of faith through your own Christian example and prayer. Pray for all children that they will grow up in godly homes, and pray for women everywhere that they will raise their children in Christian households and remain always faithful to God.

. . . . . . . . . . . . . . . . . . . . . . . . . . . . . . . . . . . . . . . . . . . . .

*Heavenly Father, shine Your light through me today*
*so that I might be an example to others. Amen.*

# DAY 131
# ONLY ONE GOD

*But for us, there is one God, the Father, by whom all things were*
*created, and for whom we live. And there is one Lord, Jesus Christ,*
*through whom all things were created, and through whom we live.*

1 CORINTHIANS 8:6 NLT

A coworker told Sue she had decided there were many ways to God. Sue knew the Bible teaches there is only one God and one way to Him. She liked and admired the woman who had spoken to her, but she was thankful she knew what God's Word says. Many voices express themselves in our world, each believing they know the right way, each wanting to convert others to their way of thinking. It's important to know the truth and to listen to the right voice.

The voices may be saying, "If you want to fit in, you need to change," "You must be more tolerant," or "That isn't politically correct." Some of these voices may sound good and we may be tempted to agree. Be careful that your good intentions don't set a trap for you. The voice of error can sound pretty good sometimes.

As Christians, we need to follow God's voice even when it makes us look politically incorrect. We can do this only by reading and knowing God's Word. Only then can we know the difference between the voice of truth and the voice of error. There is only one God, and we must know Him intimately to be able to distinguish between the voices.

· · · · · · · · · · · · · · · · · · · · · · · · · · · · · · · · · · · · · · · · · · · · · · ·

*Father, draw me close to You so I will always*
*recognize Your voice and know the truth.*

# DAY 132

## PRAYER TARGETS SELFISHNESS

*Do nothing out of selfish ambition. . . . Rather, in humility*
*value others above yourselves, not looking to your own*
*interests but each of you to the interests of the others.*
PHILIPPIANS 2:3–4 NIV

This scripture discourages selfish ambition and encourages us to look to the interests of others. As believers, God expects us to take the high road. That means, despite someone's behavior, we are called to pray. Pray for her salvation; pray for God to work on her heart and mind; pray that when approached with the truth, she will receive it with a humble, open spirit.

God targets every heart with the arrow of His Word. It travels as far as the power of the One who thrust it on its course. Prayer, coupled with God's Word spoken to the unlovable, never misses the bull's-eye.

But we must first pray to see beyond the selfishness and view the needs behind it. When we do, God equips us to pray for others. Then the arrow of transformation is launched.

* * * * * * * * * * * * * * * * * * * * * * * * * * * * * * * * * * * * * * * * * *

*Jesus, help me not only to tolerate but also to*
*pray for the ones for whom You died. Amen.*

# DAY 133

## SOLITUDE

*Very early in the morning, while it was still dark, Jesus got up,
left the house and went off to a solitary place, where he prayed.*

MARK 1:35 NIV

Where do you pray? Do you pray in a busy office, coffee in one hand and papers clenched in another? Do you pray as you scrub each finger outside the operating room, just before surgery begins? Do you pray at your desk, when the students in front of you are taking a test? Do you pray in the relative quiet of your locked bathroom, while a toddler knocks persistently on the other side?

It's strangely comforting to know that the Prince of Peace needed quiet times too. Really quiet times. Away from people. Away even from the house where people might be. Somewhere alone, still, dark. A solitary place.

We need those quiet times too. Time to focus on the Lord alone and not be distracted by what is going on around us. Certainly, it's not something that can happen on every day of the week. You must plan for it. You may even have to get up very early in the morning. But it's important to find time, every once in a while, when it can be just you and God together. No one else. No rush. Nowhere to be. Nothing else to do.

Make plans to find your solitary place today.

. . . . . . . . . . . . . . . . . . . . . . . . . . . . . . . . . . . . . . . . . . . . . . . . . . .

*Dear Lord, I need time alone with You. Help me to make that happen. Amen.*

# DAY 134
# HOW LONG HAS IT BEEN?

*Trust in him at all times, you people; pour out
your hearts to him, for God is our refuge.*
PSALM 62:8 NIV

Has it been a long time since you've completely poured out your heart to God? Not just your everyday prayers for family and friends, but a complete and exhaustive outpouring of your heart to the Lord? Oftentimes, we run to friends or spiritual counselors in times of heartache and trouble, but God wants us to pour out our hearts to Him first. He is our refuge, and we can trust Him to heal our hearts completely.

The next time you reach for the phone to call up a friend and share all your feelings, stop and pray first. Share your heart with God, and gain His perspective on your troubles. The God who created you knows you better than anyone. Let Him be your first point of contact in any situation.

* * * * * * * * * * * * * * * * * * * * * * * * * * * * * * * * * * * * * * * * * *

*Heavenly Father, help me to trust that You are here for me—to listen and
to guide me. Give me wisdom to make decisions that honor You. Amen.*

# DAY 135
# FLOOD

*The LORD has heard my weeping.*
PSALM 6:8 NIV

Flash flood alert. Psalm 6 has a rather high humidity level. The psalmist is in anguish, down to the bone. He has flooded his bed with tears and drenched his couch. Next thing you know, his friends will be filling up sandbags around him.

We've all been there. Something happens that just breaks your world apart, and the tears start coming. Then they won't stop. You think they will never stop. You think you will just go on weeping until you haven't a drop of water left in you, at which point you will be so overcome with dehydration you will just die. Then what?

Isn't it somehow comforting to see the psalmist throwing himself on his couch in utter misery? To know that thousands of years ago, bad days—really horrible ones—happened? To know that in the end, the same Lord and God who soothed and saved that poor, miserable, soaking-wet psalmist lying on his couch is the same Lord and God who soothes you today?

Our God is an expert on human suffering. He's had centuries of experience in counseling people through grief of all kinds. So next time you feel like the tears just won't ever stop, come immediately to the door of the best Counselor you could ever find. Come in prayer. Come with a box of tissues. Just come.

. . . . . . . . . . . . . . . . . . . . . . . . . . . . . . . . . . . . . . . . . . . .

*Dear God, thank You for hearing my sobs and not turning away. Amen.*

# DAY 136
# OPEN THE EYES OF FAITH

*"Therefore I tell you, whatever you ask for in prayer,*
*believe that you have received it, and it will be yours."*
MARK 11:24 NIV

Have you ever prayed for something or someone, and God seemed to turn a deaf ear? One woman prayed for her son's salvation for seven years. Each day she knelt at the foot of her tear-stained bed, pleading for her child. But God seemed silent. Yet, what she failed to understand was that the Lord had been working all along to reach her son in ways unknown to her. Finally, her son embraced the Gospel through a series of life-changing circumstances.

The world says, "I'll believe it when I see it," while God's Word promises, "Believe then see."

Someone once said, "The way to see by faith is to shut the eye of reason." When we pray, rather than ask God why our prayers remain unanswered, perhaps we should ask the Lord to close our eyes so that we might see.

. . . . . . . . . . . . . . . . . . . . . . . . . . . . . . . . . . . . . . . .

*Lord, I believe, even when my prayers go unanswered.*
*Instead, I know You are at work on my behalf. Amen.*

# DAY 137
# ENDLESS POSSIBILITIES

*"For where two or three gather in my name, there am I with them."*
MATTHEW 18:20 NIV

In our society, individual success is glorified over the benefits of a group of people working together. But if you've ever met a fund-raising goal, run a race, or completed a service project with a group, you know how fantastic it can be. To see people with different gifts join together as one unit is a beautiful thing. It can be frustrating too. The fact that it isn't always a piece of cake makes the accomplishment that much sweeter. When you are finished, you feel pride not just in the work of your own hands but in the group as a whole. Nothing seems impossible to do if you can gather enough people willing to work together.

Jesus confirms this feeling: "If two of you on earth agree about anything they ask for, it will be done" (v. 19). Does this mean that anything we pray for together we will receive? Maybe. Certainly. If Jesus says the Father will do it, then the Father will. However, God is not limited by our human designs, so how a thing gets "done" for us by the Father may look a bit different from what we had in mind. Sometimes it might even look worse. Yet the result will no doubt be infinitely better than what we could imagine.

*Dear Lord, thank You for living life with us. Amen.*

# DAY 138
## LAY IT AT THE CROSS

*"Come to me, all you who are weary and burdened, and I will give*
*you rest. Take my yoke upon you and learn from me. . .you will find*
*rest for your souls. For my yoke is easy and my burden is light."*
MATTHEW 11:28–30 NIV

Jesus gives us step-by-step guidance in how to place our difficulties and burdens at the foot of the cross. First, He invites us to come to Him; those of us who are weary and burdened just need to approach Jesus in prayer. Second, He exchanges our heavy and burdensome load with His easy and light load. Jesus gives us His yoke and encourages us to learn from Him. The word *yoke* refers to Christ's teachings, Jesus' *way* of living life. As we follow His teachings, we take His yoke in humility and gentleness, surrendering and submitting ourselves to His will and ways for our lives. Finally, we praise God for the rest He promises to provide us.

Do you have any difficulties in life, any burdens, worries, fears, relationship issues, finance troubles, or work problems that you need to "lay at the cross"? Jesus says, "Come."

*Lord, thank You for inviting me to come and exchange my heavy burden*
*for Your light burden. I praise You for the rest You promise me. Amen.*

# DAY 139

# WATCHING FROM THE REEDS

*Then she placed the child in it and put it
among the reeds along the bank of the Nile.*
EXODUS 2:3 NIV

There is very little emotion captured in the story of baby Moses. A woman has a baby. She can't hide him from the cruel government, which legislated his death, so she puts him in a basket in the river. No tears. No sound. The end.

It wasn't the end, thankfully, for baby Moses. It's hard to imagine that was the end for his mother either. Even after her daughter followed the baby boy, watching him be rescued by royalty; even after she finished nursing her son and gave him back to be raised by his adoptive family; even after the boy had grown up and fled the land—it seems likely that it wasn't the end of the story for Moses' mother.

How many mothers out there have watched from the reeds and prayed? First, that their babies might be rescued, might be saved from whatever terrible set of circumstances they were born into, and might be given a chance to grow and live. Then, that their babies might continue to thrive, to become healthy adults. Maybe one day, to know that their mothers loved them.

Say a prayer today for those mothers watching from the reeds.

. . . . . . . . . . . . . . . . . . . . . . . . . . . . . . . . . . . . . . . . . .

*Dear Lord, thank You for the gift of life. Please bless all those mothers
who have made sacrifices so their babies could survive. Amen.*

# DAY 140
# HOLY SPIRIT PRAYERS

*We do not know how to pray as we should, but the Spirit Himself*
*intercedes for us with groanings too deep for words; and He who*
*searches the hearts knows what the mind of the Spirit is, because*
*He intercedes for the saints according to the will of God.*

ROMANS 8:26–27 NASB

Many times, the burdens and troubles of our lives are too complicated to understand. It's difficult for us to put them into words, let alone know how to pray for what we need.

We can always take comfort in knowing that the Holy Spirit knows, understands, and pleads our case before the throne of God the Father. Our groans become words in the Holy Spirit's mouth, turning our mute prayers into praise and intercession "according to the will of God."

We can be encouraged, knowing that our deepest longings and desires, maybe unknown even to us, are presented before the God who knows us and loves us completely. Our names are engraved on His heart and hands. He never forgets us; He intervenes in all things for our good and His glory.

. . . . . . . . . . . . . . . . . . . . . . . . . . . . . . . . . . . . . . . . . .

*Father, I thank You for the encouragement these verses bring.*
*May I always be aware of the Holy Spirit's interceding on my behalf. Amen.*

# DAY 141

# NUDGES

*"Speak, Lord, for your servant is listening."*
1 Samuel 3:9 niv

It may be a passing memory. You think of an old friend and wonder how they are. Maybe it's a burst of inspiration. You suddenly see the solution to a problem that has been a struggle for others. It could come as a twinge of guilt. You feel you should go to someone and apologize.

The call was plain in 1 Samuel 3, but even then Samuel didn't recognize it right away. It took three times of being woken up in the middle of the night by the boy before old Eli put two and two together. He realized it was the Lord, so he told the boy to lie down again. Then, if Samuel should hear the voice calling his name again, Eli told him to answer, "Speak, Lord, for your servant is listening."

Most of us would have probably told Samuel to just ignore the voice and go to sleep, for goodness' sake. After all, isn't that what we tell ourselves?

We get a nudge from God. It comes as a whisper, a thought, a glimpse, a passing idea—maybe even a dream. We wave it away. We shrug it off. We ignore the voice.

Next time you have a thought or feeling that comes out of the blue, consider that it might not be coming out of nowhere. It might be coming from Someone.

* * * * * * * * * * * * * * * * * * * * * * * * * * * * * * * * * * * * * * * * * * * *

*Speak, Lord. I am listening. Amen.*

# DAY 142
# WHEN FEAR PARALYZES

*A young man was following Him, wearing nothing but a linen sheet over his naked body; and they seized him. But he pulled free of the linen sheet and escaped naked. They led Jesus away to the high priest; and all the chief priests and the elders and the scribes gathered together. Peter had followed Him at a distance, right into the courtyard of the high priest; and he was sitting with the officers and warming himself at the fire. Now the chief priests and the whole Council kept trying to obtain testimony against Jesus to put Him to death, and they were not finding any.*

Mark 14:51–55 nasb

Suddenly you awake at one in the morning to the sound of the doorknob being turned, followed by the sound of creaking boards. Your heart leaps into your throat. What do you do?

When John Mark, the writer of this Gospel, learned that Jesus had been captured by the Roman guards and a trial was pending, he grabbed the sheet off his bed and ran to observe the events himself.

We know John Mark escaped the threatening situation. Yet Jesus Christ remained in the eye of the storm, well aware of the situation yet in perfect sync with the Father. When fear paralyzes, help is only a prayer away.

* * * * * * * * * * * * * * * * * * * * * * * * * * * * * * * * * * * * * * *

*Lord, I believe in all that You are, both God and Man. Amen.*

# DAY 143
# WANT. ASK. GET.

*You do not have because you do not ask God.*
JAMES 4:2 NIV

It seems so simple. Want. Ask. Get. James breaks it down for us. He says, "You want something but don't get it. You kill and covet, but you cannot have what you want. You quarrel and fight. You do not have, because you do not ask God" (v. 2).

What is it you are afraid to ask for? What is it you are afraid to admit you need? Maybe you just need help. Maybe you need the truth. Maybe you need a loan. Maybe you need to be saved. Maybe you need to let go.

Want. Ask. Get.

What is it you really want? Not just a new car or more money or a nice outfit. What is it you're lacking that makes you want what others have? Do you want what God wants for you? Do you even know?

Once you know what you want, how do you ask? Do you look everywhere else first before coming to God? Do you go to Him right away? Do you come to Him humbly or as someone entitled?

You want, you ask—did you get it? If your answer's no, have you thought about why? What were your motivations? What's your reaction to not getting what you want?

If your answer is yes, have you thanked God? Have you shared what you have? Want. Ask. Get. Then give.

*Dear God, help me to make Your desires for my life my own. Amen.*

# DAY 144
# TALKING TO GOD

*One of his disciples said to him, "Lord, teach us to pray, just as John taught*
*his disciples." He said to them, "When you pray, say: 'Father, hallowed be*
*your name, your kingdom come. Give us each day our daily bread.'"*
LUKE 11:1–3 NIV

Yes, God hears—and although He knows what we need before we even ask Him, He *wants* us to pray. He even gave us instruction on how to pray. Our prayers don't have to be long or eloquent or even particularly organized. When Jesus taught His disciples to pray, the sample wasn't wordy. He simply taught the disciples to give God glory and to come to Him and ask for their daily needs.

But Luke 11 teaches us something beyond just an outline for prayer. The story shows clearly that if we ask God to teach us how to pray, He will. It's all part of the prayer—ask God to lead you, then speak to Him from the heart.

Let's make it a habit to pray every day. Like the saying goes, practice makes perfect.

. . . . . . . . . . . . . . . . . . . . . . . . . . . . . . . . . . . . . . . . .

*Dear God, teach me how to pray. Remind me that my words don't have to*
*be profound. You're just looking for earnest thoughts from the heart. Amen.*

# DAY 145
# PROTECTION, NOT ISOLATION

*"My prayer is not that you take them out of the world
but that you protect them from the evil one."*
JOHN 17:15 NIV

Through the centuries of the history of the church, there have been groups of people who concluded that the only way to stay faithful was to isolate themselves from the evils of this world. So that's exactly what they did. And the extent to which this plan was successful or not could be debated (though there's not room for that here).

But that doesn't seem to be the plan Jesus had for us. In His wonderful, revealing prayer of John 17, Jesus asked God not to "take them out of the world" (*them* referring to "those whom you gave me out of the world," v. 6), but to give the people protection from the evil one (v. 15). Jesus Himself states that, along with being "not of the world," He was indeed sent "into the world" (vv. 16, 18).

Jesus did not isolate Himself. When He was on the earth, He was walking among the people. He was living and eating and sleeping with the people, not in some fortress on His own.

We are supposed to love one another. It's hard to do that very well from behind a wall. So if you have built up barriers between you and "the world," it may be time to break those down. Don't be afraid. Ask God for help, and He will protect you.

. . . . . . . . . . . . . . . . . . . . . . . . . . . . . . . . . . . . . . . . . . .

*God, help me to reach others for You. Amen.*

# DAY 146
# REACH OUT

*But people who aren't spiritual can't receive these truths from God's*
*Spirit. It all sounds foolish to them and they can't understand it, for*
*only those who are spiritual can understand what the Spirit means.*
1 Corinthians 2:14 nlt

Unbelievers may feel confused trying to navigate the unfamiliar territory of spiritual truth. They don't have the ability to understand it because they don't have the Holy Spirit as a teacher to guide them. The Bible may not make sense to them, but don't be quick to judge. Hope isn't lost!

God likely has placed unbelievers in your life that He wants you to reach out to. Share your faith with them in words and actions they can understand. Pray the Lord opens their hearts to receive Jesus as Lord and Savior. Then the Holy Spirit will dwell with them, giving them the ability to comprehend spiritual truth. Pray that these lost "tourists" will find Jesus soon!

*Dear Lord, help me not to judge those who don't know You.*
*Instead, I pray that You intercede to show them the way. Amen.*

# DAY 147
# BARGAIN

*It is better not to make a vow than to make one and not fulfill it.*

ECCLESIASTES 5:5 NIV

"God, if You just give me a puppy, I'll be good my whole, entire life." How many children must have prayed a prayer like this one? How many of us are still praying this kind of prayer?

People make promises to God for all kinds of reasons, but most likely the biggest one of those reasons has to be to strike a deal. "God, if You'll _____, I will _____."

It is good to think of God as your friend. It is dangerous to think of God as your haggling partner.

Besides, He would be the worst person ever to bargain with. Why? He doesn't need anything. When you are trying to strike a deal, it's best to know what your counterpart needs—what they lack that you can offer.

The God who made time, who spun the earth into motion and placed the stars in the sky, does not need you. He does not need anything you have to offer. He does not need your promises. Especially the empty ones.

He does want you to come to Him. He does want to be near you. He does want to love you. He will give you everything you could ever need. Come near to God and He will come near to you. Not to negotiate a deal but just to know Him more.

. . . . . . . . . . . . . . . . . . . . . . . . . . . . . . . . . . . . . . . . . . . .

*Dear Father, if You'll love me, I will have everything I need. Amen.*

# DAY 148
# VOCALIZING A PRAYER

*"And when you are praying, do not use meaningless repetition as the
Gentiles do, for they suppose that they will be heard for their many words."*
MATTHEW 6:7 NASB

If you can remember the acrostic ACTS, you'll have an excellent formula for prayer: Adoration, Confession, Thanksgiving, and Supplication.

As we come before the Lord, we first need to honor Him as Creator, Master, Savior, and Lord. Reflect on who He is and praise Him. And because we're human, we need to confess and repent of our daily sins. Following this, we should be in a mode of thanksgiving. Finally, our prayer requests should be upheld. My usual order for requests is self, family members, and life's pressing issues. Keeping a prayer journal allows for a written record of God's answers.

Your prayers certainly don't have to be elaborate or polished. God does not judge your way with words. He knows your heart. He wants to hear from you.

. . . . . . . . . . . . . . . . . . . . . . . . . . . . . . . . . . . . . . . . . . . .

*Lord, Your Word says that my prayers rise up to heaven like incense from
the earth. Remind me daily to send a sweet savor Your way! Amen.*

# DAY 149
# EVEN NOW

*"But I know that even now God will give you whatever you ask."*
JOHN 11:22 NIV

Jesus loved Martha and Mary and Lazarus. It says so right in the Bible. Those three seemed to have a special relationship with the Lord. So it's natural that when their brother became sick, the sisters sent word to Jesus.

What do you want Jesus to do when someone you love is sick and dying?

If you've ever had the sorrow of having to wait by the bedside while someone you love is in the last stages of life, you probably know the heaviness of that experience. You start to reach in your mind for any possibility, any solution, and any chance at all to change the final outcome.

Have you ever sent word to Jesus about a friend or family member? "Jesus, the one You love is sick." "Jesus, please come." "Jesus, please heal him." "Jesus, please don't let her die."

The God who formed you in the womb and shaped you into the being you now are knows the plan for your life, including its end. As hard as it might be to understand at the time, He is with us, even in that final chapter.

When Martha spoke to Jesus after her brother's death, she declared her faith. "I know that even now God will give you whatever you ask."

Do you know God is with you even now?

* * *

*Dear Lord, I am not ready to let go. Help me*
*believe You are with me to the end. Amen.*

# DAY 150
# ANSWERED PRAYER

*Delight yourself in the LORD; and He will give you the desires of your heart.*
PSALM 37:4 NASB

Note the first part of Psalm 37:4: "Delight yourself in the LORD." A woman who truly delights herself in the Lord will naturally have the desires of her heart—because her heart desires only God and His will.

Our Father takes no pleasure in the things of this world—things that will all wither and die. Neither should we.

So what pleases God? He loves it when we witness for Him, live right, and instruct others in His Word. If those are things that we also truly desire, won't He grant us the "desires of [our] heart" and let us see people brought into the kingdom? Won't we have a life rich in spiritual growth?

*Lord, please help me see where my desires are not in line*
*with Your will so that the things that I pursue are only*
*and always according to Your own desires. Amen.*

# DAY 151

## HUMBLED

*We all, like sheep, have gone astray, each of us has turned to our*
*own way; and the LORD has laid on him the iniquity of us all.*
ISAIAH 53:6 NIV

When you come to God in prayer, do you ever feel the complete humbleness of your situation? It is a truly humiliating experience—not that God makes us feel how little we are, but that being near God makes us see how little we are.

Perhaps that's why we don't do it as often as we should. It's not comfortable to feel shame.

We are sheep. We run away. We ramble. We get off track. We lose our way. We chase after the wrong things. We fear everything. We cry out and complain. We can't find our way home. We are stubborn. We don't see well. We don't ask for help. We stumble.

Our Lord and Shepherd knows all of this and loves us still. He knows all our wrongs, and He doesn't just forget them or wipe them away. He pays for them. In blood.

That is the God to whom you say your bedtime prayers.

. . . . . . . . . . . . . . . . . . . . . . . . . . . . . . . . . . . . . . . . . . .

*Dear God, I am humbled in Your presence.*
*Help me to live a life that is worthy of Your love. Amen.*

# DAY 152
## SO, TALK!

*"No one can come to Me unless the Father who sent Me
draws him [giving him the desire to come to Me]; and I
will raise him up [from the dead] on the last day."*
JOHN 6:44 AMP

Fortunately for us human beings, God isn't easily offended. He is deeply committed to holding up His end of our relationship, and He doesn't want us to hide anything from Him. He already knows every thought we have, anyway. Why not talk to Him about those thoughts?

Every concern we have, every little thing that's good, bad, or ugly.

Our Father always wants to talk. In fact, the very impulse to pray originates in God. In his book *The Pursuit of God*, author A. W. Tozer wrote, "We pursue God because, and only because, He has first put an urge within us that spurs us to the pursuit."

So, talk!

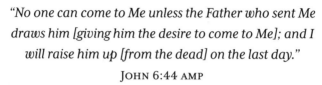

*Lord God, it boggles my mind that You want to hear from me!
And often! Your Word says that I can call out Your name with
confidence. That You will answer me! Today, Lord, I give You
praise, honor, and glory—and my heart's deepest longings. Amen.*

# DAY 153
# PRAYERS OF THE WEAK

*For when I am weak, then I am strong.*
2 Corinthians 12:10 niv

People have made different guesses as to what the "thorn" in Paul's flesh might have been. But it doesn't really matter what it was. All we need to know—all the Corinthians needed to know—is that it was something that made him feel significantly weakened. He was tormented by it—so much so that he pleaded with God to get rid of it.

What is your thorn? What's the weak spot in your armor?

Thank God today for your weaknesses. Thank Him for the times when you've had to rely on Him alone. Thank Him for the days when nothing went your way. Thank God for your failures and your falters.

For when you didn't have it all together, you had to lean on God. You had to see He was the only way out. You had to know only He could give you the resources you needed. You had to believe His words: "My grace is sufficient for you, for my power is made perfect in weakness" (v. 9).

When you have lost your strength, take a moment to be glad for God's grace and to give Him the glory.

. . . . . . . . . . . . . . . . . . . . . . . . . . . . . . . . . . . . . . . . . .

*Dear Jesus, thank You for making Your power*
*and my need for You abundantly clear. Amen.*

# DAY 154
# SUBMITTING TO HIS WILL

*"Your kingdom come, your will be done, on earth as it is in heaven."*
MATTHEW 6:10 NIV

Many times, submitting to God's will requires letting go of something we covet. We may be called to walk away from a relationship, a job, or a material possession. At other times, God may ask us to journey down a path we would not have chosen. Venturing out of our comfort zone or experiencing hardship is not our desire.

Embracing God's love enables us to submit to His will. God not only loves us immensely, but He desires to bless us abundantly. However, from our human perspective, those spiritual blessings may be disguised. That is why we must cling to truth. We must trust that God's ways are higher than ours. We must believe that His will is perfect. We must hold fast to His love. As we do, He imparts peace to our hearts, and we can say with conviction, "Your will be done."

* * *

*Dear Lord, may I rest secure in Your unconditional love. Enable me to trust You more. May I desire that Your will be done in my life. Amen.*

# DAY 155
# WHAT TO DO?

*"When the foundations are being destroyed, what can the righteous do?"*
PSALM 11:3 NIV

Anyone who has ever owned an old house knows what a worry a cracked foundation can be. Sometimes it can be repaired. But a foundation that is weak means the whole house will likely have to come down, or it will eventually fall down.

The psalmist in Psalm 11 asks a good question. What can the righteous do? When the whole stability of a world is crumbling, when the people who are supposed to be upright are being corrupted, when everything that is supposed to be true turns out to be false—what can the righteous do? What should they do?

We might come up with many answers. Worry. Shout. Look for someone to blame. Use the trouble as an excuse to give up. Hurry up and build a new house.

But the psalmist doesn't tell the righteous what to do. He tells them where to look. "The LORD is in his holy temple; the LORD is on his heavenly throne" (v. 4).

When the foundations are shaken, look to the One who cannot be shaken. Look to the Lord, who is "righteous, he loves justice; the upright will see his face" (v. 7). Turn your face to God and ask for His help. Turn your eyes toward Him, and remember who is in control.

. . . . . . . . . . . . . . . . . . . . . . . . . . . . . . . . . . . . . . . . . . . . .

*Dear Lord, help me in times of trouble to*
*remember to turn to You in prayer. Amen.*

# DAY 156

# WHEN GOD REDECORATES

*God is the builder of everything.*
HEBREWS 3:4 NIV

God—the renovator of hearts—doesn't work cautiously. When He begins renovations, He removes (or allows the removal of) all existing supports. Maybe that "support" is health—ours or a loved one's. Maybe it's our savings. Maybe it's something else. Our lives, as we know them, crash. We hurt. We don't know how we can go on.

But God knows. If we let Him, He'll replace the temporary supports we'd relied on—health, independence, ability, you name it—with eternal spiritual supports like faith, surrender, and prayer. Those supports enable us to live a life of true freedom, one abounding with spiritual blessing.

. . . . . . . . . . . . . . . . . . . . . . . . . . . . . . . . . . . . . . . . . . . .

*Lord, I am tempted to cling to the supports I've erected. When my life crashes, I'm tempted to despair. Please help me to be still and place my trust in You, the great builder of all lives. Amen.*

# DAY 157
## THE SPIRIT OF TRUTH

*"But when he, the Spirit of truth, comes, he will guide you into*
*all the truth. He will not speak on his own; he will speak only*
*what he hears, and he will tell you what is yet to come."*
JOHN 16:13 NIV

If you've ever been hiking, you know that there are some commonsense guidelines that will help to keep you safe—such as hiking with a buddy, taking a good map, wearing comfortable boots that are broken in, and taking plenty of water, just to name a few. Ignoring good hiking rules can lead to treacherous circumstances.

And just as in hiking, ignoring the good biblical guidelines that God has put before us can also be deadly. The Lord and His powerful Word are our travel guides as we journey through this dangerous passageway we call life. Without our Savior, the daily jungle gets dark and scary, and all the trails will eventually lead to destruction.

With Christ as our guide, we can feel secure since He promises to guide us into all truth. He will watch over our comings and goings. He will show us the right course to follow here on earth and the pathway to eternal life through Christ.

Pray daily that the Lord and His living Word will be our holy guide, because His way is not just a good way to go—it's the only right way.

. . . . . . . . . . . . . . . . . . . . . . . . . . . . . . . . . . . . . . . . . . . .

*Holy Spirit, give me daily direction and purpose.*
*Help me to remain within Your light and truth. Amen.*

# DAY 158
# LIFE PRESERVERS

*My comfort in my suffering is this: Your promise preserves my life.*
PSALM 119:50 NIV

In the difficulties of life, God is our life preserver. When we are battered by the waves of trouble, we can expect God to understand and to comfort us in our distress. His Word, like a buoyant life preserver, holds us up in the bad times.

But the life preserver only works if you put it on *before* your boat sinks. To get into God's life jacket, put your arms into the sleeves of prayer, and tie the vest with biblical words. God will surround you with His love and protection— even if you're unconscious of His presence. He promises to keep our heads above water in the storms of life.

. . . . . . . . . . . . . . . . . . . . . . . . . . . . . . . . . . . . . . . . .

*Preserving God, I cling to You as my life preserver.*
*Keep my head above the turbulent water of life*
*so I don't drown. Bring me safely to the shore. Amen.*

# DAY 159
# TRANSFORMING

*And we all, who with unveiled faces contemplate the Lord's*
*glory, are being transformed into his image with ever-increasing*
*glory, which comes from the Lord, who is the Spirit.*
2 CORINTHIANS 3:18 NIV

If you are like most people, you will find fault with at least one aspect of your image. It's hard to find anyone who is completely happy with the person she sees in the mirror.

It would be harder still to find anyone who is completely happy with the person she is—with all the decisions and thoughts and actions she has made in her life. Or even just today.

Thanks be to God, "where the Spirit of the Lord is, there is freedom" (v. 17). No one has to hide from the Lord. No one has to worry about the exterior image. No one has to feel alone.

If you have been running away from God for a while or just neglecting your prayer life, it's time to turn and face Him. He does not expect you to be perfect. He expects that you will need transforming. He is happy to perform that work. He wants to shape you into the best human being you can be. Come and kneel before Him; don't hide your face. He can see through any veil you might try to wear anyway. Come and stand before His image and ask Him to transform you.

. . . . . . . . . . . . . . . . . . . . . . . . . . . . . . . . . . . . . . . . .

*Dear God, I'm not happy with who I am. Please mold*
*me into the person You want me to be. Amen.*

# DAY 160
# BOARD GOD'S BOAT

*Then, because so many people were coming and going that*
*they did not even have a chance to eat, he said to them, "Come*
*with me by yourselves to a quiet place and get some rest."*
MARK 6:31 NIV

The apostles ministered tirelessly—so much so they had little time to eat. As they gathered around Jesus to report their activities, the Lord noticed that they had neglected to take time for themselves. Sensitive to their needs, the Savior instructed them to retreat by boat with Him to a solitary place of rest, where He was able to minister to them.

We often allow the hectic pace of daily life to drain us physically and spiritually, and in the process, we deny ourselves time alone to pray and read God's Word. Meanwhile, God patiently waits.

So perhaps it's time to board God's boat to a quieter place and not jump ship!

*Heavenly Father, in my hectic life, I've neglected time apart*
*with You. Help me to board Your boat and stay afloat through*
*spending time in Your Word and in prayer. Amen.*

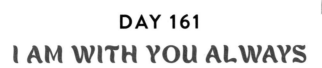

# DAY 161

# I AM WITH YOU ALWAYS

*"Do not let your hearts be troubled. You believe in God; believe also in me."*
JOHN 14:1 NIV

From the moment we emerge from our mother's womb, squalling and red and upset, until we breathe our last breath, our hearts are burdened with troubles of every kind. We know loneliness and disappointment and pain so deep that it scorches our very souls. What relief is there for us when all humans fail us—friends, doctors, family members, counselors, and sometimes even pastors?

Jesus takes us to a quiet place, and He speaks to us. He tells us that we are very dear to Him. We are His friends—His beloved children. When we fall, He picks us up. When we fail, He restores our souls. When we get discouraged, He lifts us up. When we are lost, His hand is ever near. When we walk in the darkest valleys of this life journey, burdened with many cares, He helps us carry our load. He is our strength. He is our fortress. He is all we need.

Jesus comforted His disciples with the words "Do not let your hearts be troubled. You believe in God; believe also in me." As we pray, He will speak those same words to me and to you if we listen with an earnest heart.

"Dear one, be not troubled. I am here."

. . . . . . . . . . . . . . . . . . . . . . . . . . . . . . . . . . . . . . . . . .

*Lord Jesus, I give to You the burdens of my heart. I cast
my anxiety onto You because I know that You care for me—
more than I could possibly imagine. Amen.*

# DAY 162
## IS ANYONE LISTENING?

*"And I will ask the Father, and He will give you another
Helper (Comforter, Advocate, Intercessor—Counselor,
Strengthener, Standby), to be with you forever."*
JOHN 14:16 AMP

The Greek translation for "comfort" is *paraklesis* or "calling near." When we are called near to someone, we are able to hear his or her whisper. It is this very picture that scripture paints when it speaks of the Holy Spirit. God sent the Spirit to whisper to us and to offer encouragement and guidance, to be our strength when all else fails. When we pray—when we tell God our needs and give Him praise—He listens. Then He directs the Spirit within us to speak to our hearts and give us reassurance.

Our world is filled with noise and distractions. Look for a place where you can be undisturbed for a few minutes. Take a deep breath, lift your prayers, and listen. God will speak—and your heart will hear.

* * * * * * * * * * * * * * * * * * * * * * * * * * * * * * * * * * * *

*Dear Lord, I thank You for Your care. Help me
to recognize Your voice and to listen well. Amen.*

# DAY 163

## HOW YOU SHOULD PRAY

*"When you pray, do not be like the hypocrites."*
MATTHEW 6:5 NIV

There are not that many places in the Bible that spell out exactly how people should perform the Christian disciplines of faith. Jesus' words in Matthew's Gospel come as a welcome relief to those who are seeking to know exactly how to behave as a follower of Christ.

First, He paints a picture of what not to do. Don't pray to be seen. Don't use prayer as a step on the faith success ladder. Don't think you have to be seen for the Father to hear your words. Don't look for any reward or praise outside of the glory that comes from God Himself.

Do not babble on, using words as a weapon of power or as a show of strength. Don't think that God desires quantity over quality. Don't make the mistake of thinking God needs to hear you speak at all.

Instead, pray quietly. Pray on your own. Pray in private. Pray with words that show God respect, that show you know His power. Thank God for His provision. Ask Him to forgive what you lack. Request His guidance and His salvation. Ask Him for His will to be done, even if you have no idea what that is just yet.

Then go out and live as you pray. Be forgiving, knowing your Father has forgiven you time and time again for all the small and big ways you have stumbled.

- - - - - - - - - - - - - - - - - - - - - - - - - - - - - - - - - - - - - - - -

*Our Father in heaven, let Your will be done. Amen.*

# DAY 164
# ANSWERED KNEE-MAIL

*The prayer of a righteous person is powerful and effective.*
JAMES 5:16 NIV

The concept of the power of prayer is familiar, but sometimes we forget what it means. Prayer is a powerful tool for communicating with God, an opportunity to commune with the Creator of the universe. Prayer is not something to be taken lightly or used infrequently. Yet, in the rush of daily life, we often lose sight of God's presence. Instead of turning to Him for guidance and comfort, we depend on our own resources.

But prayer isn't just a way to seek protection and guidance; it's how we develop a deeper relationship with our heavenly Father. We can access this power anywhere. We don't need a Wi-Fi hotspot or a high-speed modem. We just need to look up. He's connected and waiting.

* * * * * * * * * * * * * * * * * * * * * * * * * * * * * * * * * * * * * * * * * * *

*Father, thank You for being at my side all the time. Help me
to turn to You instantly, in need and in praise. Amen.*

# DAY 165
# HOW DO I LOVE GOD?

*Jesus replied: "'Love the Lord your God with all your heart and with all your soul and with all your mind.' This is the first and greatest commandment."*
MATTHEW 22:37–38 NIV

If you love your mom and dad—hopefully you do—do they know it? Really know it, all the way to the depths of their hearts? Do you say the words "I love you" often to them, or are you neglectful, hoping that saying it on birthdays and holidays is enough? Do you show your love for them in your actions?

Showing God that we love Him has some similarities to loving our parents. If we love the Lord with all our heart and soul and mind, does He know it? Or are we neglectful in saying, "I love You"? Do we show our love for Jesus with our actions? Do we relish spending time with Him? The Lord cherishes our fellowship, and He hopes for our love and devotion as well.

Other ways to show God that we love Him would be through other gifts of the heart, such as repentance, respect, obedience, and thanksgiving. This can be our grateful response to His great love, His daily tender mercies, and His abundant grace.

How will you show the Lord today that you love Him? What will you say?

. . . . . . . . . . . . . . . . . . . . . . . . . . . . . . . . . . . . . .

*Heavenly Father, I love You. Thank You for first loving me. Help me to show my love for You through my lifestyle and attitude. Amen.*

# DAY 166
# FAST

*"When you fast, do not look somber."*
Matthew 6:16 niv

People engage in all kinds of fasting fads these days. Juice fasts. Cleansing fasts. TV fasts. Fasting has become a status symbol of sorts. It's a true sign of a society that has plenty to choose as a fast.

For other people in the world, fasting is sadly just a way of life.

Yet fasting was meant to be a kind of prayer. The idea is to deliberately go without something (usually food) to focus on God and on His will for your life. It's a time to be reminded of who provides everything we eat and drink. It's a time to be reminded who we depend on and who we can trust with all our needs and desires. Often, it is meant to be a time to bring a particular desire or concern before God.

The fasting is not for God. It is not a show for others. The fasting is a very personal decision to engage in a small act of sacrifice, and in so doing remind yourself of the much greater sacrifice God has made for you.

So if you do fast, don't make a show of it. Don't advertise it. Do it with a right heart and mind, and God will certainly honor your efforts.

. . . . . . . . . . . . . . . . . . . . . . . . . . . . . . . . . . . . . . . . . . . . . . .

*Dear God, help me to focus on You more,
no matter what else is going on in my life. Amen.*

# DAY 167

## WHAT IS YOUR REQUEST?

*And pray in the Spirit on all occasions with all kinds of prayers and
requests. With this in mind, be alert and always keep on praying.*
EPHESIANS 6:18 NIV

Be patient. What we may view as a nonanswer may simply be God saying,
"Wait" or "I have something better for you." He *will* answer. Keep in mind that
His ways are not our ways, nor are His thoughts our thoughts.

God knows what He's doing, even when He allows trials in our lives.
We might think that saving a loved one from difficulty is a great idea—but
God, in His wisdom, may decide that would be keeping them (or us) from an
opportunity for spiritual growth. Since we don't know all of God's plans, we
must simply lay our requests before Him and trust Him to do what is right.
He will never fail us!

* * *

*Father God, here are my needs. I lay them at Your feet, walking away
unburdened and assured that You have it all under control. Thank You! Amen.*

# DAY 168
# IT MAY HAPPEN LIKE THIS

*You, Lord, keep my lamp burning; my God turns my darkness into light.*
PSALM 18:28 NIV

That nighttime routine with your child may happen like this. You've spent the last hour trying unsuccessfully to get little Penelope to go to sleep. First is a story, then a glass of water. Then she needs an extra hug. Then she wants to go to the bathroom. When all is finally as quiet as a sleepy mouse, you tiptoe away.

Then comes the big howling cry, "There's a monster under my bed!" What do you do? You talk away her fears, say a prayer, and kiss her forehead.

Haven't you too been afraid of the dark? Those times you felt more comfortable singing when passing through a dark passage? Or the times you rushed to a light switch and felt such a surge of relief when the light came on? With God by our side, there is no reason to fear the dark, or the enemy, or anything the world can do to us. Those words in Psalm 18 are so comforting, aren't they? The Lord will keep our lamp burning brightly, and He will turn our darkness into light!

The Lord's light can never be diminished, and that light is brighter than any sun, more holy than any other being, and more beautiful than anything we have ever known.

When we pray, we step into that holy light. What do we have to fear?

* * * * * * * * * * * * * * * * * * * * * * * * * * * * * * * * * * * *

*Lord, You are the source of all light and all that is good.*
*Bring me into Your holy presence. Amen.*

# DAY 169
# PUT ON A HAPPY FACE

*He restoreth my soul: he leadeth me in the*
*paths of righteousness for his name's sake.*
PSALM 23:3 KJV

Be encouraged. The Lord has promised He hears our pleas and knows our situations. He will never leave us. He will guide us through our difficulties and beyond them. In *Streams in the Desert*, Mrs. Charles E. Cowman states, "Every misfortune, every failure, every loss may be transformed. God has the power to transform all misfortunes into 'God-sends.' "

Today we should turn our thoughts and prayers toward Him. Focus on a hymn or a praise song and play it in your mind. Praise chases away the doldrums and tips our lips up in a smile. With a renewed spirit of optimism and hope, we can thank the Giver of all things good. Thankfulness to the Father can turn our plastic smiles into real ones, and as the psalm states, our souls will be restored.

- - - - - - - - - - - - - - - - - - - - - - - - - - - - - - - - - - - - - - -

*Father, I'm down in the dumps today. You are my unending*
*source of strength. Gather me in Your arms for always. Amen.*

# DAY 170
## MARY'S GLORY

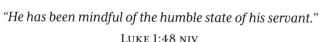

*"He has been mindful of the humble state of his servant."*
LUKE 1:48 NIV

What is striking about Mary's prayer in Luke 1 is the confidence. Here is Mary, a young girl in a completely unheard-of situation. She is carrying the child of God in her womb. Strange and wonderful things are happening around her. People are having experiences and dreams and hearing from God in ways they never have. Mary receives Elizabeth's blessing with all the composure of a woman five times her age.

It is clear to see this confidence does not come through the mind of a teenager, ruled by emotions and hormones. It comes from a deeper place. "My soul glorifies the Lord and my spirit rejoices in God my Savior" (vv. 46–47). Mary knew she was not anything special on her own. She knew also, from deep within, that God was doing something great not just for her but for generations. In the same way she had heard as a child the stories of the amazing things He had done for her ancestors, she could see with certainty the Lord's hand at work now in her own time, her own village, her own body.

Let us come to God and praise Him with the same certainty Mary had. Let us read His Word and remember His marvelous works. Then let us pray with a humble heart and ask Him to open our eyes to the work He is doing today in our world, in ourselves.

. . . . . . . . . . . . . . . . . . . . . . . . . . . . . . . . . . . . . . . . .

*My soul glorifies You, my Lord. Amen.*

# DAY 171
# HOLD ON!

*Let us not become weary in doing good, for at the proper
time we will reap a harvest if we do not give up.*
GALATIANS 6:9 NIV

When Elijah fled for his life in fear of Jezebel's wrath, depression and discouragement tormented him. Exhausted, he prayed for God to take his life, and then he fell asleep. When he awoke, God sent an angel with provisions to strengthen his weakened body. Only then was he able to hear God's revelation that provided the direction and assistance he needed.

God hears our pleas even when He seems silent. The problem is that we cannot hear Him because of physical and mental exhaustion. Rest is key to our restoration.

Just when the prophet thought he could go on no longer, God provided the strength, peace, and encouragement to continue. He does the same for us today. When we come to the end of our rope, God ties a knot. And like Elijah, God will do great things in and through us if we will just hold on.

- - - - - - - - - - - - - - - - - - - - - - - - - - - - - - - - - - - - - - - -

*Dear Lord, help me when I can no longer help myself. Banish
my discouragement, and give me the rest and restoration
I need so that I might hear Your voice. Amen.*

# DAY 172

# CONSIDER THE SOURCE

*The heart of the discerning acquires knowledge,*
*for the ears of the wise seek it out.*
PROVERBS 18:15 NIV

Joy asked her eight-year-old daughter why she had tried to climb the tree that she fell from. Lily looked up from the cast on her broken arm and tearfully admitted that the neighbor boy had told her to climb the tree, so she thought it would be okay. Joy explained to Lily the importance of considering the source of information before making a decision. Although the neighbor boy was two years older, Lily would have been wise to double-check with an adult. Lily was suffering the consequences of being gullible.

Like Lily, we need to consider the source of information. In the current age of twenty-four-hour news coverage, the same story is reported over and over. It's easy to believe that it must be true when we hear or read a story repeatedly. However, we need to listen with care to what is actually said. People can stretch or omit parts of the truth to sensationalize or distort a story. Discerning listeners use their minds and available resources to verify information before they accept its truth. At a minimum, an internet search engine can be used for research.

We don't need to doubt the Word of God; we need to doubt the words of man. We need to take time to consider the source of information and wisely seek its confirmation.

*Lord, thank You for giving us the ability to wisely discern true*
*knowledge and not be gullible to false information. Amen.*

# DAY 173
# KNOW MY HEART

*Search me, God, and know my heart; test me and know my anxious thoughts.*
*See if there is any offensive way in me, and lead me in the way everlasting.*
PSALM 139:23–24 NIV

If you know anything about rodents, you know they like to run and hide in dark corners. They don't generally come out and present themselves in the bright light.

Sometimes our hearts are so full of wrongdoing that we tend to have a few rodential habits of our own. When our actions and thoughts are not so holy, then we hope they aren't placed under a spotlight.

In Psalm 139, it encourages us to do the opposite. We should ask God to search our souls, to know us intimately, to test us, and know even our worries. We are to take it a step further and ask Him if there is any offensive way in us and to lead us in the way everlasting.

This biblical directive and divine scrutiny don't sound easy, since to voluntarily step into His light to be judged isn't on the top of our list of fun things to do. We are deeply concerned that He will find some offensive ways in us.

Perhaps one could ponder the scripture in this light: Wouldn't it be better to endure the Lord's discipline and become faithful and lovely in spirit than to enjoy the evil applause of Satan and lose our very souls?

How shall we then pray?

*Holy Spirit, please break down the walls around my heart and sweep out the dusty, dark places that harbor sin, bitterness, and distrust. Amen.*

# DAY 174
# WHEN PRAYER SEEMS IMPOSSIBLE

*Lord, save us! Lord, grant us success! Blessed is he who comes in
the name of the Lord. From the house of the Lord we bless you.*
PSALM 118:25–26 NIV

Sometimes the last thing on earth we feel like doing is praying.

We're angry. We're scared. We're exhausted, and we're world weary.

Maybe we've just had an argument with a close friend. Maybe we've just been admitted to the hospital with yet another debilitating illness. Maybe we are bone tired from working two jobs and still not making the rent. Maybe we feel as though our prayers are never heard. That we are truly alone. That life seems hopeless.

What in the world do we do?

Pray.

Yes even then. The book of Psalms is full of every manner of heart cry to the Almighty. Nothing is held back. Every tear is shed in those passages. Every weary thought is revealed. Every doubt and misery expressed. And what happened? God listened. He came near. He became the people's rescuer and redeemer. As in Bible times, God may not choose to lift us out of every storm, but when we cry out, He will be there with us, whether it's in a howling gale or still, blue sea.

Prayer is mighty because the One to whom we pray is mighty. Let us never forget.

*Savior, please be with me in my hour of need and bring me hope. Amen.*

# DAY 175

# SILENCE

*He was oppressed, and he was afflicted, yet he opened not his mouth; like a lamb that is led to the slaughter, and like a sheep that before its shearers is silent, so he opened not his mouth.*

ISAIAH 53:7 ESV

Jesus' silence can teach us important lessons. Underneath His silence was an implicit trust in His Father and His purposes. Christ knew who He was and what He had come to do.

Perhaps He was praying silently as He stood before Pilate. It is often in the stillness of our lives that we hear God best. When we take time to think, meditate on scripture, pray, and reflect, we find that we can indeed hear the still, small voice. Many of us avoid quiet and solitude with constant noise and busyness. But important things happen in the silence. The Father can speak; we can listen. We can speak, knowing He is listening. Trust is built in silence, and confidence strengthens in silence.

. . . . . . . . . . . . . . . . . . . . . . . . . . . . . . . . . . . . . . . . . .

*Lord Jesus, help me to learn from Your silence. Help me to trust You more so that I don't feel the need to explain myself. Give me the desire and the courage to be alone with You and learn to hear Your voice. Amen.*

# DAY 176
# BE INSPIRED!

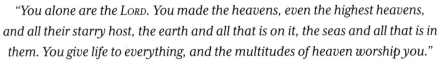

*"You alone are the Lord. You made the heavens, even the highest heavens, and all their starry host, the earth and all that is on it, the seas and all that is in them. You give life to everything, and the multitudes of heaven worship you."*
NEHEMIAH 9:6 NIV

When you wake up each morning, know that the One in charge is not only the Maker of all but a lavish and mystifying and beautifully beguiling Creator being.

His works stir our souls. Reach out of us. Embrace us. Delight us. Surprise us. He crafts such magnificent objects we cannot replicate them or even fully understand them, such as the mysteries of frost flowers, the northern lights, glowing plankton, moonbows, meat-eating plants, and red lightning—just to name a very few.

To think, we are made in His image—the One who created all the wonders of the earth, including you and me. We too have that imprint on us—that passion to create. We have the need to interact with the One who gave us those gifts. Jesus came to give us that connection to our Creator. Jesus came to give us eternal life and abundant life, which includes time spent with Him in creating marvels.

What can you create with God today as Father and daughter? Not *for* Him but *with* Him as collaborators in this supernatural dance?

Just ask Him, "Father, what can we do today?"

* * *

*Creator God, You are truly awesome and inspiring.*
*Thank You for the ability to create. Amen.*

# DAY 177

# FAITH, THE EMOTIONAL BALANCER

*But that no man is justified by the law in the sight of God,*
*it is evident: for, The just shall live by faith.*
GALATIANS 3:11 KJV

Emotions mislead us. One day shines with promise as we bounce out of bed in song, while the next day dims in despair and we'd prefer to hide under the bedcovers. One moment we forgive; the next we harbor resentment.

The emotional roller coaster thrusts us into mood changes and affects what we do, what we say, and the attitudes that define us.

It has been said that faith is the bird that feels the light and sings to greet the dawn while it is still dark. The Bible instructs us to live by faith—not by feelings. Faith assures us that daylight will dawn in our darkest moments, affirming God's presence so that even when we fail to pray and positive feelings fade, our moods surrender to song.

. . . . . . . . . . . . . . . . . . . . . . . . . . . . . . . . . . . . . . . . . . . . . . .

*Heavenly Father, I desire for my faith, not my emotions, to*
*dictate my life. I pray for balance in my hide-under-the-covers*
*days so that I might surrender to You in song. Amen.*

# DAY 178

# I WILL GIVE YOU REST

*The LORD replied, "My Presence will go with you, and I will give you rest."*
EXODUS 33:14 NIV

The world is full of clamor and shouts and unsavory whispers. Our attention is stolen at every turn. Even Christians can absorb and reflect the noise if they're not careful. They can take in that frenzy, that panic. That soul-wrenching fright.

Christ did not come to give us a spirit of fear. He did not come to condemn but to save. He came to give us a rich life in spirit and truth. He came with healing in His hands. He came with redemption and mercy, love most abundant.

Let us rest in these truths—rest in Him.

The Lord reaches out to you. He will take you by your outstretched hand and lead you to a restful place. By still waters that lap gently to the shore. A place that is far from the roaring crowds. Far from the clamor of fear. From the whispers of temptation. From the accusing cries of the enemy.

Yes, the Lord says, "My presence will go with you, and I will give you rest." Can you hear His gentle voice? He's calling us to sit a spell. To visit. To rest.

*Father, amid my trials and frustrations today, give me rest and peace in You. No matter how difficult my circumstances may be, help me to remember that You are more than capable and sufficient for me. Amen.*

## DAY 179

# FOLLOW THE LORD'S FOOTSTEPS

*"Come, follow me," Jesus said, "and I will send you out to fish for people."*
MATTHEW 4:19 NIV

Jesus asked His disciples to follow Him, and He asks us to do the same. It sounds simple, but following Jesus can be a challenge. Sometimes we become impatient, not wanting to wait on the Lord. We run ahead of Him by taking matters into our own hands and making decisions without consulting Him first. Or perhaps we aren't diligent to keep in step with Him. We fall behind, and soon Jesus seems so far away.

Following Jesus requires staying right on His heels. We need to be close enough to hear His whisper. Stay close to His heart by opening the Bible daily. Allow His Word to speak to your heart and give you direction. Throughout the day, offer up prayers for guidance and wisdom. Keep in step with Him, and His close presence will bless you beyond measure.

- - - - - - - - - - - - - - - - - - - - - - - - - - - - - - - - - - - - - - - - -

*Dear Lord, grant me the desire to follow You.*
*Help me not to run ahead or lag behind. Amen.*

# DAY 180
# PEPPER WITH SALT

*"You are the salt of the earth. But if the salt loses its saltiness,
how can it be made salty again? It is no longer good for anything,
except to be thrown out and trampled underfoot."*
MATTHEW 5:13 NIV

Gabby never said no when asked to help a good cause. As a stay-at-home mom, she felt obligated to be available whenever possible. Gabby had two teenage children active in after-school activities with booster clubs and fund-raisers. Plus, she volunteered at church and for two charities.

Her husband, Mark, believed Gabby did so much volunteer work that she had become overcommitted. He asked to sit down and discuss his concerns. Mark acknowledged that Christians should willingly give of their time and resources in salty service to others. However, he told Gabby that she was so busy trying to do good works that it might be hurting her effectiveness. He referred to Matthew 5:13 when he told Gabby that if she overextended herself, she would lose her saltiness and no longer be good for anything.

Gabby defensively explained how she juggled all her volunteer tasks with her family responsibilities. Mark reminded Gabby they had agreed to make their kids her first priority. They made sacrifices to have her at home because it was valuable to their family.

Gabby finally admitted that she had probably taken on more than she could do well. She liked her husband's suggestion that she sparingly pepper her life with service so that she could preserve her salty effectiveness.

* * * * * * * * * * * * * * * * * * * * * * * * * * * * * * * * * * * * * * * * * *

*Lord, thank You for showing me how to balance my
responsibilities with my salty service to others. Amen.*

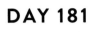

# DAY 181
# REMEMBERING HIS PROMISES

*Tell everyone about God's power. His majesty shines down on Israel; his strength is mighty in the heavens. God is awesome in his sanctuary. The God of Israel gives power and strength to his people. Praise be to God!*
PSALM 68:34–35 NLT

Do you ever find yourself dreaming of a place of safety? A place where you can close your eyes, rest your head, and let go of the stress and angst that follow you around like a shadow? It rarely matters what kind of season you are in—busy or calm—you always seem to feel an inner longing to find a place where there is nothing but peace.

Before you move on to the next thing on the list, take a moment to close your eyes. Don't reach for a book. Refuse to look at your phone. Keep your thoughts from wandering away. And simply fix your heart on the One who loves you. Think about His compassion. Dwell on His promises. Consider His majesty and the army of angels He commands. Have faith in the One He sent so you can forever be with Him.

Whether you need comfort, encouragement, or protection, He is the answer. Look first in His direction for clarity and understanding. He is close at hand and forever unchanging.

· · · · · · · · · · · · · · · · · · · · · · · · · · · · · · · · · · · · · · · · · · ·

*Lord, thank You for showing me that You are my everything. Through every day, through every year, I need only to fix my eyes on You—the author and perfecter of my faith. Amen.*

## DAY 182
# NO REGRETS

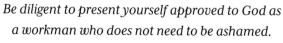

*Be diligent to present yourself approved to God as
a workman who does not need to be ashamed.*
2 TIMOTHY 2:15 NASB

Bonnie Ware nursed patients in the last twelve weeks of their lives. She recorded their dying epiphanies and compiled this top-five list:

1. I wish I'd had the courage to live a life true to myself, not what was expected of me.
2. I wish I hadn't worked so hard.
3. I wish I'd had the courage to express my feelings.
4. I wish I had stayed in touch with my friends.
5. I wish that I had let myself be happier.

God has given us a great gift—life. Some use it well and others waste it.

William Borden was a college freshman when he started a prayer group with three young men. It grew to thirteen hundred by his senior year. He cared for widows, orphans, and drunks and sought hard souls who needed the Gospel. He later pursued missions to Chinese Muslims, but Borden contracted spinal meningitis and died at age twenty-five. Inside his Bible, he had written: "No reserves. No retreats. No regrets."

In the parable of the sower, the master referred to the one who buried his money as a "wicked servant." But to the one who invested, he said, "Well done." Consider the investment of your life. If today was your last, would you be able to say, "No reserves. No retreats. No regrets"?

*Lord, I want to live my life to its fullest potential in the
kingdom so that when my time comes, I'm ready. Show
me how best to use the time You've given me. Amen.*

# DAY 183

# CHAPEL BELLS, TOLLING FOR THEE

*"They sing to the music of timbrel and lyre;*
*they make merry to the sound of the pipe."*
JOB 21:12 NIV

Stained-glass, arched windows and a steeple adorn a pure white chapel on a distant hill. How beautiful. How peaceful. How heartening. And the bells, oh how pretty are those chapel bells that ring out through the vales and through the villages to gladden every heart who hears their music.

It is a reminder to see beyond the mundane. Downturned faces will once again rise from the daily tedium and toil and witness the firmament—the swirling clouds, azure sky, and stars of night that shout His glory!

The tolling bells call to me and to you—as a reminder to gather together in worship, to seek, to fellowship, to share communion, to praise, to pray. To return to all the things—and the One—that are easily forgotten, easily set aside.

The bells ring of hope. Those in Christ have great reason to make merry, to shout in joy, to sing to the music of all kinds of instruments.

When we hear the chapel bells, let us remember to look up. To gather in worship. To raise our voices in song. To embrace the hope. And to prayerfully and excitedly share that hope with all who will listen.

. . . . . . . . . . . . . . . . . . . . . . . . . . . . . . . . . . . . . . .

*Lord, You are worthy of all praise. I want to worship*
*You every day, every hour, and every moment. Amen.*

# DAY 184
# A DIFFERENT CUP TO FILL

*O God, thou art my God; early will I seek thee.*
PSALM 63:1 KJV

King David resided over the nation of Israel and all that that entailed. Yet he found time to seek the counsel, mercy, and direction of God daily. The more responsibilities he assumed, the more he prayed and meditated on God's precepts. Well before David was inundated with worldly concerns, nagging obligations, and his administrative duties, the Bible suggests that he sought the Lord in the early morning hours.

If the king of Israel recognized his need to spend time with God, how much more should we? When we seek our heavenly Father before daily activities demand our attention, the Holy Spirit regenerates our spirits, and our cups overflow.

• • • • • • • • • • • • • • • • • • • • • • • • • • • • • • • • • • • • • • • •

*Dear Lord, I take this time to pray and spend time with You before I attend to daily responsibilities. Fill my cup with the presence and power of Your Spirit. Give me the wisdom and direction I need today. Amen.*

# DAY 185
# CAN'T YOU HEAR HIM WHISPER?

*He says, "Be still, and know that I am God."*
PSALM 46:10 NIV

Our society is so fast paced there is little time to take care of our mental and physical health, let alone our spiritual health. We are beings created for eternity, and we are made in the image of a supernatural God, and yet paying attention to our spiritual journey gets put off and off and off.

Until something terrible happens. Like a financial crisis. Or infidelity in our marriage. Or bad news at the doctor's office. Or a death in the family. Then we do far more than pause. We go into a full-body panic mode, drenched in fear, racing around, grasping at anything and everything, desperate for answers. For peace.

But had we been in close fellowship with the Lord all along, we wouldn't be so frantic, our spirits so riddled with terror. What we need to do is to be still and know that He is God. Know that He is still in control even though we think the bad news is in control. It's not. God is.

Life would be more peaceful, more focused, more infused with joy if we were already in the midst of communion with God when troubles come.

Can't you hear Him whisper to you, "Be still, and know that I am God"?

. . . . . . . . . . . . . . . . . . . . . . . . . . . . . . . . . . . . . . . . . .

*Lord, help me to want to spend time with You every day*
*of my life—in fair weather as well as stormy. Amen.*

# DAY 186
# REMEMBER

*"In the future your children will ask you, 'What do these stones mean?'*
*Then you can tell them, 'They remind us that the Jordan River stopped*
*flowing when the Ark of the Lord's Covenant went across.' These stones*
*will stand as a memorial among the people of Israel forever."*

JOSHUA 4:6–7 NLT

After God did this miraculous thing for the Israelites, He instructed them to build a memorial so that what He did for them would be remembered for generations. Future generations would remember that God took care of His people. The memorial would serve as a symbol of His power and faithfulness and would give hope to those in the future.

What has God done for you? It is just as important for us to build memorials in our lives—memorials that declare the goodness of God. These things remind us that, during hard times, God is still the same yesterday, today, and forever. They remind us in times of plenty that it is because of His goodness we can shout and dance with joy.

There is no one right way to remember what God has done. It can be through journaling or a photograph. It could be a vase sitting in your living room filled with little slips of paper with the ways God has provided written on them. Each of these ways is a means to an end, and that end is remembering the faithfulness of God.

*You have been so good to me, Lord! As I go through today,*
*remind me. Remind me of the big and the little things, that*
*my faith in You may grow and my joy increase. Amen.*

# DAY 187
## SWEET TO THE SOUL

*If we confess our sins, he is faithful and just and will forgive
us our sins and purify us from all unrighteousness.*
1 JOHN 1:9 NIV

A boy sneaks a big sugar cookie from Mom's cookie jar just before suppertime.

Does the boy sit at the table, calmly looking around, munching on the sweet treat innocently?

Probably not.

Most likely—since he knows his mother asked him not to eat a cookie before dinner because she loves him and wants him to eat a healthy dinner first—the boy will do what many boys do and hide in his room with his guilty pleasure.

The boy's mother—since she already knows about the incident because she really does have eyes in the back of her head—hopes that he will confess his folly. Would it really be that hard to come to her and say, "I'm sorry, Mom. I shouldn't have eaten the cookie. Will you forgive me?"

Repentance may feel uncomfortable but only for a short time. Usually Mom will forgive with a gentle warning and a hug.

God's love is far beyond our own, so we are safe in His perfect justice and mercy. We need not run and hide in our folly but go to Him instead. He is faithful and just and will forgive us our sins. Yes, repentance is such sweetness to the soul.

. . . . . . . . . . . . . . . . . . . . . . . . . . . . . . . . . . . . . . . . . . .

*Father God, I come to You now with all my sins both intentional
and unintentional. Thank You for Your unlimited grace. Amen.*

# DAY 188
## POWER UP

*The Spirit of God, who raised Jesus from the dead, lives in you.*
ROMANS 8:11 NLT

It's natural to want to do things on our own. We all want to be independent and strong. When faced with a challenge, the first thing we do is try to work it out in our own skill and ability—within our own power. But there's another way.

We don't have to go it alone. Our heavenly Father wants to help. All we have to do is ask. He has already made His power available to His children. Whatever we face, wherever we go, whatever dreams we have for our lives, let's take courage and know that anything is possible when we draw on the power of God.

. . . . . . . . . . . . . . . . . . . . . . . . . . . . . . . . . . . . . . . . . . . . . .

*Father, help me to remember that You are always*
*with me, ready to help me do all things. Amen.*

# DAY 189
## AS PURE AS RAINWATER

*Hatred stirs up conflict, but love covers over all wrongs.*
PROVERBS 10:12 NIV

Have you ever seen a rain barrel filled after a good storm? That water is clean and refreshing. But if you take a big stick and whip up the contents, soon the dregs will rise and whirl. Suddenly, what was clean is now a dirty mess. That visual is a good one for Proverbs 10:12, which reminds us that hatred stirs up old quarrels.

When we choose to hold on to grudges, hatred seeps into our hearts. It's like we're carrying around a big stick, and we're more than ready to whip up some dregs by bringing up an argument from the past. This is a common way to live but not a godly or healthy one.

What's the answer?

Love.

When we love others, we will overlook insults whether they were intended or not. Does that seem like an impossible task using these feeble shells of ours?

It is impossible in our own humanness.

But with the supernatural power of the Holy Spirit, we can overcome this need to stir up trouble, and we can forgive freely and love abundantly—just as Christ has done for us. So let us come not with a big stick but with a spirit as refreshing and as pure as rainwater.

* * * * *

*Holy Spirit, please take away any tendency in me to bicker.*
*Make me into a woman who loves with my whole heart*
*and who is an instrument of Your peace. Amen.*

# DAY 190
# BOLDLY WE COME

*God's free gift leads to our being made right with God,*
*even though we are guilty of many sins.*
ROMANS 5:16 NLT

Why do you think it is that, as a general population of people, we often assume that God is out to get us? We tend to jump immediately to the notion that God is angry with us and ready to bring down the hammer. We become afraid to go to church or read the Bible—thinking that as soon as we enter the building or crack the cover, we will drown in waves of guilt and condemnation.

We even become too afraid to pray.

This must be one of the devil's most effective schemes—to convince us to fear talking with God—when talking with God is what will ultimately transform us from the inside out. Indeed, prayer is what we were created for. We were created for a relationship with Him—the entire Bible is the story of our being restored to that relationship.

The next time you are afraid to pray, refuse the fear. Know in confidence that, unlike the devil, you are covered by the blood of the Lamb and can enter freely into His presence. You can enter freely because He chose to open the way to you.

. . . . . . . . . . . . . . . . . . . . . . . . . . . . . . . . . . . . . . . . . .

*I will enter into Your presence and sit and talk with You.*
*I can feel You restore my soul, because this is what I*
*was made for. This is what I've been missing. Amen.*

# DAY 191
# WORDS GONE BAD

*May these words of my mouth and this meditation of my heart*
*be pleasing in your sight, LORD, my Rock and my Redeemer.*
PSALM 19:14 NIV

There's a fuzzy, ripe peach in the grocery store, and it has your name on it. It's juicy, fragrant, and sweet as candy. You tenderly bring it home and set it in the bottom of your crisper in the fridge. And then you promptly forget about it.

Uh-oh.

Well, that same luscious, fuzzy peach will soon be covered with the ugliest and fuzziest green monster-mold you have ever seen, making it impossible to eat. Impossible for anything of good use. That is the way of words gone bad.

Once our words are spoken, once they have tumbled out of our mouths, we can never get them back. They are like the water that plunges from a cliff into the sea. It just keeps on going, flowing and changing everything it touches. That water cannot come back. Our words cannot come back into our mouths. Yes, we can apologize and make amends. We can ask the Lord to forgive us, and He will keep His promise. Yet the sting of those thoughtless remarks can sometimes last a lifetime in the recipient's heart as well as in our own spirits.

A helpful daily prayer would be to ask the Lord to temper our words with wisdom and love. That what we say will not go bad like a rotten piece of fruit. But that our words will be pleasing and good and usable in His sight!

* * * * * * * * * * * * * * * * * * * * * * * * * * * * * * * * * * * * * * * * * * * * * * * * * *

*God, help my words to always be kind, compassionate, and uplifting. Amen.*

# DAY 192

# GOD'S MOUNTAIN SANCTUARY

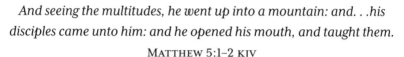

*And seeing the multitudes, he went up into a mountain: and. . .his*
*disciples came unto him: and he opened his mouth, and taught them.*
MATTHEW 5:1–2 KJV

Jesus often retreated to a mountain to pray. There He called His disciples to depart from the multitudes so that He could teach them valuable truths—the lessons we learn from nature. Don't fret; obey God's gentle promptings, and simply flow in the path He clears.

Do you yearn for a place where problems evaporate like the morning dew? Do you need a place of solace? God is wherever you are—behind a bedroom door, in your favorite chair, or even at a sink full of dirty dishes. Come away and enter God's mountain sanctuary.

• • • • • • • • • • • • • • • • • • • • • • • • • • • • • • • • • • • • • •

*Heavenly Father, I long to hear Your voice and to flow in the path You clear*
*before me. Help me to find sanctuary in Your abiding presence. Amen.*

# DAY 193
# HIS LOVING EYE IS ON YOU

*I will instruct you and teach you in the way you should*
*go; I will counsel you with my loving eye on you.*
PSALM 32:8 NIV

Imagine you are asked to walk through a long hallway, but then as you travel along, you discover that the hallway is more like a maze with many passageways to choose from. Then you discover that the farther you go into those corridors, the more they are shrouded in darkness. You can't tell for sure which way to go. The shadows become sinister. You hear whispers, but they don't sound encouraging or helpful. Feeling frightened and alone, you frantically run this way and that. You stumble in the darkness and cry out to God.

Suddenly, someone switches on all the lights, and you can see clearly. Warm, pure light vanquishes the darkness. Now as you walk along, you can maneuver around the perilous choices and see which path will take you on your way. Your footing becomes stable and your heartbeat steady.

So it goes with prayer. It lights our path. It is a way for God to guide us through life so we will know which course to take—in fact, His will for us.

Have you spent time in prayer today? God's loving eye is on you, and He will counsel you in the way you should go.

. . . . . . . . . . . . . . . . . . . . . . . . . . . . . . . . . . . . . . . . . . .

*Lord, help me to remember to spend time in prayer*
*every day so I might know Your will. Amen.*

# DAY 194
# BEAUTIFULLY IMPERFECT

*Yet I am confident I will see the Lord's goodness*
*while I am here in the land of the living.*
PSALM 27:13 NLT

Being in process is not pretty. In fact, sometimes it's downright ugly. When life gets too busy and overwhelming, oftentimes we snap. There is only so much our minds can sort through and only so much our tired bodies can handle.

Remember—we must give ourselves grace. We must allow ourselves to be imperfect. Yes, we want to handle every situation with finesse and poise, but sometimes trying to achieve that goal only makes the situation worse. We are exhausted in every way, and we cannot handle it the way we want. If we are completely honest, we only show our worst to one, maybe two people we trust. Everyone else gets the dressed-up version and the still-smiling face.

We are imperfect, so let's find some comfort in that. We can accept that we are broken and work from there. A lot of the time, we stress ourselves out by trying to be flawless. But when we put that type of obsessive striving aside, we can sort through the pieces with a clear head because we're not hindered by trying to do it "just right." There is freedom in giving ourselves permission to be imperfect.

*Oh God, I need You more than ever. I am broken into a thousand pieces. I will find comfort in Your peace that passes understanding and in Your love that knows no limits. Amen.*

# DAY 195
# NO SHRINKING VIOLETS HERE

*"Have I not commanded you? Be strong and courageous. Do not be afraid; do not be discouraged, for the Lord your God will be with you wherever you go."*
JOSHUA 1:9 NIV

When the world says, "Boo," do you jump? It's very hard not to. Right? Our days can be arduous and our nights riddled with terrors. Our spirits grow bone-weary and our hearts skittish and faint. So, when people mean to harm us or Satan comes to attack us, we feel like running to hide in a safe little closet or crawling in bed and pulling the covers over our heads for a day.

Or a month.

Until we sense that life has decided to settle down. But the problem is, just as soon as the wave of suffering is over, we see another storm brewing on the horizon. How can we ride these relentless storms for a lifetime and make it safely to the shores of heaven?

Reading God's Word, staying connected to a Bible-believing church, and praying are the only answers in these perilous times. If we remain faithful to following Christ, we will be able to rise up and say to the world with confidence, "Lord, I will be courageous. I will not fear what the world can do to me. I will not become discouraged, since I know You will be with me wherever I go."

. . . . . . . . . . . . . . . . . . . . . . . . . . . . . . . . . . . . . . .

*Father, I have complete victory through You. With You on my side,*
*I have nothing to fear. Help me to fully trust in You. Amen.*

# DAY 196
# STAND IN THE GAP

*"I looked for someone among them who would build up the*
*wall and stand before me in the gap on behalf of the land*
*so I would not have to destroy it, but I found no one."*
EZEKIEL 22:30 NIV

Each prayer request you offer up to God is important to you, and when you ask others to pray, you're counting on them to help carry you through the tough times.

It's easy in the busyness of life to overlook a request someone else has made. Maybe you don't know the person very well or you don't really understand what he or she is going through. Perhaps the request came in an email that you quickly glanced at and then deleted.

Don't delay. Take time right when you receive a request to talk to the Lord on the requester's behalf. Be the bridge that carries that person through the valley of darkness back to the mountaintop of joy.

. . . . . . . . . . . . . . . . . . . . . . . . . . . . . . . . . . . . . .

*Heavenly Father, help me to have a heart of compassion for those I*
*know and even for those I don't know who need Your comfort and*
*love. Help me never to be too busy to pray for them. Amen.*

# DAY 197

# REMEMBER THE MIRACLES

*He came to Jesus at night and said, "Rabbi, we know that*
*you are a teacher who has come from God. For no one could*
*perform the signs you are doing if God were not with him."*
JOHN 3:2 NIV

People today are cynical about miracles. Even some Christians wonder if miracles are perhaps a Bible-times phenomenon and no longer part of modern-day life. Disbelief and cynicism are easy emotions. In fact, some of the Israelites felt this way even after they had witnessed many signs and wonders from God. How many miracles does it take for humanity to finally have faith? The kind of belief that doesn't wobble like a tower of Jell-O?

If we look, we will see miracles—even daily. Miracles come in all shapes and sizes. And when they do come, thank God for them. Tell others about them so that they too might be uplifted. Write them down. Memorize them and keep them close to your heart. That way, when hardships come—and they will come eventually—you can remember all that God has done for you.

Then when the enemy of your soul comes to tempt and discourage you, you will be able to stand strong. You will keep hold of joy. You will live with victory.

Acknowledging and celebrating these wonders from God is part of a contented Christian life. What miracles will you praise God for today?

*God, help me to remember all the miracles*
*in my life, both big and small. Amen.*

# DAY 198
# YOUR FIRST LOVE

*"And you shall love the Lord your God with all your heart, and with
all your soul, and with all your mind, and with all your strength."*
MARK 12:30 NASB

Remember when you first fell in love with your significant other? Every minute apart seemed like an eternity! You couldn't wait until the next time you could be together. You thought about him all the time. You talked about him all the time. Everything reminded you of him. Just hearing his name made you smile. Face it, you were obsessed with him, right?

Well, that's how we should feel about Jesus! After all, He is our first love, yet it's easy to lose sight of that fact in the busyness of everyday life. So if you've lost that "loving feeling" when it comes to your Lord and Savior, then it's time to fall back in love. How do you do that? Bottom line: The more time you spend with Jesus, the more time you'll want to spend with Him. Having your devotional/prayer time shouldn't feel like an obligation; rather, it should be exciting and wonderful. You should look forward to it!

And here's the best part. The God of this universe is looking forward to spending time with you! He can't wait to reveal things to you in His Word. He adores you, and He has been waiting for you.

* * * * * * * * * * * * * * * * * * * * * * * * * * * * * * * * * * * * * * *

*Lord, I love You. Help me to always keep You in first place in my life. Amen.*

# DAY 199
# HE HOLDS THE BLUEPRINT

*"And even the very hairs of your head are all numbered."*
MATTHEW 10:30 NIV

We spend our lives searching for someone to understand us, to "get" us. Don't we? When we find it, what a blessing! Yet the understanding we long for comes freely from the Almighty. Even though there are billions of humans on our planet, no two people are just alike. Not even identical twins. We each are uniquely and wonderfully made. It is our loving Creator who holds that blueprint—which He considers precious—that has your name on it.

Imagine God so loving the world—loving us—that His "knowing" extends to the number of hairs on our heads. He knows every single thing about us. The kind of friends we enjoy. Our favorite ice cream, favorite pets, and favorite hobbies. The things that tickle our funny bones. The things that make us cry at the movies. Every secret we've hidden. Our deepest longings. Our worst nightmares. Yes, the Lord knows every nuance and detail about us. He loves us dearly.

Knowing these truths will help us to pray, since being loved and understood by the One to whom we are praying makes all the difference in the way we begin, "Dear Lord. . ."

· · · · · · · · · · · · · · · · · · · · · · · · · · · · · · · · · · · · · · · ·

*Thank You for knowing and loving every single part of me.*
*Help me to run to You when I feel misunderstood or forgotten. Amen.*

# DAY 200
# AVAILABLE 24/7

*I call on you, my God, for you will answer me;*
*turn your ear to me and hear my prayer.*
PSALM 17:6 NIV

We've all felt the frustration of that black hole called voice mail. It is rare to reach a real, honest-to-goodness, breathing human being the first time we dial a telephone number.

Fortunately, our God is always available. He can be reached at any hour of the day or night and every day of the year—including weekends and holidays! When we pray, we don't have to worry about disconnections, hang-ups, or poor reception. We will never be put on hold or our prayers diverted to another department. The Bible assures us that God is eager to hear our petitions and that He welcomes our prayers of thanksgiving. The psalmist David wrote of God's response to those who put their trust in Him: "He will call on me, and I will answer him" (Psalm 91:15 NIV). David had great confidence that God would hear his prayers. And we can too!

*Dear Lord, thank You for always being there for me. Whether I am*
*on a mountaintop and just want to praise Your name or I need*
*Your comfort and encouragement, I can count on You. Amen.*

# DAY 201

# LAUGHING AT THE DAYS TO COME

*She is clothed with strength and dignity; she can laugh at the days to come.*
PROVERBS 31:25 NIV

You mean a woman of God can laugh at the days to come? Really? Wow. Most of the world wakes up each morning under a black cloud of regret and a debilitating fear of the future. That sounds more realistic, right? To laugh at the future is hard to imagine. To see hope instead of futility? Promise in the pain? What would that kind of woman look like? Sound like?

Perhaps a woman of God as described in Proverbs 31 doesn't necessarily have a lot of confidence in herself but rather in God. Perhaps she trusts so implicitly in His divine plan and goodness that she can sleep deeply. She can wake up refreshed each morning.

And this woman of God knows some truths—that God will indeed work everything for good in her life. That He is watching over her comings and goings, and nothing will befall her that He can't handle. She knows that this earthly life is temporary. That heaven is not only for real but forever. Knowing these truths all the way to her soul gives her peace and joy, and it shows in her countenance. Yes, and even in her laugh.

. . . . . . . . . . . . . . . . . . . . . . . . . . . . . . . . . . . . . . . . .

*Jesus, help me trust in You every hour of every day, and let me be*
*so full of peace that I too can laugh at the days to come. Amen.*

## DAY 202
# THE RIGHT TOOLS FOR THE JOB

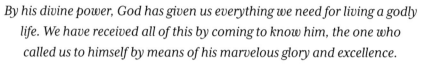

*By his divine power, God has given us everything we need for living a godly life. We have received all of this by coming to know him, the one who called us to himself by means of his marvelous glory and excellence.*

2 PETER 1:3 NLT

Have you ever tried to hang a picture without a hammer? Or make a dress without a sewing machine? Or bake a pie without an oven? Trying to do a job without the right tools can be difficult, inefficient, and even impossible. Having the right tools for the job can mean the difference between frustration and success.

As we journey through the Christian life, we may feel frustration. We may feel like we lack the patience to deal with a difficult spouse or the forgiveness to let go of anger toward someone who has hurt us. We may become tired and discouraged, lacking the energy to continue the Lord's work. But the Bible promises us that God has already given us everything we need. From time to time, the tools we need may not seem readily available, but we can hold tight to the truth that His divine power has made them available to us. The more we come to know Him, the more we realize our calling. We can be assured that He will equip us with everything we need to do His work.

. . . . . . . . . . . . . . . . . . . . . . . . . . . . . . . . . . . . . . . . . . .

*Father, thank You for Your divine power and for giving me everything I need to live the Christian life. When I feel discouraged, remind me to seek to know You more so that I can experience Your great and perfect promises. Amen.*

# WHERE SHALL I PRAY?

*But Jesus often withdrew to lonely places and prayed.*
LUKE 5:16 NIV

Are you searching for the best place to talk to God? One might think of a great cathedral or perhaps a hometown chapel. Or maybe you'd like to be near a quiet stream or sitting under a favorite willow tree with the breeze giving sway to the leaves. What about one's front porch early in the morning before everyone rises or the solitary space of a prayer closet? Fortunately, all of these places work because God is omnipresent. Since the Lord is all around us, He can hear our pleas and our praises wherever we happen to be—in a crowded bus or a stadium full of people or even an airport terminal bustling with noisy travelers.

We know from God's Word that Jesus often withdrew to quiet places to pray. The culture during Jesus' time—even without anything fast-paced or high-tech—could still have created enough "busy" to make seeking out a solitary place important. Vital, really.

So, even though we can pray anywhere and everywhere, let us also seek solitary places to talk to God. We can regain our sense of peace—His peace. To hear His words of guidance. To remember that His power is sufficient for every day, every task.

Where is your favorite quiet place to talk to God?

. . . . . . . . . . . . . . . . . . . . . . . . . . . . . . . . . . . . . . . . .

*Lord, help me to carve out pockets of time to seek You in quiet,*
*solitary prayer. You deserve my complete, undivided attention. Amen.*

# DAY 204
## RUN THE RACE

*Therefore, since we are surrounded by such a great cloud of witnesses,*
*let us throw off everything that hinders and the sin that so easily entangles.*
*And let us run with perseverance the race marked out for us.*

HEBREWS 12:1 NIV

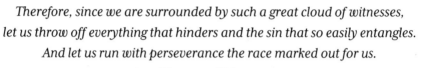

A Christian's journey is much like a marathon. The road isn't always easy. Spiritual training is required to keep going and finish the race. Train by reading and obeying God's Word. Discipline yourself to keep your eyes on Jesus at all times. Be determined to spend time in prayer.

The writer of Hebrews reminds us that others are watching. Let their cheers bring encouragement. Let their presence inspire and motivate. Be quick to confess sin in order to run the race unhindered. Persevere. Jesus waits at the finish line. The reward will be well worth it!

*Dear Lord, help me run this Christian race with perseverance. Amen.*

# DAY 205
# REFRESHMENT

*A generous person will prosper; whoever refreshes others will be refreshed.*
PROVERBS 11:25 NIV

Maybe you've hit a low point in your year already. Things aren't going as planned. You feel stuck at your job or stifled in a relationship. Maybe you're having a bad year. Or even just a bad hair day.

At any moment when you feel disappointed or unlucky or down, try this: Find someone who is in need—maybe someone who is also feeling knocked down—and do something for them. It doesn't have to be a big something. A fountain drink, a small bouquet, a bar of chocolate, a good book. Maybe just call and say hi or send a card.

The person doesn't even have to be someone you know. Go to a nursing home and read to someone who can't see anymore. Just spend some time listening to a person's story. Go to a bus stop and hand out free bottles of water. Go to the grocery store and offer people help with carrying groceries. Buy someone's coffee in the drive-through line at the coffee shop.

Once you've done some act of kindness or generosity, stop and note how you feel. Is life a little bit brighter? If it isn't, try again. And if it is, try again. You will soon find that the more you give to others, the better you get at it and the more you will feel refreshed by God.

. . . . . . . . . . . . . . . . . . . . . . . . . . . . . . . . . . . . . . . . . . .

*Dear Giver of all good things, thank You for Your blessings. Help us to see them all around us, especially in our service to others. Amen.*

# DAY 206

## EMBRACING PAIN

*But he said to me, "My grace is sufficient for you, for my power is
made perfect in weakness." Therefore I will boast all the more gladly
about my weaknesses, so that Christ's power may rest on me.*

2 CORINTHIANS 12:9 NIV

Theologians have speculated on the nature of Paul's thorn in the flesh. We
don't know much about it except that it must have tortured him. Paul says in
Corinthians that he begged God—three times—to remove this thorn from him.

God always answers prayer but often not in the way we want Him to.
God could have healed Paul of this thorn, but He chose not to. Why? So His
power could be felt profoundly—"so that Christ's power may rest on me," Paul
says. Physical and emotional pain have a way of quickening our hearts toward
God. When we are pain-free and trouble-free, we tend to think we can handle
things on our own. We acquire a false sense of strength. On the other hand,
pain gets our attention. If you are in pain, whether physical or emotional, be
reminded that God hears your prayer. Our pain can be a reminder to trust in
God's strength.

. . . . . . . . . . . . . . . . . . . . . . . . . . . . . . . . . . . . . . . . .

*Father, I confess that I don't like pain. Like Paul, I have often begged
You to remove my weakness. I long for comfort and to live a pain-
free life. But I know that, as my Father, You know what's best for
me. Help me to rest in Your power when I feel weak. Amen.*

# DAY 207
# A FACE LIT WITH JOY

*Do not be anxious about anything, but in every situation, by prayer and petition, with thanksgiving, present your requests to God. And the peace of God, which transcends all understanding, will guard your hearts and your minds in Christ Jesus.*

PHILIPPIANS 4:6–7 NIV

Sometimes when we bow our heads, we feel a little hesitant in addressing God, knowing He is the Creator of all things. It's certainly not the same as approaching our earthly father or our boss, teacher, or pastor. So, we sometimes approach God with trepidation.

Fortunately, God's Word gives us direction even in prayer. First, we are not to spend our lives wringing our hands in worry. If we have concerns and requests, we should present them to God and trust Him with the answer. His response might not be what we asked for or on our timetable, but He will be faithful because He loves us.

We are also to make our appeals with a thankful heart, rather than with a muttering and grumbling spirit, since the Lord is good and He knows how to give good gifts to His children. When we follow these divine instructions, the Lord will give us peace, a peace that is beyond human understanding. It is the kind of calm and sweet serenity that will make all those who meet us ask, "What gives your heart courage, and what is it that makes your face light up with joy?"

• • • • • • • • • • • • • • • • • • • • • • • • • • • • • • • • • • • •

*Lord, I surrender to You every worry, fear, and burden. You are more than sufficient for me. Amen.*

## DAY 208

# LEARNING AS WE GROW

*"But I am only a little child and do not know how to carry out my duties."*
1 KINGS 3:7 NIV

When King David died, Solomon became the king of Israel. Just like a child who does not yet know how to put away his toys, Solomon confesses that he does not know how to carry out his duties as king of Israel. Instead of sitting down on his throne in despair, though, Solomon calls on the name of the Lord for help.

As Christians, we are sometimes like little children. We know what our duties as Christians are, but we do not know how to carry them out. Just like Solomon, we can ask God for help and guidance in the completion of our responsibilities. God hears our prayers and is faithful in teaching us our duties, just as He was faithful to Solomon in teaching him his.

· · · · · · · · · · · · · · · · · · · · · · · · · · · · · · · · · · · · · · · · · · · ·

*Dear Lord, thank You for being willing to teach me my Christian responsibilities. Help me to learn willingly and eagerly. Amen.*

# DAY 209
# EXPECTATIONS

*"But love your enemies, do good to them, and lend
to them without expecting to get anything back."*
LUKE 6:35 NIV

Do you feel entitled to a certain kind of treatment from others? Think about that for a minute. Think about some of the most annoying things that happen to you on a regular basis. You have to wait in line longer than you like at the so-called fast-food restaurant. You order something online, and the store sends you the wrong thing. You do a good deed, and no one notices. You give generously (so you think), and no one pays you back.

How much do you expect from others? from strangers? from friends? from enemies? from God?

Whatever your level of expectation, take a step back and evaluate what that says about your relationship with that person. It may be a good thing—for example, you expect faithfulness from your spouse because of the vows you've taken. But it may be that you have placed too much importance on your part in this equation. Should you get something simply because you have given something? Is that the requirement? Or rather is the requirement to give cheerfully, with or without a reward?

Jesus came to turn the "eye for an eye" kind of justice on its head. He came to say that loving God with all your heart, soul, mind, and strength means giving differently. Giving big. And quite likely getting *nothing* back.

* * * * * * * * * * * * * * * * * * * * * * * * * * * * * * * * * * * * * * * * * *

*Dear Lord, help me to give with a heart like Yours. Amen.*

## DAY 210
# THE PATH TO GOD'S WILL

*All the paths of the Lord are lovingkindness and truth to*
*those who keep His covenant and His testimonies.*
PSALM 25:10 NASB

It's an age-old question: What is God's will for my life? It's easy to agonize over this question, pondering which path to take and fearfully wondering what will happen if we take a wrong step. But God's will is not necessarily a matter of choosing precisely the right step in each and every situation. This verse teaches that we should focus on God's covenant and His testimony. As we do so, the journey becomes part of the destination.

God doesn't always give us a clear road map, but He does clearly ask us to keep His covenant and His testimonies. When we do so, our individual steps will become clearer, and we will find ourselves more and more in step with His will. As He guides us closer to our destination, we will find much joy in the journey.

*Lord, when I agonize over which way to take, help me to focus*
*on Your covenant and Your testimonies. Help me to trust You*
*to lead me on the paths You want me to take, knowing that*
*when I follow Your Word, I am always in Your will. Amen.*

# DAY 211

# A SPECIAL WINDOW OF OPPORTUNITY

*Then people brought little children to Jesus for him*
*to place his hands on them and pray for them.*
MATTHEW 19:13 NIV

People are very willing to tell you their troubles. Over coffee. Over the fence. Over the counter. Over everything. Friends, family, acquaintances, even strangers will sometimes tell you the most private details of their ongoing ailments and travails. Rarely will they refuse you if you say you're willing to pray for them during your quiet time with the Lord. This can be a divine appointment that can be a multifaceted opportunity.

Think of the unbeliever and how an offer of prayer might lead the discussion to spiritual matters and then provide an opening to mention the good news of the Gospel.

Jesus showed us by example how important it is to intercede for others. Let us pray for ourselves, yes, but let's not neglect the needs of others. A habit of praying for others will cause us to think beyond our own lives, and it will help us lead a more Christ-centered life. The scriptures tell us that the prayer of a righteous person is powerful and effective. What encouragement! What divine assurance!

Who might you pray for right now?

*Father, I lift up in prayer the people I have forgotten in the midst*
*of my own concerns. Grant me compassion as I seek those*
*who are hurting and bring their burdens to You. Amen.*

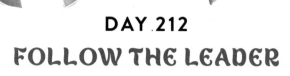

## DAY 212
# FOLLOW THE LEADER

*Lead me, Lord, in your righteousness because of
my enemies—make your way straight before me.*
PSALM 5:8 NIV

The psalmist offers us hope for learning to live as Christians in an environment that does little to help us. He reminds us to ask the Lord to lead us in righteousness. Too often we believe in Him for our eternal salvation but go about trying to live our daily lives as if being righteous is something we have to figure out on our own. Christ is the righteousness of God embodied for us. In Him, we have been accepted by the Father and given the Spirit, who enables us to live in right relationship to God and others. Daily and hourly, we can pray for Christ's leading, asking Him to keep us focused on Him and mindful that we are following Him. He has a path that He desires to walk with each of us, guiding us each step of the way.

*Lord, help me remember to ask for Your leading. Show me the path
You have designed for my life and give me clear direction. Amen.*

# DAY 213
## YET

*"Though he slay me, yet will I hope in him."*
JOB 13:15 NIV

There are many who know the meaning of these words better than the rest of us.

The family living in Tornado Alley whose house has been torn to shreds no fewer than five times in the last fifteen years.

The mother whose sons and husband were all lost on the field of battle.

The family of the woman who survived a long, wearying struggle with cancer only to be sent back into the hospital by a megavirus.

Have you ever felt under attack? Have you ever felt perhaps God was testing your mettle? How do you hold on to hope when there seems to be no reason to do so? What does that even look like?

Though his case seems extreme, it's unlikely that many of us would react much differently than the course Job took. People going through difficult periods of their lives cycle through anger and bitterness, anguish and sorrow, resignation and confusion, just as Job did. Though they probably don't sit and cover themselves with ashes, they may hole up in their bedrooms with quilts over their heads.

But in the end, what leads Job to hope is God. God is still there. Even through all of Job's complaints and cries and angry accusations, God does not leave. God does not change. God provides no excuses. Bad things will come. But so will God.

* * * * * * * * * * * * * * * * * * * * * * * * * * * * * * * * * * * * * * * * *

*Dear Lord, thank You for holding on to*
*me when I can't hold on to hope. Amen.*

# DAY 214
# AN ANCHOR FOR THE SOUL

*But when you ask him, be sure that your faith is in God alone.
Do not waver, for a person with divided loyalty is as unsettled
as a wave of the sea that is blown and tossed by the wind.*

JAMES 1:6 NLT

Imagine being on a life raft in the middle of the ocean. When the storms come, the seemingly weightless raft is picked up and tossed wherever the wind chooses to take it. There is no ability to steer, no sail to work with the wind, certainly no protection from the storm. When the storm ends, the raft's destination is really left up to chance.

James tells us that this is how unstable we become when we do not have a strong foundation. When our loyalty is divided—between serving God and pleasing others, for example—we are as unstable as a raft in a storm on the raging sea. The writer of Hebrews speaks of our hope in Jesus as "a strong and trustworthy anchor for our souls" (Hebrews 6:19 NLT). Faith in God anchors us and braces us against the raging storm. When we are firmly anchored, the winds may whip us around, but ultimately we cannot be moved. Anchor your faith and loyalty on Him.

. . . . . . . . . . . . . . . . . . . . . . . . . . . . . . . . . . . . . . .

*Lord Jesus, You are the anchor for my soul. Help me to hold firmly to
You, to keep my loyalty focused on You and You alone. Thank You
for the promise that You will keep me steadfast and strong. Amen.*

# DAY 215
# GRANDSTANDING

*"But when you pray, go into your room, close the door
and pray to your Father, who is unseen. Then your Father,
who sees what is done in secret, will reward you."*
MATTHEW 6:6 NIV

*Grandstanding.* What a word. It can mean showing off. Yes, we humans are forever trying to impress others and get that spotlight to swivel over to us on that grand stage of life. Even as little tykes, we begin the process of learning how to get attention. We wail and wiggle and giggle and coo and shout and sing and sigh and stomp and put our little fists on our hips—anything to be in the limelight and show how important we are. Then we grow up and do adult versions of the same thing.

Bottom line? Humans love attention.

It's safe to say that showing off isn't a deed that is promoted in the Bible. In fact, Jesus says, "But when you pray, go into your room, close the door and pray to your Father, who is unseen. Then your Father, who sees what is done in secret, will reward you."

It's a simple directive. Should be easy, right? It's not that easy. Perhaps we need a prayer to preface our other prayers and ask God to make us prayer warriors who carry the sword of truth rather than the trumpet of pride.

• • • • • • • • • • • • • • • • • • • • • • • • • • • • • • • • • • • • • • • • • • • • •

*God, help me to remember that, when I pray, I should not be seeking the
approval or admiration of others—I should be seeking You alone. Amen.*

# DAY 216
# RECONCILED TO GOD

*Ezra wept, prostrate in front of The Temple of God. As he prayed and confessed, a huge number of the men, women, and children of Israel gathered around him. All the people were now weeping as if their hearts would break.*
EZRA 10:1 MSG

Satan loves to remind us of our sins to make us feel guilty. He adores it when we wallow in them. But God never intended for us to do that. Instead, God wants us to confess our sins—daily or hourly if need be!—receive His forgiveness, and move on to live with renewed fervor.

What sins have separated us from God today? Let's draw near the throne of grace so we can receive His pardon. He longs for us to come near to Him, and He will cover us with Jesus' robe of righteousness so that we don't have to feel guilt or shame anymore.

. . . . . . . . . . . . . . . . . . . . . . . . . . . . . . . . . . . . . . .

*Lord, forgive me for the sins I've committed today. Make me ever aware of Your grace and forgiveness so that I may share Your love with others. Amen.*

# DAY 217
# FLOWERS FALL

*"The grass withers and the flowers fall,*
*but the word of the Lord endures forever."*
1 Peter 1:24–25 niv

It's funny how people try to make things last that were never meant to do so. For example, people hold on to mementos of special occasions, sometimes keeping the flowers that were worn on the day or that decorated the scene. They will press flowers, dry them, and preserve them in various ways. And when that isn't enough, they have silk renditions created. Or they take photographs and hold on to those instead.

We want good things to last. We want people to live long lives and relationships to endure hardships. We root for the long-suffering hero who finally wins in the end. We hold detailed ceremonies to remember those we have lost.

Though these bodies of ours were not meant to continue forever, when we have accepted Jesus as our Savior and Redeemer, we become "born again, not of perishable seed, but of imperishable, through the living and enduring word of God" (v. 23).

It's this contradiction—forever souls bound in temporary houses—that makes us long for all good things to never die. But peace and contentment—a cure of sorts for that longing—can be found in the enduring Word of God. The more time we spend there, the more we realize we have all the time in the world.

* * *

*Thank You, Lord, for giving us Your Word to guide and*
*sustain us as we walk in this temporary home. Amen.*

# DAY 218
# PRAYING FOR YOU

*With this in mind, we constantly pray for you, that our God may make
you worthy of his calling, and that by his power he may bring to fruition
your every desire for goodness and your every deed prompted by faith.*
2 THESSALONIANS 1:11 NIV

When we share prayer requests, we often pray for health and for healing, maybe
an open door for a job opportunity or safety or protection. But throughout 1
and 2 Thessalonians, Paul shares his prayers for the church at Thessalonica. His
prayers are not for health and healing but that God would make them worthy
of His calling. That He would bring to fruition their hearts' good desires. This
is not to say that prayers for healing and health are not important; James 5:14
instructs us to pray this way. However, there is more to prayer than asking for
healing or comfort. By following Paul's example in 1 and 2 Thessalonians, our
prayers can take on more substance and spiritual meaning.

Take a moment to read through the books of 1 and 2 Thessalonians, noting
the way Paul prays for his fellow believers. Deepen your prayer life. Make a
commitment to pray for others on a spiritual rather than superficial level.

* * * * * * * * * * * * * * * * * * * * * * * * * * * * * * * * * * * * * * * *

*Heavenly Father, thank You for my friends. Help me to
pray for them regularly and expansively. Thank You
for all that You do to show us Your presence. Amen.*

# DAY 219
# THE BLACK FLOOD

*Out of the depths I cry to you, L*ord.
P*salm* 130:1 *niv*

Those black nights. When loneliness becomes like a living thing. When disaster strikes unexpectedly. When you can't seem to draw another breath because the sense of failure or grief or pain seems to consume the very air. The night. The last drop of your hope.

What can you do? Who can you turn to?

God.

He alone is all you need for life and hope on those black nights. He is mighty and powerful and living hope. He is the One who made you, so He knows exactly what you need. Cry out to Him on those black nights. Cling to Him when the world comes crashing in and everyone has fled. When you feel your sin is beyond redemption. When every last drop of hope seems to have dried up. His promises are real. His grace is sufficient. His mercy endures forever. His Word stands. Pray and believe.

He is right here with you. He will never leave you or forsake you. No burden is too great for Him. No sin too dark that He cannot wash it away. He will forgive. He will cradle you in His love. He will reach down and touch your cheek because He considers you to be His precious child.

Cry out to God.

He is right here.

- - - - - - - - - - - - - - - - - - - - - - - - - - - - - - - - - - - - - - - - - - - - - - - - - -

*Heavenly Father, help me to cling to You in times of despair*
*and hopelessness. Wrap me in the safety of Your arms and*
*soothe me with the peace of Your presence. Amen.*

# DAY 220
# JONAH'S PRAYER

*"In my distress I called to the Lord, and he answered me. From deep in*
*the realm of the dead I called for help, and you listened to my cry."*
JONAH 2:2 NIV

Jonah's prayer is distinctive because he's praying from the belly of a large fish—a seemingly hopeless situation. The response you might expect is "Lord, get me out of here!" Instead, Jonah praises God for listening to and answering him! He prays with gratitude and praise as well as with contrition.

Jonah's example is helpful to Christians today. He teaches us that, even in our worst situations, we need to approach God with both repentance and thanksgiving. No matter our experiences, we serve a powerful God—One who deserves all honor and praise.

. . . . . . . . . . . . . . . . . . . . . . . . . . . . . . . . . . . . . . . . . . . .

*Dear Lord, thank You for hearing my prayers.*
*Thank You for having mercy on me. Amen.*

# DAY 221
# SINGING TREES

*Let the fields be jubilant, and everything in them; let all the*
*trees of the forest sing for joy. Let all creation rejoice before*
*the Lord, for he comes, he comes to judge the earth.*

PSALM 96:12–13 NIV

What are your favorite worship songs? Are they slow and soft or fast and bright? Do they bring peace or excitement? What would you do if your favorite song was performed by a chorus of trees?

It would certainly make for an interesting service. No one would sleep through that one.

But the interesting thing about this idea from Psalm 96 is not just the singing trees and fields. It's why they are so joyful that seems intriguing. They are rejoicing before the Lord because He is coming to judge the earth.

Judging doesn't sound like much fun. Judging sounds like something that might be followed by the word *sentence*, *punishment*, or *penalty*. And there's nothing joyful about any of that.

But the writer of this psalm is rejoicing in this event because of two things he is sure of: (1) his place before the Creator of the earth and (2) the truth that God is a just and righteous judge.

Are you sure of these two things? Do you trust God to judge fairly? Could you sing with joy about your judgment to come? If you answer no, what can you do today to start trusting God more? What do you need to do to be sure of your position before God?

. . . . . . . . . . . . . . . . . . . . . . . . . . . . . . . . . . . . . . . . . .

*Dear God, I know You are a just and*
*righteous judge. Help me honor You. Amen.*

# DAY 222
# THE WORLD IS WATCHING

*How great is the goodness you have stored up for those who fear you. You lavish it on those who come to you for protection, blessing them before the watching world.*
PSALM 31:19 NLT

We humans tend to focus on what we don't have. We lament not having enough money or time. We become frustrated with our physical limitations and fret about things not turning out the way we wanted them to. We're even good at whining about these things. But remember, the world is watching. You may not think much of a whine here and there, but others are watching to see how we respond to this God who we say is so loving and good.

One of the ways God demonstrates His love to a hurting world is to lavish His love upon His children. When we whine and complain about little things, we diminish God's blessing to us before a watching world. It's important for us to respond appropriately to all of God's blessings and to demonstrate how deeply our heavenly Father loves us.

. . . . . . . . . . . . . . . . . . . . . . . . . . . . . . . . . . . . . . . . . . . .

*Father, You have blessed me abundantly. I confess that I sometimes miss those blessings and spend more time focusing on what is lacking than on what You have provided. Help me to be grateful before a watching world. Amen.*

# DAY 223

# BIG TALK

*Then he continued, "Do not be afraid, Daniel. Since the first day that you
set your mind to gain understanding and to humble yourself before your
God, your words were heard, and I have come in response to them."*

DANIEL 10:12 NIV

They say everything is bigger in Texas, but you don't have to live in that big state to experience big pick-up trucks. Big hair. Big beef. Big talk. Oww. That last one is as common as mosquitoes in summer and just as welcome. Ever been around someone with BIG talk? When that person Won't. Stop. Talking? It's unnerving. And maddening. After a while your brain goes numb, your eye begins to twitch, and your feet get the itch to run.

There are a lot of people in the world who have this problem. They love the sound of their own voices. They believe their words are a spring of wisdom when they're really a fount of NOISE. Even with a pickax, you couldn't chisel your way into the conversation. You begin to wonder, with so many people talking, is there anybody out there listening?

God is.

Yes, your words will be heard. He will respond. That is a promise.

What will you say to God?

· · · · · · · · · · · · · · · · · · · · · · · · · · · · · · · · · · · · · · · · · · · · ·

*Lord, thank You for listening to me better than anyone ever could.
When there is a lack of attentive ears, help me to turn to You
instead of despairing. I have found a friend in You. Amen.*

# DAY 224

# A FAITHFUL EXAMPLE

*"Surely your God is a God of gods and a Lord of kings and a revealer*
*of mysteries, since you have been able to reveal this mystery."*
DANIEL 2:47 NASB

Maybe you have a friend, coworker, or family member who has not yet put his or her faith in God. Perhaps you have been praying about it for many years. Don't give up hope! Daniel's faith allowed God to demonstrate His power to the king, and while the king did not immediately bow down to God, he saw that God was real and powerful.

Our faithful example is important. When we trust in God, those around us will see His power in us. Through our actions, others will come to know God and proclaim that He is a God of gods and a Lord of kings.

. . . . . . . . . . . . . . . . . . . . . . . . . . . . . . . . . . . . . . . . . . . .

*Dear Lord, be with my friends who don't know You. Help me to plant seeds*
*of faith in their hearts. Let me trust that You will make them grow. Amen.*

# DAY 225

# THIS IS THE DAY THAT THE LORD HAS MADE... AND I JUST MESSED UP!

*This is the day which the LORD has made; let us rejoice and be glad in it.*
PSALM 118:24 NASB

Have you ever wondered how a perfectly good day can get so messed up?

The answer can usually be laid down to human behavior. All it takes is a sharp word to a family member or an unhelpful attitude or an unkind action, and the situation quickly degenerates. Personal failure has odd tentacles. The guilty feeling from knowing the problem was self-instigated fosters a desire to shift the blame and then in the end leads to self-incriminating despair at again being the cause of strife.

Human relationships, while having the strength to withstand much trauma, are remarkably fragile when it comes to insult. Friends and spouses and children can be hurt greatly when we are careless with our words and attitudes. So how do we fix the day?

We can turn to our God, who is the essence of redemption. Since He sent Jesus to redeem our souls, He is able also to redeem even the smallest earthly concern. Coming to Him for mercy is the first step in righting the wrong. Exchanging our failure for His grace reminds us that all is not lost. The day is His, after all, and He offers the hope we need to live it through to the end.

. . . . . . . . . . . . . . . . . . . . . . . . . . . . . . . . . . . . . . . . . . .

*Father God, thank You for Your abundant mercy and constant grace. Redeem my failures today, and help me not to repeat them. In Jesus' name, amen.*

# DAY 226
## SET APART

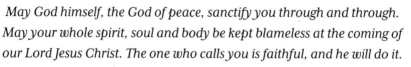

*May God himself, the God of peace, sanctify you through and through.*
*May your whole spirit, soul and body be kept blameless at the coming of*
*our Lord Jesus Christ. The one who calls you is faithful, and he will do it.*
1 Thessalonians 5:23–24 niv

*Sanctification* is a big word that means "to be set apart" for a specific purpose. The Bible teaches that as Christians we are sanctified, or set apart, for God's purposes. This act is initiated by God. There is nothing we can do to set ourselves apart. But if you have ever tried to change the diaper of a squirming baby, you know how important cooperation is for a person to be changed.

God has already done the work. He has made your spirit, soul, and body blameless through the death and resurrection of Jesus Christ. This work is done. Paul expresses to the Thessalonians the importance of being kept blameless. This is the work of cooperation—our need to trust and obey God in every situation. We can cooperate with His setting-apart work in our lives by reading and studying His Word, by praying to Him, and by sharing our knowledge with other believers.

How have you been set apart for God? He has called you. He is faithful. *He* will do it.

* * * * * * * * * * * * * * * * * * * * * * * * * * * * * * * * * * * *

*Father, thank You for Your sanctifying work through Jesus on the cross.*
*Thank You for choosing me and setting me apart for righteousness.*
*Help me to trust and obey this work You are doing in my life. Amen.*

# WHEN WE THINK OF GOD

*For you make me glad by your deeds, LORD; I sing for joy at what your hands
have done. How great are your works, LORD, how profound your thoughts!*
PSALM 92:4–5 NIV

Do you ever feel the flatness of life—as if you were one of those cartoon characters who's been bopped on the head with a mallet and your head now meets your knees? Do you approach the day with words like these: *One-dimensional. Dull. Gray. Dreary. Stale. Tedious. Humdrum.*

The God of the universe wants us to start our day with a different mindset. There is nothing about God and His creation that is humdrum. Nothing. He made the elegant silhouette of a swan. The shimmer of a sunrise on a pristine glacier. The whispers of tropical wildlife still unknown to man.

When we think of God and His creation, our words should be transformed. They might become: *Mysterious. Exotic. Breathtaking. Radiant. Exhilarating. Enlivening. Miraculous.* Prayer is connecting with that mind. That heart. That brilliance. That life and color. That perfection.

Let us come into His presence with thanksgiving and praise. Let us come to know the One who is extraordinary beyond compare. And through that communion, let us see His world and His people as they were meant to be.

* * * * * * * * * * * * * * * * * * * * * * * * * * * * * * * * * * * * * * * *

*Creator God, open my eyes to the richness and vibrancy of
life. I want to encounter each day with the freedom and
joy that is abundant in a relationship with You. Amen.*

# DAY 228
# CHRIST IS INVOLVED

*Being confident of this very thing, that he which hath begun a*
*good work in you will perform it until the day of Jesus Christ.*
PHILIPPIANS 1:6 KJV

Christ wants you to grow in your faith. He wants to help you flee the temptations that you will inevitably face. He wants to give you strength to be joyful even as you go through trials. His ultimate desire is to help you become more like Him.

Do you allow Jesus to be as involved in your life as He wants to be? Unfortunately, a lot of people accept Him in order to get into heaven, but then they want little more to do with Him. Why not choose now to let Him be a part of everything you do and every decision you make? Go to Him in prayer. Seek answers from His Word and from the Holy Spirit. He will do a great work in your life. He will be faithful to complete what He started in you—and you will become like Him.

. . . . . . . . . . . . . . . . . . . . . . . . . . . . . . . . . . . . . . . . . .

*Dear Jesus, thank You for wanting to help me be like You. Thank You for*
*being involved in my life and not leaving me to my own designs. Amen.*

# DAY 229
# UNFADING BEAUTY

*You should clothe yourselves instead with the beauty that comes from within,*
*the unfading beauty of a gentle and quiet spirit, which is so precious to God.*

1 PETER 3:4 NLT

Perhaps Sarah was the only elderly woman who was so beautiful that an Egyptian pharaoh wanted her for his harem! Most of us don't have to worry about that. We know that whatever physical beauty we possess is fleeting. Despite the commercials and the boutique counters in the department stores and the advances of Botox and collagen, aging happens to every woman.

God understands that our bodies pay a heavy price for the brokenness caused by sin. He knows that we grieve as we see our youth slipping away. Yet He does not want us to make this temporal body the focus of our living. After all, the body only houses the spirit, and one day we will exchange this primitive model for a glorified one.

I love vintage photos and am intrigued by the youthful beauty seen in the picture albums of the elderly. Looking at them in younger days, full of life and vitality, and then glancing at them today brings one to the stark reality that beauty fades and only a shadow of the former glory exists.

That's why God's Word tells women to spend most of their effort on beautifying the spirit, which can grow lovelier with every passing year. For only eternity will reveal the glories yet to come.

· · · · · · · · · · · · · · · · · · · · · · · · · · · · · · · · · · · · · · · ·

*Father, let me not mourn the passing of time as a foolish woman.*
*Rather, let me beautify my spirit for Your glory. In Jesus' name, amen.*

# DAY 230
# NO WORRIES

*"So don't worry about tomorrow, for tomorrow will bring
its own worries. Today's trouble is enough for today."*
MATTHEW 6:34 NLT

It has been said that today is the tomorrow you worried about yesterday. Isn't it true? And how many of the things you worry about actually happen? Worry is a thief. It robs us of the joy of the moment and plants us firmly in the future, where we have absolutely no control. Instead of focusing on the problems that this day brings, we propel ourselves into an unknown tomorrow. In living this way, we miss out on all the little moments that make life precious.

The antidote to worry is to focus on today—this hour, this moment in time. What is happening now? Experience it with all five of your senses. Allow the wonder of today to touch your heart and settle it down. Sure, there is trouble today, and there are problems to solve, but Jesus is right here with us. We have the gift of the Holy Spirit, who can counsel and comfort us and help us get through any and every situation. There is nothing you can't face without Jesus by your side. When you focus on what He can do instead of what you can't do, you will experience a deep and abiding peace that comes only from Him.

*Lord, worry is such a part of who I am! When I'm not worried,
I worry that I'm missing something. Please help me not to worry
about tomorrow. Help me to focus on today, on what is happening
now, and to let You take care of all my trouble. Amen.*

# DAY 231

## LIVING IN THE SHADOWS

*"Who can hide in secret places so that I cannot see them?"*
*declares the Lord. "Do not I fill heaven and earth?" declares the Lord.*
JEREMIAH 23:24 NIV

Evil lurks in shrouded places, the murky crevices of life. It hates the light. So sin tries to conceal itself.

We might think we're hiding our secret little sins from God, but there is no such thing as secrets from God. He sees all. And to believe that some sins are small is a lie we create to make ourselves feel better. Hiding from God? It is the dream that we wouldn't want to come true.

Still, we try to live in the shadows, fearful of stepping into the light of heaven—His light. Once bathed in His divine illumination, we can never see sin the same way again. As something livable. Doable. Acceptable. In that light, we see that we are naked just as Adam and Eve did after their disobedience. We see what must be changed. Our hearts. Our minds. All of our being. In that holy light, we see love in a new way. We long for goodness. We desire to be clothed in righteousness. We can see our way to heaven.

Let us step out of the dark corners of sin and into the light of Christ, where we can confess our sins and accept His love and forgiveness. Where eternal life will be ours.

. . . . . . . . . . . . . . . . . . . . . . . . . . . . . . . . . . . . . . . . . .

*Savior God, give me the strength to step into Your holy, cleansing light. Amen.*

# DAY 232
# LOYALTY TO FAMILY

*Then Orpah kissed her mother-in-law goodbye, but Ruth clung to her.*
RUTH 1:14 NIV

Orpah went back to her homeland, but Ruth remained with her mother-in-law. Naomi urged her to leave, but Ruth wouldn't go.

Ruth refused to worry about the future or to look out only for her own good. She put a high priority on the welfare of her mother-in-law. She stood by her in her time of need.

Do you have a family member who needs your loyalty? Maybe it is your spouse, a parent, child, sibling, or an in-law. Perhaps there is someone in your family who has been a blessing to you and whom you can bless in return. Or maybe you have a relative who has let everyone down, someone who truly does not even deserve your faithfulness but who desperately needs it. Pray that God will show you the Naomi in your life. He will honor your faithfulness to family.

. . . . . . . . . . . . . . . . . . . . . . . . . . . . . . . . . . . . . . . . . .

*Father, help me to be faithful to my family. Amen.*

# ARE YOU AWARE OF STRESS?

*You will keep in perfect peace all who trust in you,*
*all whose thoughts are fixed on you!*
ISAIAH 26:3 NLT

I suppose there aren't enough months in the year to focus on all our ailments and national concerns, so the calendar makers piggyback them to give everyone a fair hearing. Are you ready for this? April is also Stress Awareness Month. And as you might guess, during this month, health-care professionals try to increase awareness of the causes and cures for what is called our "modern stress epidemic."

We're all aware that stress is widespread and affects us in many ways. And stress management is difficult to implement. Taking a vacation only helps a few weeks out of the year. Relaxing on the weekend only increases the anxiety of Monday morning. Displaying beachfronts on our computer desktops only reminds us that we are office-bound. And talking with a therapist is only a release valve for continuing pressure. Yes, stress is a problem, and it is here to stay.

For Christians, stress seems to fly in the face of Jesus' promise of peace and abundant joy. Yet the peace He gives keeps the stress from destroying us. He keeps the threads of our sanity from unraveling. But He expects us to do what we can to help ourselves. This month, take a good look at your schedule and your routines, and ask God for wisdom so you can appropriately manage your stress.

. . . . . . . . . . . . . . . . . . . . . . . . . . . . . . . . . . . . . . . . . .

*God, grant me the serenity to accept the things I cannot change, courage*
*to change the things I can, and wisdom to know the difference. Amen.*

## DAY 234
# A GOOD WORD

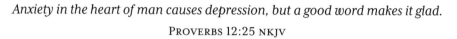

*Anxiety in the heart of man causes depression, but a good word makes it glad.*
PROVERBS 12:25 NKJV

As most of us know, anxiety and depression are two sides of the same coin. According to this verse, keeping anxiety in our hearts causes depression. We are anxious about what might happen, and we become depressed about what didn't. Anxiety and depression create a vicious cycle, keeping us bound to the past and paralyzed about the future.

But this proverb reminds us that "a good word makes [the heart] glad." Where can you get a good word? Philippians 4:8 (NLT) tells us to "fix [our] thoughts on what is true, and honorable, and right, and pure, and lovely, and admirable. Think about things that are excellent and worthy of praise." This is a good word! We know it to be true experientially, and studies prove that reading the Bible, singing praise songs, and hearing encouraging words from friends can literally change our brain's chemistry and lift a dark mood. These good words replace the anxiety and depression in our hearts with joy and peace in the Holy Spirit.

- - - - - - - - - - - - - - - - - - - - - - - - - - - - - - - - - - - - - - -

*Father, my heart is sometimes weighed down by anxiety. I know what it feels like to be depressed. Thank You for Your Word and the reminder that I don't have to settle for these feelings. Thank You that I can trust You to bring joy back to my soul. Amen.*

# DAY 235

# PRAYING THE SCRIPTURES

*All Scripture is God-breathed and is useful for teaching,*
*rebuking, correcting and training in righteousness.*
2 TIMOTHY 3:16 NIV

Have you ever needed a little help with your prayers? You wanted to say more that was on your heart, but you couldn't quite put it into words? Since the entire Bible is God-breathed, and it is valuable in many ways, using the scriptures to help you to pray is a wonderful way to speak the truth and get right to the heart of what you're trying to say.

Here's an example from Psalm 103:1–5 (NIV). In this passage, the second person reference has simply been changed to first person. But to repeat the psalms or any other scripture in this way is not to be thought of or used as a chant as some people do in other religions. Nor are we to think that there is supernatural power in the words themselves, for it is God who is all-powerful and who hears and responds to our petitions.

Try infusing your prayers with a helping from God's holy Word.

> *Praise the LORD, my soul; all my inmost being, praise his holy name.*
> *Praise the LORD, my soul, and forget not all his benefits—who*
> *forgives all [my] sins and heals all [my] diseases, who redeems*
> *[my] life from the pit and crowns [me] with love and compassion,*
> *who satisfies [my] desires with good things so that [my] youth is*
> *renewed like the eagle's.*

* * * * * * * * * * * * * * * * * * * * * * * * * * * * * * * * * * * * *

*Lord, infuse my prayers with passion, sincerity, and praise.*
*May our communion be beautiful and strong. Amen.*

# DAY 236
# ATTENTION AND PRAYER

*Pray in the Spirit at all times and on every occasion. Stay alert*
*and be persistent in your prayers for all believers everywhere.*
EPHESIANS 6:18 NLT

Paul must have known how difficult prayer could be. He realized the kind of prayer he describes in Ephesians is demanding, but he also knew that it is the most fulfilling and valuable type of prayer. Paul encourages us to work hard at prayer, being constant, alert, and attending to Christians everywhere.

Persistence and consistency are difficult, but possibly Paul's most challenging instruction is to pray for all Christians everywhere. In today's society, getting wrapped up in our own lives is all too easy to do. Even when we look outside ourselves, we often limit prayer to our family and friends, or at most our local church family. We must look further, though. Praying for Christians everywhere requires us to engage in a world we might not always be involved with, but God wants us to love and pray for our Christian family whether they are around the corner or around the world.

* * * * * * * * * * * * * * * * * * * * * * * * * * * * * * * * * * * * * *

*Dear Lord, teach me to pray according to Your will. Help me*
*to be consistent in my prayers, and help me to remember to*
*pray for my Christian family throughout the world. Amen.*

# THE GIFT THAT KEEPS ON GIVING

*Just as people are destined to die once, and after that to face
judgment, so Christ was sacrificed once to take away the sins
of many; and he will appear a second time, not to bear sin,
but to bring salvation to those who are waiting for him.*
HEBREWS 9:27–28 NIV

After we've been Christians awhile and traveled down the road of our spiritual journey, it's easy to lose sight of what started us on our way. Christ's blood paid the price for our sins and is the cost of our spiritual journey. From His death, we receive several benefits.

We get forgiveness of sins. Not only did Jesus pay the price for everything we ever have done or ever will do wrong, but God annuls our sins. He treats them as if they never happened. And this means we are rescued from the judgment we deserve for our sinful rebellion. In addition, we get brought into God's family.

After Jesus rose from the dead, He made a promise to return and give us a permanent place in heaven. He sent the Holy Spirit to live inside us and to act as the deposit on the contract that He will return one day to fulfill.

The journey of faith is not free, but Jesus has paid the price. And we receive freedom now and hope for the future.

. . . . . . . . . . . . . . . . . . . . . . . . . . . . . . . . . . . . . . . . .

*Precious Jesus, thank You so much for paying the penalty for
our sins. May we never become complacent and forget the
price You paid. Help us to be continually grateful. Amen.*

# DAY 238
# THE SPIRIT OF TRUTH

*"If you love me, keep my commands. And I will ask the Father, and he will give you another advocate to help you and be with you forever—the Spirit of truth. The world cannot accept him, because it neither sees him nor knows him. But you know him, for he lives with you and will be in you."*
JOHN 14:15–17 NIV

Turn the other cheek. Love your enemies. Do good to those who hurt you. Give generously. Don't be anxious. Store up treasures in heaven. In the Sermon on the Mount (Matthew 5–6), Jesus presents a perspective on living that must have confused many of His listeners.

For those who don't know or recognize the Holy Spirit, Jesus' teachings don't make any sense. They are countercultural and go against the grain of natural instinct. When Christians are able to forgive those who have hurt them, give generously, or refuse to follow the latest trends and fashions, the world gets confused. To those who don't have the Holy Spirit, these seemingly extraordinary actions must seem unreal, impossible even. Knowing the Holy Spirit makes all the difference. When the Holy Spirit lives in us, we can finally see truth. We have the advocacy and the help we need to follow Jesus' commands—and they make all the sense in the world.

. . . . . . . . . . . . . . . . . . . . . . . . . . . . . . . . . . . . . . . . .

*Jesus, thank You for the gift of the Holy Spirit. My life would be so meaningless and confusing without this precious Comforter, Advocate, and Friend. Help me to follow Your commands and shine Your light to a watching world. Amen.*

# DAY 239

## EXPECT A MIRACLE

*You turned my wailing into dancing; you removed*
*my sackcloth and clothed me with joy.*
PSALM 30:11 NIV

How do you rise up from your prayer time with the Lord? Be honest. As if nothing will really happen? As if your words have flowed from your heart and will spill into nothingness? Or perhaps you go away from your prayers with enthusiasm and heartfelt faith, but by the afternoon you are weary and disheartened again. In a world that doesn't believe in the supernatural, it is easy to make assumptions that a miracle is impossible. That miracles only happened in biblical times. Or the assumption that miracles seem to be for everyone but you.

And yet that is not the truth.

God does hear our prayers. He does listen. He will respond. He already knows our every need. Know that in His timing our tears will turn to joy. That our hobbling, stumbling, pain-filled steps will turn to dancing. It will be in His way, His timing. Don't struggle in this truth, but rest in its beauty. The Lord's timing is perfect, and His answers are full of mercy and justice and love.

Pray.

Expect a miracle.

Keep the faith.

* * *

*Sovereign God, forgive my unbelief and give me great faith.*
*Help me to trust in Your plans and remember that in all things,*
*You work for the good of those who love You. Amen.*

# DAY 240
# PRAYING FOR LOVED ONES

*"Therefore I tell you, whatever you ask for in prayer,
believe that you have received it, and it will be yours."*
MARK 11:24 NIV

One of the best things a woman can do for her loved ones is pray for them. And while we don't find one simple formula for effective prayer in the Bible, *how* we pray may be just as important as *what* we pray.

Do we beseech God with faith, believing that He can do anything? Or do we pray with hesitation, believing that nothing is going to change? God is honored and willing to work when we pray with faith.

The most beneficial times of prayer often come when we make time to listen to God, not just talk "at" Him. He can give us wisdom and insights we would never come up with on our own.

Though we can't always see it, He is at work in our loved ones' hearts and in ours.

* * * * * * * * * * * * * * * * * * * * * * * * * * * * * * * * * * *

*Lord, thank You for Your concern for my friends and family
members. I know You love them even more than I do. Amen.*

# DAY 241

# GREAT IS HIS FAITHFULNESS

*Because of the LORD's great love we are not consumed, for his compassions
never fail. They are new every morning; great is your faithfulness.*
LAMENTATIONS 3:22–23 NIV

Have you ever felt you were being consumed? Consumed by rage, hurt,
jealousy, pain, loneliness, grief, fill-in-the-blank? Have you ever said, "One
more thing, and I'll fall to pieces. I can't handle this"?

The good news is we don't have to handle it. God's compassion never fails.
He is greater than anything that threatens to consume us. His mercy never
runs out. It is new every morning.

When the Israelites were wandering in the desert because of their disbelief
in God's ability to deliver the Promised Land into their hands, God was still
faithful. He fed them manna daily. But they had to go out of their tents and
gather it. And it was only good for a day.

In the same way, God is faithful to us regardless of what we have done.
And like the manna that came every morning, new mercies are available to us
every day. We just have to ask for them. We can't let our pain, shame, anger,
fill-in-the-blank keep us from running to God daily for new mercies to sustain
us. He will not let us be consumed. He is faithful.

* * * * * * * * * * * * * * * * * * * * * * * * * * * * * * * * * * * * *

*Oh Lord our God, we are such faulty, frail humans. You know that
we are but dust. We thank You that we don't have to do anything
but run to You and receive Your mercies that never run out. Help
us not to let anything keep us from running to You. Amen.*

# DAY 242
# NEW EVERY MORNING

*This I recall to my mind, therefore I have hope. Through the Lord's*
*mercies we are not consumed, because His compassions fail not.*
*They are new every morning; great is Your faithfulness.*
LAMENTATIONS 3:21–23 NKJV

For many people, one of the most difficult times of the day is nighttime. We fall into bed physically exhausted, grateful to finally be done with the activity of the day. Suddenly, our brains are awake and alert with swirling thoughts. Thoughts of today lead to thoughts of yesterday and ten years back. We think of things we should have said but didn't and things we shouldn't have said but did. We rehearse bad decisions and mistakes and worry anxiously about the future. The thoughts that keep us awake some nights can be daunting, to say the least. These thoughts can consume us with worry, fear, and regret, robbing us of peace and sleep. We feel hopeless and exhausted.

But God's Word says we don't have to be consumed by regrets from the past or fears of the future. Every morning with the rising of the sun comes a new measure of His mercy, compassion, and faithfulness. So let your worrisome thoughts go, and replace them with hope. His mercy and compassion will never fail.

*Father, when I can't sleep, bring Your mercy and compassion to*
*my mind. Give me hope in Your faithfulness. Thank You for the*
*promise of the new morning, and help me to rest in You. Amen.*

# DAY 243

## SPA DAY FOR THE SOUL

*One of those days Jesus went out to a mountainside*
*to pray, and spent the night praying to God.*
LUKE 6:12 NIV

We women enjoy going to the spa—relaxing with a hot stone massage or getting our toenails painted the color of red-hot candies. Or indulging in a facial that sends us into orbital bliss. Gotta love it, eh?

We like to spoil our bodies in every way. But what about pampering our spirits? We tend to neglect what can't be seen, and yet we are made of spirit as well as flesh. So, what about having a spa day for the soul? Talk about rejuvenating. We would come away with a new outlook, a smile on our lips, and a song in our hearts. Our spirits might even feel ten years younger.

When Jesus walked among us, He showed us how important prayer was. It says in God's Word that Christ "went out to a mountainside to pray, and spent the night praying to God." He knew how powerful and vital prayer was and how He needed it to stay the course.

So, are you ready to schedule a spa day for your soul? A day of prayer and communion with your Lord? Or even an hour on Sunday? The luxury of this refreshment is gratis, and its beautification will be a lift to the body and spirit.

. . . . . . . . . . . . . . . . . . . . . . . . . . . . . . . . . . . . . . . . . . . . .

*Lord, help me to remember to regularly refresh my spirit through*
*prayer. My soul needs You as much as my body needs oxygen. Amen.*

# DAY 244

## PRAYERS FOR BOLDNESS

*Pray that I may declare [the Gospel] fearlessly, as I should.*
EPHESIANS 6:20 NIV

In Ephesians 6:20, Paul asks the Ephesians to pray for him. He realized that without the prayers of the saints and the faithfulness of God, he would not be an effective ambassador for Christ.

In today's world, proclaiming our faith can be difficult. Our family, friends, and coworkers can make us feel shy about sharing the Gospel. We might feel unworthy to talk about our faith, or we may be worried that we will not use the right words. Paul's request for prayer should encourage us. Paul too worried about his ability to effectively communicate the Gospel to those around him. He relied on his brothers and sisters in Christ to lift him up to God. In the same way, we should rely on our brothers and sisters to pray for us, that we may declare the Gospel fearlessly, as we should.

*Dear Lord, thank You for Your Word. Surround me with people who will pray for me, and place people in my life for whom I can pray. Together let us boldly proclaim Your name. Amen.*

# THE WARRIOR SINGS

*"The LORD your God is with you, the Mighty Warrior who saves.*
*He will take great delight in you; in his love he will no longer*
*rebuke you, but will rejoice over you with singing."*

ZEPHANIAH 3:17 NIV

What kind of picture does this verse create in your mind? The Lord is a mighty warrior who leads the armies of angels. Yet He is with us. One of Jesus' names is Immanuel, literally "God with us." And He takes delight in us. He doesn't rebuke us. He rejoices over us with singing.

This verse from Zephaniah is like a sampler of God's attributes. Look them over again. How does each of these characteristics show up in your relationship with Him? What attribute do you need to know more about? Which do you struggle with?

We sing worship songs to God, but have you thought about His joy over you being so great He bursts out into song? Or maybe He sings you a sweet lullaby like a parent does to a small child. Next time you sing a worship song, think about what kind of song God would sing about you. Let that fuel your worship of Him and deepen your relationship with the One who loves you so greatly.

. . . . . . . . . . . . . . . . . . . . . . . . . . . . . . . . . . . . . . . .

*Heavenly Father, it is almost too much for us to comprehend that*
*You, the Creator of the universe, could sing about us. We want to*
*understand that, even in just the small way our minds can handle.*
*Show us Your love, and help us to love You more deeply. Amen.*

## DAY 246
# PLANTED BY THE WATER

*"But blessed are those who trust in the L*ORD *and have made the*
L*ORD their hope and confidence. They are like trees planted along*
*a riverbank, with roots that reach deep into the water. Such trees*
*are not bothered by the heat or worried by long months of drought.*
*Their leaves stay green, and they never stop producing fruit."*
JEREMIAH 17:7–8 NLT

While trees don't get to choose where they're planted, the ones growing by the riverbank have it made. Their roots are free to reach deep in the water. They never have to worry about drought or blistering hot days. They are in the ideal position for growth.

This familiar analogy, also found in Psalm 1, paints a beautiful picture of what it means to stand steadfastly with the Lord. Trees don't get to choose where they're planted, but we do, and we must choose carefully. For maximum growth, we must plant ourselves near a source of living water. . .close to the body of Christ. We must immerse ourselves in prayer, feed ourselves with God's Word, and be fertilized and challenged by the companionship of other believers. When we do this, we can be assured that we will stay healthy and never stop producing fruit.

*Father, Your Word paints such beautiful pictures. Thank You for*
*the image of a tree by the riverbank and for the peace it gives me*
*to imagine being planted so close to You. Help my roots to grow*
*deep as I learn more and more to depend on You. Amen.*

## DAY 247
# THE HARDEST PRAYER

*Going a little farther, he fell with his face to the ground
and prayed, "My Father, if it is possible, may this cup
be taken from me. Yet not as I will, but as you will."*
MATTHEW 26:39 NIV

When we pray, asking God for help, we have a good idea of what we want. We might even think, "This is my life. I'm the one living it, and I know exactly what I need."

Yet we don't. We can't possibly know. We are human and more than a little fallible. Only God knows exactly what we need. So, when we pray, we should end our petitions with "Your will be done." Hmmm. We've got to put a bit of thought into that part of the prayer. It means we'd have to trust God for our every need. All the time. Night and day. Uh-oh. Do we really trust Him that much?

Even Jesus, on the night before His crucifixion, when He knew He would be betrayed by His followers and die a brutal death on the cross, still ended His prayer with "Your will be done." Yes, Jesus did ask God for a way out—in other words, was there another way for redemption to come to man other than His death on the cross? In fact, Christ asked God this question three times. But in the end, our Lord said the words "Your will be done."

Jesus trusted. And so should we.

*God, even when I am discouraged and afraid, help me to trust
in Your will for my life. You know what's best. Amen.*

# DAY 248
# A WOMAN WHO FEARS THE LORD

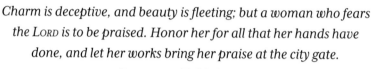

*Charm is deceptive, and beauty is fleeting; but a woman who fears the LORD is to be praised. Honor her for all that her hands have done, and let her works bring her praise at the city gate.*
PROVERBS 31:30–31 NIV

Charm and beauty are not the attributes that God values in His daughters. Clearly, it is a healthy and holy respect for the Father that sets apart believers from the lost. Through Bible study and prayer, we get to know God better. In the Old Testament, He is a God of order, a jealous God. In the New Testament, He is consistent and faithful, offering up His great sacrifice in His Son, Jesus.

Ask the Lord to help you develop a true reverence for Him. He wants us to call Him *Abba* Father ("Daddy"), but He also demands respect, reverence, and a holy fear. He is the God of the universe—the same yesterday, today, and tomorrow.

. . . . . . . . . . . . . . . . . . . . . . . . . . . . . . . . . . . . . . .

*God, make me a woman who respects You deeply, I pray. Amen.*

# DAY 249
# DAY OF PRAYER

*I call on you, my God, for you will answer me;*
*turn your ear to me and hear my prayer.*
PSALM 17:6 NIV

Have you ever tried calling someone's name in a crowded room? You yell and wave until everyone else is looking at you except the person whose attention you're trying to get. Or you call, leave a voice mail, text, and send an email, all without getting an answer. Is anything more frustrating?

With God, we can be confident that He hears us. He stands ready to listen to us all the time. In fact, He welcomes our prayers. He encourages us to pray to Him and pour out our hearts, our concerns, our praises, and our dreams. Prayer connects us deeply to God. Just as you would have a weak relationship with a friend who only called when she needed something, our relationship with God grows and deepens through regular prayer.

One simple way to organize your prayer time is with the simple acrostic ACTS. A—Adoration. Tell God how much you love Him and why. C—Confession. Confess areas in which you've fallen short and messed up. T—Thanksgiving. Thank God for the many ways He has shown you His love. S—Supplication. An old-fashioned word that simply means to ask for something. Whether or not you use this format, take time to regularly connect with God throughout your day.

* * *

*Lord, thank You for listening to us when we pray. You are*
*never too busy to hear the smallest request. Help us to*
*remember to come to You with everything. Amen.*

# DAY 250
# CONFIDENCE

*Let us then approach God's throne of grace with confidence, so that*
*we may receive mercy and find grace to help us in our time of need.*
HEBREWS 4:16 NIV

Do you have a robe-and-slippers friend? Someone who could just show up at your door on a Saturday morning, and you'd be in your robe and slippers, and she wouldn't care? It's a wonderful thing to have a friend so close you know you could approach her at any time of day, in any state, and no matter what, she'd make time for you.

It is an even more wonderful thing to know that our God, the King of kings and Lord of lords, allows us—invites us—to approach His throne with confidence. He tells us to have confidence for two reasons. The first is that He understands. He has experienced everything we have and more. He knows what it is like to be us—He has felt the weakness of the human form and the vulnerability of the human heart. The second reason is that He overcomes. He has experienced all of this and yet not succumbed to the sinful will. He was obedient even to death.

So this is our God. He understands and overcomes and lives today. He invites us to come to Him fully trusting that He will accept us as we are.

Even in our robe and slippers.

. . . . . . . . . . . . . . . . . . . . . . . . . . . . . . . . . . . . . . . . . . . . .

*Lord God, I bow in awe of Your grace and mercy.*
*Let me learn how to live for You. Amen.*

# DAY 251
## SOUL-CRAVINGS

*As the deer pants for streams of water, so my soul pants for you, my God.*
*My soul thirsts for God, for the living God. When can I go and meet with God?*
PSALM 42:1–2 NIV

Our hearts have some indefinable yearnings. We look for fulfillment from people, titles, achievement, chocolate. We may attempt to squelch the longings with distractions of busyness, fashion, an extra drink, motherhood, or even church work. But the longing is a thirst for intimate connection with our God. Our souls pant for Him! He alone quenches our needs.

The Spirit knows our subtle moods, our hearts' aches, and our soul-cravings. We must turn to Him in transparent prayer, mulling the Word over in our minds, allowing it to penetrate the hidden recesses of our souls.

. . . . . . . . . . . . . . . . . . . . . . . . . . . . . . . . . . . . . . . . . . . . .

*God, You are the headwaters of life for me. Reveal the substitutes I*
*look to for fulfillment. Help me to drink deeply from Your Word and*
*Your abiding Spirit, that I might be complete in You. Amen.*

# DAY 252
# JOY AND THANKFULNESS

*Then Hannah prayed and said: "My heart rejoices in the Lord; in the Lord my horn is lifted high. My mouth boasts over my enemies, for I delight in your deliverance. There is no one holy like the Lord; there is no one besides you; there is no Rock like our God."*

1 Samuel 2:1–2 niv

Hannah had prayed for years for a child. In those days, not bearing a child was a sign of disgrace, a sign that you had somehow displeased God. Hannah felt this stigma keenly.

God answered her prayers, and she followed through on her vow to deliver the child, Samuel, to live at the temple in service to the Lord. The name Samuel means "heard by God." And while it is difficult to imagine how a mother could give up her only child in this way, Hannah is rejoicing.

Hannah's focus is not on herself. She is praising God. She is telling others what He has done for her. She has surrendered all that is precious to her to the Lord and is trusting in Him.

How hard it is for us to do this! We worry and we fret and we wonder where God has gone when we don't see Him answering our prayers in the way we think it should happen. Let's follow Hannah's example and praise the Lord. And let's tell others how He is working in our lives.

• • • • • • • • • • • • • • • • • • • • • • • • • • • • • • • • • • • • • • • • •

*Lord, we so often forget to praise You and thank You for all that You have done for us. Help us to remember to keep our trust in You. Amen.*

# DAY 253
# AN OFFERING

*May my prayer be set before you like incense; may the
lifting up of my hands be like the evening sacrifice.*
PSALM 141:2 NIV

It is not entirely clear exactly why or when the custom of burning incense as a part of religious practices came to be. Perhaps it was a way to mask the odor of the dead animals killed and burned as sacrifices to God. Perhaps it was a way to both literally and figuratively clear the air between the people and God. Or perhaps it was just that people like nice-smelling things.

For whatever reason, the burning of incense continues to this day to be an important part of many religious services. It is an expression of something from us going up to heaven. An aromatic love letter to God.

The offerings of old given to God had to be pure, clean, and whole. So we should try to come before God either in that form or ready to submit to Him making us so.

"May my prayer be. . .like incense"—strong and sweet words, full of life. "May the lifting up of my hands be like the evening sacrifice"—empty of self and wholly devoted to the will of the Lord.

. . . . . . . . . . . . . . . . . . . . . . . . . . . . . . . . . . . . . . . . . . .

*Lord, make me a living sacrifice. Amen.*

# DAY 254

# PRAYER REVEALS OUR DEPENDENCE

*Then Jesus went with his disciples to a place called Gethsemane,*
*and he said to them, "Sit here while I go over there and pray."*
MATTHEW 26:36 NIV

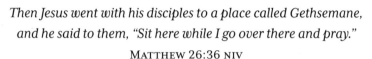

Jesus was humble. He conceded that He needed help. He admitted His human weakness. He acknowledged His struggle in the garden of Gethsemane. Confiding in His disciples, He revealed His anguish and pain. Then He turned to His heavenly Father. Jesus knew He needed God's help to endure the cross. Prayer revealed Jesus' utter dependence on God.

How much do you really need God? Your prayer life reveals your answer. If an independent attitude has crept into it, prayer may seem a ritualistic exercise. But if you realize your weakness and acknowledge your need, then prayer will become vital to your existence. It will become your sustenance and nourishment—your lifeline. Prayer reveals your dependence on God. How much do you need Him?

*Dear Lord, I truly need You. May my prayer life*
*demonstrate my dependence on You. Amen.*

# DAY 255
# EVERYTHING YOU NEED

*You can be sure that God will take care of everything you need,*
*his generosity exceeding even yours in the glory that pours from Jesus.*
PHILIPPIANS 4:19 MSG

Have you ever gone through a period in your life when you were completely dependent on God to supply everything for you? Perhaps you lost your job or had an extended illness. It can be humbling to be unable to provide for yourself and your family.

The Israelites faced similar circumstances when God freed them from slavery in Egypt. As He led them through the desert toward the Promised Land, He provided water and food in miraculous ways. Every morning, one day's supply of manna would appear. Any attempt to save it until the next day was futile; the manna would rot. God wanted them to rely on Him daily for their provision. Yet the Israelites' response wasn't to be grateful but to complain they didn't have enough variety!

God often takes us through the desert before we get to the Promised Land. It's in the desert that we learn the lessons we will need to use in the Promised Land, most of which involve trusting Him. It's in the desert that we learn God is who He says He is. It's in the desert that we learn to obey Him not because He says to but because it's what will ultimately give us the life we were designed to live.

* * *

*Lord, we don't always live our lives as if all of our provision comes from You.*
*Remove our fear, and help us to trust in You and take You at Your word. Amen.*

# DAY 256
# MY MORNING PRAYER

*Let me hear Your lovingkindness in the morning; for I trust in You;*
*teach me the way in which I should walk; for to You I lift up my soul.*
PSALM 143:8 NASB

Do mornings excite or depress you? "Good morning, Lord!" or "Good Lord, it's morning!" When David wrote Psalm 143, he probably dreaded the sun coming up because that meant his enemies could continue pursuing him and persecuting his soul. "The enemy. . .has crushed my life to the ground" (v. 3). "My spirit is overwhelmed within me; my heart is appalled" (v. 4).

What did David do when he didn't know which way to turn? He turned to the Lord. He stayed in prayer contact with God and meditated on God's faithfulness and righteousness (v. 1), God's past work in his life (v. 5), and His loyal love (vv. 8, 12). He also took refuge in God (v. 9) and continued serving Him (v. 12).

No matter what our day holds, we can face it confidently by practicing verse 8. Let's look for God's loving-kindness and keep trusting Him no matter what. Ask Him to teach and lead us in the way He wants us to go. We have the privilege of offering up our souls (thoughts, emotions, and will) to Him anew each morning. Have a good day.

- - - - - - - - - - - - - - - - - - - - - - - - - - - - - - -

*Good morning, Lord. You are my loving Father, secure refuge, and trustworthy*
*God. Deliver me from my enemies, and show me Your loving heart as I trust in*
*You. Help me to please You today in my decisions and goals, in my attitudes*
*toward circumstances, and in the way I respond to people around me. Amen.*

# DAY 257
# CALL TO ME

*"Call to me and I will answer you and tell you*
*great and unsearchable things you do not know."*
JEREMIAH 33:3 NIV

The word *unsearchable* seems a near impossibility in today's technological age. Is there anything that Google cannot search for? Apparently so.

God tells us to call to Him and He will answer. That arrangement is a miracle in itself—that the Lord of the universe would even want us to speak to Him. But even more amazing is the idea that God would let us in on His secrets—that He would take the time and effort to be our teacher.

This relationship with God, this closeness, is reflected again and again in scripture. It's there in Abraham staring at the stars, it's there in Moses on the mountain, and it's there in Mary's womb. God wants us to know, to be certain of the fact that He is with us, in us, through us.

God wants more from us than a Q and A session. He wants a constant conversation. He wants more than what we might "ask Siri." He wants to know the deepest questions of our souls—the ones that keep us up at night or frighten us with their proportions.

Oswald Chambers said in *My Utmost for His Highest*, "We look upon prayer as a means of getting things for ourselves; the Bible's idea of prayer is that we may get to know God Himself."

. . . . . . . . . . . . . . . . . . . . . . . . . . . . . . . . . . . . . . . . . . . . . . .

*Dear Lord, thank You for the chance to know You more. Amen.*

# DAY 258
# THE BLUES

*Why, my soul, are you downcast? Why so disturbed within me?*
*Put your hope in God, for I will yet praise him, my Savior and my God.*
PSALM 42:11 NIV

Has your soul ever felt weighed down? Everyone experiences times when frustrations seem to outweigh joy, but as Christians, we have an unending source of encouragement in God.

*That's great*, you may think, *but how am I supposed to tap into that joy?* First, pray. Ask God to unburden your spirit. Share your stress, frustrations, and worries with Him. Don't hold back; He can take it. Make a list of the blessings in your life, and thank the Provider of those blessings. Choose to not focus on yourself; instead, praise Him for being Him.

Soon you'll feel true, holy refreshment—the freedom God wants you to live out every day.

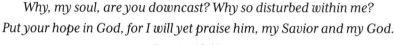

*Rejuvenate my spirit, Lord! You alone can take away the burden*
*I feel. You are my hope and my redeemer forever. Amen.*

## DAY 259

# ENCOURAGEMENT FROM THE SCRIPTURES

*For everything that was written in the past was written to teach*
*us, so that through the endurance taught in the Scriptures and*
*the encouragement they provide we might have hope.*

ROMANS 15:4 NIV

You know those days when nothing goes right? And sometimes those days stretch into weeks and months? You don't get the promotion. Your car breaks down. Someone you love gets sick. Disappointment settles in and brings its brother, Discouragement. Things are not going according to your plan, and you may wonder if God even hears your prayers.

Looking at the heroes of the Old Testament, you'll see that God's plan for those people wasn't smooth sailing either. Joseph was sold into slavery, falsely accused by Potiphar's wife, and unjustly imprisoned. Moses tended flocks in the wilderness for forty years after murdering a man and before leading God's people out of slavery. David was anointed king but had to run for his life and wait fifteen years before actually sitting on the throne.

Those stories give us hope and encouragement. Our plans are quite different from God's plans, and His ways of doing things are quite different from what we would often choose. We see how things worked out for the people of the Old Testament. We can take encouragement from the fact that the same God is at work in our lives.

• • • • • • • • • • • • • • • • • • • • • • • • • • • • • • • • • • • • • • • •

*Heavenly Father, it can be difficult to have hope during trying times.*
*Remind us to trust in You and cling to Your Word for encouragement. Amen.*

# DAY 260
# ANYTHING

*"You may ask me for anything in my name, and I will do it."*
JOHN 14:14 NIV

Anything. Ask anything. That's what Jesus said. And Jesus doesn't lie.

Humans are funny creatures. God gave us the gift of speech, and we just can't seem to stop getting tripped up on words. The God who knows every tongue is not so concerned with words—His concern is meanings.

So Jesus says, "Ask anything," and visions of cars, houses, and perfect hair pop into our heads. But the sentences before and after help us to understand the meaning. "I will do whatever you ask in my name, so that the Father may be glorified in the Son" (v. 13). The point of the "whatever" here is that it needs to be something that would bring glory to God. How do you do that? Read verse 15: "If you love me, keep my commands." By being obedient to Jesus, we will do what is needed to love God and love others—bringing glory to God in the process (and not to ourselves).

If we are busy keeping Jesus' commands and thinking about glorifying God, there's a good chance we won't ask for just "anything." We'll ask for what we need to fulfill those commands. We'll ask for what we need to glorify God. Peace. Faith. Grace. Mercy. Love. Courage. We'll ask for the things that count.

Anything.

*Dear Father, help me know what to ask for. Amen.*

# DAY 261
# FAITHFULNESS AND OBEDIENCE

*"O Lord, God of Israel, there is no God like you in all of heaven
and earth. You keep your covenant and show unfailing love
to all who walk before you in wholehearted devotion."*
2 Chronicles 6:14 nlt

After seven years of hard work, thousands of workmen, and unfathomable amounts of money, Solomon finally completed the temple. The priests carried the ark of the Lord's covenant into the inner room of the sanctuary, and suddenly, the presence of God appeared in the form of a cloud. The people were overjoyed, and Solomon led them in this prayer of thanksgiving and praise.

Sometimes, as God's people, we can be overwhelmed by the requests God makes of us. We may not be expected to build a temple, but God certainly asks us to obey Him in other ways. Thankfully, when we feel overcome with panic, we can rely on God's loving faithfulness to see us through our challenges. We simply must acknowledge God's power and eagerly obey His will.

. . . . . . . . . . . . . . . . . . . . . . . . . . . . . . . . . . . . .

*Dear Lord, truly You are the one true God in all creation. Thank You for Your
faithfulness and unfailing love. Teach me to eagerly obey Your will. Amen.*

# DAY 262
# SUSTAINER AND PROVIDER

*My flesh and my heart may fail, but God is the*
*strength of my heart and my portion forever.*
PSALM 73:26 NIV

As we grow older, we realize there are limits to our physical bodies. Our minds aren't as sharp as they used to be. An injury weakens a body part. Loss breaks our hearts. This life is hard.

Fortunately, we have more than this life to sustain us. God provides more than just what we need physically. He strengthens our hearts and walks with us, even during the difficult times.

Psalm 73 was written by a Levite, who was supported by the offerings worshippers brought to the temple. And he is saying that the Lord is more than any portion someone could bring in. He is the sustainer and preserver of all who trust in Him. He is far more than any earthly provision, and there is no limit to His ability to provide for us physically and emotionally. He never gets tired. He never runs out of resources.

When we go through difficult times, we may have trouble trusting God for a solution we can't see. But His Word promises He will sustain us. And we can tie the anchors of our hearts to this hope during the blowing storms of life.

. . . . . . . . . . . . . . . . . . . . . . . . . . . . . . . . . . . . . . . . . . . . .

*Lord God, we thank You that You are not limited by earthly*
*resources or physical barriers. You love us with a limitless*
*love, even when we cannot see it. Help us to see Your love*
*today to encourage our hearts and give us hope. Amen.*

# DAY 263
# WITH AUTHORITY

*"Therefore I tell you, whatever you ask for in prayer,*
*believe that you have received it, and it will be yours."*
MARK 11:24 NIV

The scene in Mark 11 brings to mind any stereotypical mob boss out for a stroll. If the big guy doesn't get what he wants, he just "takes care" of things. Ba-da-boom, ba-da-bing, no more problems.

Jesus was hungry. And apparently a little grumpy. He spies a fig tree with leaves on it—but no figs. What gives? (Never mind that it wasn't fig season. A good tree bears fruit, right?) So Jesus curses the tree.

His fellas hear all this, but no one's gonna be a tree hugger. They continue on their way to Jerusalem, where Jesus goes into one of the most glorious rages ever described in the Bible. (Told you He was grumpy.) He literally puts the fear of God into the rival gang (the chief priests and teachers of the law).

The guys are walking back home from all this excitement when they come upon a black, gnarled stump of a tree—the fig tree, withered right down to its roots. Jesus tells them that if they believe what they say will happen in prayer, it will be done.

Who could have questioned Him? No one. And that's the point of Mark 11.

Jesus was not just another teacher or nice guy. Jesus was God. When God says your prayers will make things happen, you better believe Him.

. . . . . . . . . . . . . . . . . . . . . . . . . . . . . . . . . . . . . . . .

*God, help me make things happen for Your kingdom. Amen.*

# DAY 264
# SKINNIER TIMES

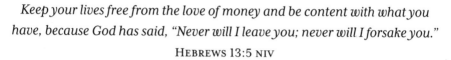

*Keep your lives free from the love of money and be content with what you have, because God has said, "Never will I leave you; never will I forsake you."*
HEBREWS 13:5 NIV

It can seem like God has left when you are bone-weary, working for meager earnings, giving all you've got, and the creditors are banging at the doors of your deficit account. You ask, "Where are You, God?"

Life's richest lessons come from our hard times. It is *there* that we are stripped of our self-sufficiency. We can see life from a perspective we miss in cushy-comfort times, when we feel less of a need to come to God in prayer. When we have need, we cry out to Him. In those times, He becomes our sufficiency, and we learn His resources are inexhaustible. His presence and comfort are irreplaceable. These lessons from skinnier times deepen our walk with Christ, bringing more contentment for what we have.

*God, You've promised to never leave or forsake me. Help me to remember that in the sparse times, You are there with me. I can be content because it all flows from Your hand. Amen.*

# DAY 265
# HOPE FOR THE SOUL

*We have this hope as an anchor for the soul, firm and secure.*
*It enters the inner sanctuary behind the curtain.*
HEBREWS 6:19 NIV

In just a few words, this verse paints a rich word picture to comfort us. "This hope" refers to the verses before where God secures His promise by swearing by Himself, giving us two trustworthy things to place our hope in: His Word and Himself.

Anchors are also a symbol of hope. During a storm, a strong anchor locked into a solid foundation keeps the boat from being blown off course or onto the rocks. Sailors' hope during a storm is the anchor.

"The inner sanctuary behind the curtain" would be familiar to these Jewish Christians—the audience of the book of Hebrews—as the Holy of Holies, where the high priest went once a year, after the sin sacrifices were offered, to enter the presence of God. When Christ died on the cross, the curtain separating the two areas tore from top to bottom, symbolizing direct access to God for all believers. So instead of anchoring into solid rock, like a ship would, we anchor our hope directly to God.

Our hope is founded in the unshakable character of God, who loves us so much He sent His Son to die for us. His Word is true. He will do what He says He will do.

. . . . . . . . . . . . . . . . . . . . . . . . . . . . . . . . . . . . . . . . . . .

*Heavenly Father, we are grateful for the sacrifice of Your Son, which made it possible for us to have a relationship with You. Remind us we can trust You completely, and help us to rest in that truth. Amen.*

# DAY 266
## CURE FOR DISCONTENT

*Always giving thanks for all things in the name of*
*our Lord Jesus Christ to God, even the Father.*
EPHESIANS 5:20 NASB

Do you struggle with being satisfied with your current situation in life? Discontent is a heart disease that manifests in comparing, coveting, and complaining. What is the cure? The habit of gratitude. Thanking God for everything—the good and the bad—means we accept it as His will even if we don't like it.

Sometimes we receive birthday or Christmas gifts we have no desire for, but we still thank the giver. God is the good giver of every perfect gift (James 1:17). Failing to thank Him is rebellion against His wisdom and ways. If we expect Him to do things the way we want or to give us more, we forget that God owes us nothing.

When God commands thanksgiving, He is not mandating our feelings but rather our submission. However, because thankfulness changes our attitude and outlook, it does affect our feelings. Discontent and resentment cannot coexist with humble acceptance of what happens to us. Therefore, thanking God must become our lifelong habit. When we turn out the light every night, we can review our day and thank God for each event—good and bad—because He allowed it, and He is good. We can be satisfied with that.

. . . . . . . . . . . . . . . . . . . . . . . . . . . . . . . . . . . . . . . . . . .

*Bountiful Father, I'm sorry I often rebel against Your sovereign plan*
*for me. Thank You for doing all things well. Your essence is love,*
*and every mark You make in my life is a love mark, conforming*
*me to Christ. I accept Your will and Your ways. Amen.*

# DAY 267
# LADY PERSISTENCE

*"Will not God bring about justice for his chosen*
*ones, who cry out to him day and night?"*
LUKE 18:7 NIV

Sometimes—admit it—you feel like giving up. You have a chronic illness that just never seems to get any better. You have a workload that never lets up. You have some family struggle that just cannot be resolved, no matter how hard you try.

Keep praying.

You keep trying to learn a new thing, but your grades don't show your effort. You want a relationship to work, but you don't know what to do. You keep looking for a job, but no one seems to be hiring.

Keep praying.

Jesus painted the picture for us of a widow bringing a complaint before a judge. She wanted justice. The uncaring judge wanted to be left alone. But the widow kept coming, no matter how many times he refused her. Finally, he gave in and actually did the right thing.

Jesus pointed out that if unjust judges here on earth can decide cases to bring about justice, then God certainly can and will do the same for His children. He won't keep putting them off. He will always see that justice gets done.

* * * * * * * * * * * * * * * * * * * * * * * * * * * * * * * * * * * * * * * *

*Dear Judge of all, please help to bring justice*
*and peace to the situation on my mind. Amen.*

## DAY 268
# REMEMBER

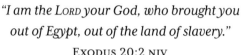

*"I am the LORD your God, who brought you
out of Egypt, out of the land of slavery."*
EXODUS 20:2 NIV

Just before God gave the Israelites the Ten Commandments, He reminded them that He had brought them out of slavery in Egypt. It is easy for us to read this verse and wonder why the Israelites needed reminding. After years and years of harsh treatment and manual labor in Egypt, wouldn't they always be grateful to the Lord for delivering them from slavery?

Establish for yourself some reminders of God's blessings. Start a prayer journal where you can record your prayer requests and God's answers. Review the pages of your prayer journal when you face a hardship. Thank God for taking care of you in the past, and ask Him to increase your faith. He wants you to trust that He will never leave you or forsake you.

Like the Israelites, we forget. God is faithful in *all ways* for *all days*. Remember that today.

. . . . . . . . . . . . . . . . . . . . . . . . . . . . . . . . . . . . . . . . . . . . . . .

*You are faithful, Father. You have freed me from the gates of
hell and given me an abundant life with the promise of eternity
with You. Grow my faith. Help me to remember. Amen.*

# DAY 269

# JOY IN TRIALS

*Consider it pure joy, my brothers and sisters, whenever you face
trials of many kinds, because you know that the testing of your
faith produces perseverance. Let perseverance finish its work so
that you may be mature and complete, not lacking anything.*

JAMES 1:2–4 NIV

James begins his letter by encouraging his brothers and sisters in Christ to find joy in their trials. The word *consider* tells us to move this discussion about trials out of our emotions and into our heads.

Stop and think about this for a minute. Trials are going to come. That is a fact of this life. We can't waste our time trying to avoid them. So instead, let's remember we have the ultimate victory in Christ. Nothing that happens on earth will take away our heavenly reward and the joy we will have in heaven.

With Christ, the fruit of our trials can be growth, maturity, peace, and the fruit of the Spirit instead of despondency, discouragement, depression, and hopelessness. Ask God for wisdom for the next step. Draw close to Him. Let perseverance finish its work to increase your maturity. Take real steps of obedience and faith because the key to joy is obedience.

. . . . . . . . . . . . . . . . . . . . . . . . . . . . . . . . . . . .

*Lord, as hard as it is, help us to find joy in the difficult things that
come our way, because we know You have given us the ultimate
victory. And in the process, we can become more like You. Amen.*

# DAY 270
# GUILT REMOVAL

*If we confess our sins, He is faithful and just to forgive us
our sins and to cleanse us from all unrighteousness.*
1 John 1:9 nkjv

Sometimes we don't feel forgiven. Even though we have believed that Christ's death and resurrection paid the penalty for all our sins and we now have eternal life, we still sin. First John 1:9 tells us believers to confess our sins to God, and He cleanses us. What if we still feel guilty? Some people say we should forgive ourselves. This is not a biblical concept, but it probably means accepting God's forgiveness. If feelings of guilt return every time we recall what we have done, perhaps we are still grieving the losses a particular sin has caused. Sin can be forgiven, and restitution can be made, but most consequences are permanent. Something broke like an egg when we sinned, and it cannot be fixed in this life. Yet God can redeem it for good. Failures can keep us dependent on Him and give us empathy for others.

Two things will help us "feel" forgiven: (1) Thanking God for His promise that we are cleansed "from all unrighteousness." The promise is as sure as God is. (2) Meditating on Galatians 5:1 (nkjv): "Stand fast therefore in the liberty by which Christ has made us free, and do not be entangled again with a yoke of bondage." Stand victorious in the truth that Christ has freed us from our sin and guilt. It cannot enslave us again unless we let it.

. . . . . . . . . . . . . . . . . . . . . . . . . . . . . . . . . . . . . . . . . .

*Dear Lord, although I don't deserve Your mercy and grace,
I gratefully accept Your complete forgiveness. Amen.*

# DAY 271

## REFRESH

*"Repent, then, and turn to God, so that your sins may be wiped out, that times of refreshing may come from the Lord."*
ACTS 3:19 NIV

Surely one of the prayers most often prayed is "God, I'm sorry." It must be right up there with "God, help!"

Prayer is a profound and essential part of repentance. You cannot repent without coming before God. In our present time, you cannot come before God without prayer.

Certainly it's not anyone's favorite prayer to say. To come before the Holy One and declare the ways in which you have been most definitely not holy is uncomfortable, to say the least. For some the encounter could even be sickening.

You cannot get rid of a wound without exposing it and cleaning it out. You cannot repent and start to heal without exposing your heart to God.

Let God wipe away your sins. Let God forgive you so you can know how to forgive others. Start over. Start fresh.

Then don't take the same steps when you walk away. Try something new. Walk a different way. Set up a new routine. Make sure prayer is part of your daily schedule. Not just one part. Let prayer prepare you for your day, let prayer be a time of rest throughout your day, and let prayer end your day with thanksgiving. If you do this, the times of refreshing will come.

- - - - - - - - - - - - - - - - - - - - - - - - - - - - - - - - - - - - - - - -

*Dear Lord, refresh my spirit and renew my heart. Amen.*

# DAY 272
# SKEPTICS AND CYNICS

*For ever since the world was created, people have seen the earth and sky.*
*Through everything God made, they can clearly see his invisible qualities—his*
*eternal power and divine nature. So they have no excuse for not knowing God.*

ROMANS 1:20 NLT

There are skeptics and cynics in our world. They love to question the possibility of a divine Creator. They have seemingly sound arguments based in logic and science. We can share testimonials, blessings, and miracles from our personal lives and from scripture. But these are often met with disbelief and tales of big bangs and evolution.

In order for a skeptic to be changed to a seeker, Jesus must grab his attention, often using His children to do that. Take time to really consider the miraculous works of God that prove His existence. Pray for wisdom and compelling words to lead cynics to the throne.

. . . . . . . . . . . . . . . . . . . . . . . . . . . . . . . . . . . . . . . . . . . .

*Father, help me to be a good witness of You and Your miraculous wonders.*
*Give me the words to convince even the most hardened skeptic. Guide me*
*to people, according to Your will, so that I can make a difference. Amen.*

# DAY 273
# NO MORE TEARS

*" 'He will wipe every tear from their eyes. There will be no more death' or*
*mourning or crying or pain, for the old order of things has passed away."*
REVELATION 21:4 NIV

This world is sadly full of sorrow and disappointment. But God doesn't allow our pain to be purposeless. It helps us need Jesus more. It drives us to a closer, more dependent relationship with Him, even when we can't possibly understand the reason for the pain we are experiencing.

Pain, especially when it's seen in our rearview mirror rather than in front of our faces, helps us have greater compassion for others' suffering. It also gives us common ground to give comfort and empathize with others who are in painful circumstances.

It won't always be like this. Someday we will live with Jesus in a perfect life with no sorrow, pain, or disappointment. And we get a "no more tears" promise that is greater than any baby shampoo could deliver. Someday we will have joy greater than anything this earth can offer because it won't be tinged by sin and death. And that is a promise we can hold on to.

*Heavenly Father, thank You so much for defeating death and sin*
*so we can have a glorious future with You in heaven, where we will*
*truly have no more tears. Help us to cling to Your promises and to*
*comfort others who are going through painful situations. Amen.*

# DAY 274
# SPIRITUAL CPR

*How long, O LORD? Will You forget me forever?*
*How long will You hide Your face from me?*
PSALM 13:1 NASB

Our feelings do not determine our relationship with God. Since euphoria is not necessarily spiritual joy, feeling numb is not a sign of unspirituality—it's a grief emotion. Nevertheless, Psalm 13 gives a formula for times when we feel like God is gone—two verses each for Complaints, Petition, and Resolve (CPR!).

While we should not question God as if He goofed, it is okay to ask God questions. He may not answer, but He can handle our complaints. The writer asks God how long his suffering will continue. He feels like God is absent, his heart is filled with sorrow every day, and his enemies are winning.

So he petitions God to hear and answer, to put light back into his eyes, or else he will continue to feel dead, and his enemies will gloat over him. He *complains*, he *prays*, and then he *resolves* to trust God now as he has in the past. By remembering God's loving-kindness and rejoicing in the way God will deliver him, he can count on God's bountiful nature.

Two exercises will help us when afflicted—rejoicing in the Lord and singing to the Lord (vv. 5–6). List things you are thankful for or think about God's attributes A to Z. Choose a praise song to play or sing throughout the day.

Suffering can cause doubt and fear to attack our hearts, but performing CPR will revive our weak faith.

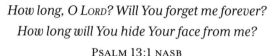

*Oh Lord, I cast all my cares upon You because You care for me. Amen.*

# DAY 275
# LIKE AN EAGLE

*Like an eagle that stirs up its nest and hovers*
*over its young. . . . The Lord alone led him.*
DEUTERONOMY 32:11–12 NIV

It is good to remember the kind of Person we are addressing when we pray. God is mighty like the ocean and strong like the wind. God is unending like the sky and enduring like the mountains. God is peaceful like a quiet sea and patient like shore rocks that take the waves. God is all-powerful, all-knowing, always with us.

God is big and unsearchable in many ways. Yet He lets us know Him and learn about Him. God is a whispering voice in our souls, and yet His Word shouts truth.

God is huge and grand and impossible to fathom. He is our Father— deliverer of justice, ruler of peace, rescuer, and redeemer.

God is like the eagle, which nurtures its eggs, turning them over at just the right time and keeping them at just the right temperature for proper growth. God is like the eagle, which protects its young chicks, covering them with its wings. God is like the eagle, playing with its young, letting them take chances and then always being there to catch them when they fall.

God is like the eagle, teaching us to fly and carrying us high over the hard parts.

This is the God we call on when we pray.

*Dear God, thank You for Your tender, caring love. Amen.*

# DAY 276
## THE NEARNESS OF YOU

*Come near to God and he will come near to you.*
JAMES 4:8 NIV

"Come near to God," we hear. And we think, *I can do that.* So we take our notebooks and buy the most inspirational Bibles complete with ribbon bookmarks and study notes, we create quiet-time nooks, we go sit under trees, we spiritually retreat and. . .find we are no closer. We don't feel closer to God; we feel tired.

So we follow the rest of James's instructions. We pray, pour our hearts out, and maybe even cry. We humbly admit our faults to God. Finally, James says, "*Now, you've got it!*" Because it was never about us making ourselves any better. We are messed-up people. Even our best efforts at doing better are going to get us nowhere in the end. Once we humbly admit that fact, God will lift us up. And *that's* how we get nearer, by realizing we can't do anything without Him.

. . . . . . . . . . . . . . . . . . . . . . . . . . . . . . . . . . . . . . . . . .

*My God, my Friend, my Savior. Humble me so You can lift me up. Amen.*

# PEACE BEYOND COMPREHENSION

*Do not be anxious about anything, but in every situation, by prayer and petition, with thanksgiving, present your requests to God. And the peace of God, which transcends all understanding, will guard your hearts and your minds in Christ Jesus.*

PHILIPPIANS 4:6–7 NIV

Within the first hours of the day, many of us can find opportunities to worry. But as we learn to take every situation to God, He exchanges our worries for His peace.

We come before God and bring Him our needs, knowing He is the only One who can grant our request. And we are to do this with thanksgiving. When we remember all God has done for us and provided for us, the worries that cause us to focus on what we don't have slip away in the presence of our mighty God.

God has compassion on us and knows we have many things to worry about. He tells us many times to come to Him. In 1 Peter 5:7, He tells us to give Him our cares. In Matthew 6:25, He tells us He will provide for us and meet our needs.

God promises that peace will permeate both our hearts, where our feelings can churn painfully, and our minds, where we can turn situations over endlessly. Along with giving us His peace, God takes our minds into protective custody, cutting off worries before they can enter.

*Lord Jesus, thank You for giving us Your supernatural peace. Remind us to bring all of our cares to You and to thank You for everything You've done for us. Amen.*

# DAY 278
# DO NOT FEAR

*"Do not fear, for I am with you; do not anxiously look about you,*
*for I am your God. I will strengthen you, surely I will help you,*
*surely I will uphold you with My righteous right hand."*
ISAIAH 41:10 NASB

Fear can seep into our lives so easily. We fear the unknowns of the future. We fear we didn't handle a certain situation as well as we should have. We fear we are too inadequate, or too busy, or too unmotivated to handle the things being thrown at us in the present.

But in this verse, God tells you not to fear. This isn't just an idle "Don't worry, you'll be okay" kind of statement. In fact, He *commands* you not to fear. How can He be so confident that you are completely safe so that He can command you not to fear? Because He is with you. The God who created, sustains, and governs this entire world is with you. With that perspective, what is there to fear?

Stop looking anxiously around you at all the burdens, worries, and fears of your life. Instead, focus on your God. He promises to strengthen and help you. Nothing in this world is so overwhelming that you cannot overcome it with almighty God's strength. And even when you feel that you have fallen with no strength to get up, He promises to hold you up with His hand.

• • • • • • • • • • • • • • • • • • • • • • • • • • • • • • • • • • • • • •

*Lord, help me to fully understand that You are with me,*
*strengthening me, helping me, and holding me in Your hands. Amen.*

# DAY 279

# NEAR

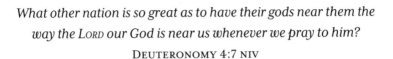

*What other nation is so great as to have their gods near them the way the Lord our God is near us whenever we pray to him?*

DEUTERONOMY 4:7 NIV

Moses makes a rather undeniable point in his speech to the Israelites. He reminds them what God has done for them and the way in which God has spoken to them. He reminds them of these things as a warning to them not to try to make a form to fit God—not to worship idols of their own making.

Look around at the people who were living at the time, and it's not hard to see why this warning was needed. Many people worshipped other gods, which were often linked with the seasons or natural elements. For every god they had, they had a form. It was common for people to create shapes and pictures and statues to represent their gods. People like to have something to hold on to—a way of understanding something that they can't understand.

Moses reminds the people that they need not do that. They don't have to paint a picture or shape a statue. God is right there with them. They can know Him by His voice, by the commands He has given them, and by the promises He has made to them. They can be sure of Him by remembering all He has done for them and telling these stories to the next generation so they remember too.

God is near. No other god comes close.

*Dear God, thank You for coming near. Amen.*

# DAY 280
# ALL TOO FAMILIAR

*"God, I thank you that I am not like other people."*
LUKE 18:11 NIV

Have you ever said this prayer? Or one like it? "Thank God, we aren't that bad." "Good heavens, I'm glad no one I know is like that!" "Well, we might not be perfect, but at least we've never _____!" (Fill in the blank with an appropriate sin.)

Perhaps you've never said such words or even thought them, but could it be that you have, somewhere in a small corner of your mind, felt just a little bit better than other people? A little more worthy? A little more deserving?

Jesus sets us straight. It was the other guy who "went home justified" (v. 14). The tax collector. The guy who wouldn't even look up. The guy who stood at a distance, beating the words out of his chest: "Have mercy on me, a sinner" (v. 13). The two prayers could not have been more different. The two pray-ers? They had a lot in common.

*God, if I ever start thinking of myself as better*
*than someone else, show me the truth. Amen.*

# TAKING JESUS AT HIS WORD

*The royal official said, "Sir, come down before my child dies." "Go," Jesus replied, "your son will live." The man took Jesus at his word and departed.*
JOHN 4:49–50 NIV

The royal official must have been desperate. He had probably made offerings to the many Roman gods, but his son was still sick. He'd heard about a prophet the local Galileans called Jesus. Everyone was looking to see what miracles He would perform.

The official found Jesus and begged Him to come heal his son. But Jesus didn't do the expected. He didn't go to heal the man's son. Instead, He simply said that the son would live. The man may have had a moment of confusion at the unexpected turn of events, but he did take Jesus at His word. He believed that Jesus' word could heal his son even though he'd expected that Jesus would have to touch his son to heal him. And when he arrived home and found his son well, he and his whole household believed.

Sometimes we are like this official. We look to Jesus as a last resort, and then we expect Him to act in a certain way. But as we look through the Gospels, we see that Jesus healed in a variety of ways. Still today He works any way He chooses, not just the way we expect.

Are you looking for Jesus to act in a certain way to answer a prayer? Ask God to open your eyes to the unexpected ways He is working.

. . . . . . . . . . . . . . . . . . . . . . . . . . . . . . . . . . . . . .

*Lord Jesus, thank You for being intimately involved in our lives. Remind us to trust You for everything. Amen.*

# DAY 282
# A PRAYER FOR PASTORS

*Pray also for me, that whenever I speak, words may be given me*
*so that I will fearlessly make known the mystery of the gospel.*
EPHESIANS 6:19 NIV

How often do you pray for pastors? Pastors may be paid or not, but they are people who devote the majority of their lives to the teaching, development, care, counseling, and nurturing of God's flock. They serve in one of the hardest and most stressful jobs a person can have. Why? Because their job 100 percent of the time is dealing with people—and most often people in some kind of physical, spiritual, mental, or emotional need.

So pray for your pastors. Pray that they will be able to endure long nights and long phone calls. Pray that they have time to study and be refreshed. Pray that they have clear understanding of God's Word and ability to speak truth well.

Pray for courage. Pray that they will not be afraid to stop someone from a life of destruction. Pray that they will be confident in God's love for them. Pray they will be strong in fighting off temptation.

Pray for wisdom. Pray that they will be able to pick their battles. Pray that they will know when to be silent. Pray that their understanding of people will be strengthened by experience and by prayer.

Pray for an unending well of energy. Pray for the ability to share unconditional love. Pray for an eternal life with God.

Pray for your pastors.

*Dear God, thank You for Your servants.*
*Please help me to build them up. Amen.*

# DAY 283
## FAMILY PICTURE

*How wonderful, how beautiful, when brothers and sisters get along!*
PSALM 133:1 MSG

What do you think the church's family picture would look like? If we could somehow manage to get all the people in all the congregations around the world to sit still and look nice for just ten seconds, what would happen? Would the photo be all lovely and Olan Mills perfect? Or would it show fingers pointing in accusation, someone getting knocked over, someone's feelings getting hurt, tears, bruises. . .anarchy?

It's highly unlikely we can do much about the world's Christian population in general, but what can we do in our own communities to make a better family photo? What can we do to become a better family?

Pray to promote peace, love, and unity among our brothers and sisters, beginning with ourselves.

* * *

*Dear God, let me be an instrument of Your peace.*
*Help me, in whatever conversations or relationships I*
*develop, to build up unity among Your followers. Amen.*

# DAY 284

# THE BATTLE BELONGS TO THE LORD

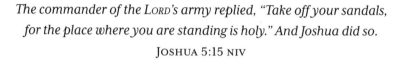

*The commander of the Lord's army replied, "Take off your sandals,*
*for the place where you are standing is holy." And Joshua did so.*
JOSHUA 5:15 NIV

Joshua has some big sandals to fill. Moses is gone, and Joshua is in charge of the nation of Israel. Surrounded by enemies, the tiny nation has its first battle for the Promised Land coming up. And even though he's seen God work in miraculous ways, Joshua must be at least a little afraid.

And then he hears the same message his predecessor, Moses, did. "Take off your sandals. You're on holy ground."

Moses heard it coming from a burning bush. Joshua hears it from the commander of the Lord's army. If he wasn't scared before, he certainly is now. But ultimately this messenger and his message give comfort to Joshua. He has been anointed to be Israel's leader in the same way Moses had been. The battle isn't Joshua's to win or lose. He just needs to be faithful. The battle is God's. And He's already won it. Joshua just needs to follow orders.

We can have the same comfort that Joshua had. Whatever battle or challenge we may be facing, we don't face it alone. God is with us every step of the way. He will never leave us or forsake us.

* * * * * * * * * * * * * * * * * * * * * * * * * * * * * * * * * * * *

*Heavenly Father, thank You for always being beside us. Remind us of Your*
*presence, and help us to bring all of our cares and concerns to You. Amen.*

# DAY 285
## DAUGHTER

*And He said to her, "Daughter, your faith has made
you well; go in peace and be healed of your affliction."*
MARK 5:34 NASB

The woman in this passage had suffered greatly from an affliction that made her ceremonially unclean; she was an outcast, not able to participate in society. In an act of desperation, she pushed through the thick crowd to Jesus and touched His garments. When Jesus turned around and asked who had touched Him, she fell in fear and trembling at His feet. This woman had probably been in shameful hiding for many years and now, in front of a large crowd, recounted her humiliating story. Probably some of the spectators were repulsed by her story, and yet Jesus, in front of the whole crowd, called her "daughter." Can you imagine how it must have felt to this rejected and shamed woman to hear herself called "daughter"—a term of belonging and love?

You also have been adopted and called a daughter of God. Don't hide your shame and struggles from Him. In circumstances where you can hardly stand up under the weight of your burden, fall at His feet as this woman did. You will not be rejected or shamed by Him. He calls you daughter. He loves you and is able to heal you.

* * * * * * * * * * * * * * * * * * * * * * * * * * * * * * * * * * * * * * * * * *

*Lord, may I have the same faith that this woman had.
Thank You that You have made me Your daughter. Amen.*

# DAY 286
## SON THOUGH HE WAS

*He offered up prayers and petitions with fervent cries*
*and tears to the one who could save him from death.*
HEBREWS 5:7 NIV

There's an amazing description of Jesus in Hebrews 5. It's not long, and it's not poetically written (like the oft-quoted passages in Isaiah). It's striking in the depiction of our Savior as our brother.

Jesus walked on this earth with us. He was born and died like we are born and will die. He suffered more than we could ever know. Just as there come days when we lift up desperate prayers to God through tears, Jesus prayed and cried too. Just as we sometimes have to face hard things and are not given an easy out, Jesus didn't get the easy way out either. He prayed and asked, "God, please, if. . ." But He did not get the "if." He got the "Thy will be done" part instead.

Son though He was, His burdens were not taken away.

Son though He was, He was not rescued in a daring last-minute escape.

Son though He was, He did not triumph over His captors. At least not that time.

Instead, Son though He was, He "learned obedience from what he suffered" and, then when he had fulfilled the prophecies and conquered death, he "became the source of eternal salvation for all who obey him" (vv. 8–9).

Why should we expect answers to our prayers to be different from His—Son that He is?

· · · · · · · · · · · · · · · · · · · · · · · · · · · · · · · · · · · · · ·

*Dear God, help me to accept Your will. Amen.*

# DAY 287

# GRIEF-WORN

*Heal me, LORD, for my bones are in agony. My soul
is in deep anguish. How long, LORD, how long?*
PSALM 6:2–3 NIV

We struggle to find ways of expressing the bone-crushing weariness of grief. Sometimes it feels as though if we could just put it into words, maybe we could get past the sorrow.

But the psalmists have given us words: "I am worn out from my groaning. All night long I flood my bed with weeping and drench my couch with tears. My eyes grow weak with sorrow; they fail because of all my foes" (vv. 6–7).

It is somehow comforting to know that souls from thousands of years ago can speak to us about the same feelings we have today. And that even though there is still pain and trouble and sorrow, there is also still our Lord God, who never changes: "The LORD has heard my weeping. The LORD has heard my cry for mercy; the LORD accepts my prayer" (vv. 8–9).

. . . . . . . . . . . . . . . . . . . . . . . . . . . . . . . . . . . . . . . .

*Dear God, hear me when I am sad and feel alone. Show me
You are with me and that my grief will not go on forever. Amen.*

# DAY 288
# THE BLESSING BLUES

*Bless those who persecute you; bless and do not curse.*
ROMANS 12:14 NIV

"Roger's not even part of the family. He's adopted! He shouldn't get part of Mother's property!" Rena complained. "I want my share and everything else I deserve!"

Normally calm, Roger was rattled. Chosen by their mother for his financial expertise, he was astonished when his stepsister stopped probate. Now that their mother's house was in escrow, Rena stopped the sale. Her actions hurt all the family, including her children.

The next morning, Roger prayed, "Lord, get her good!" Then he realized his mistake in Jesus' words: "Love your enemies, do good to those who hate you, bless those who curse you, pray for those who mistreat you" (Luke 6:27–28 NIV).

"You're kidding, Lord. I've got the blessing blues, and You want me to pray good things for her!" He began with clenched teeth, "Lord, bless Rena and her attorney. Let this come out Your way." As he asked God for a blessing on Rena day after day, Roger felt his own resentment melt away. He could smile. His sense of humor returned. He became willing to let God handle the situation entirely. He let go of worry and let God manage the issue.

Blessing those who mistreat you is impossible—except with God. In His strength, we can overcome.

. . . . . . . . . . . . . . . . . . . . . . . . . . . . . . . . . . . . . . . .

*Lord, I ask You to strengthen me as I pray with a sincere heart for You to bless those in my life who may be dishonoring or mistreating me. Amen.*

# DAY 289

# PRAYER OF A RIGHTEOUS PERSON

*Therefore confess your sins to each other and
pray for each other so that you may be healed.*
JAMES 5:16 NIV

James is a clear, practical writer. In chapter 5 of his message, James tells the hearers when to pray. "Is anyone among you in trouble?" Pray. "Is anyone happy?" Praise God. "Is anyone among you sick?" Gather your church elders and let them pray over you (vv. 13–14).

He gives you the results with complete confidence as well. "And the prayer offered in faith will make the sick person well; the Lord will raise them up. If they have sinned, they will be forgiven" (v. 15). He urges people to pray for each other so they can receive healing, for "the prayer of a righteous person is powerful and effective" (v. 16).

Why is the prayer of righteous people so powerful and effective? There are at least three reasons: (1) the faith they have; (2) the faith people have in them; (3) the faith they don't have yet. A righteous person is a faithful person—a person who knows God and whose hope is consistently settled on God. When they pray, God knows they mean it. The people who hear them know it too. They see the righteous person's life and who their hope is in, and this strengthens their faith.

Lastly, the prayer of the righteous is powerful because of what they lack. God's strength shines in their weakness.

*Dear Lord, thank You for righteous people who trust in You. Amen.*

# DAY 290
## ENFORCED GRATITUDE

*They were also to stand every morning to thank and praise the L*ORD.
1 C<small>HRONICLES</small> 23:30 <small>NIV</small>

David appointed the Levites to help Aaron's descendants with the service of the temple of the Lord. One of their jobs was to "stand every morning to thank and praise the L<small>ORD</small>." They did this in the evening as well.

They also had thank offerings. It seems it would be far easier at times to offer a thank offering to burn—would handmade sweaters work?—than to actually say words of thanks, and far, far simpler than actually feeling thankful.

But for every awkward gift we receive or uncomfortable moment in life we endure, there must be at least a hundred good things our Father gives us that we can and should feel thankful for.

So try it. . . Appoint yourself to be your own Levite. Get up and stand every morning and thank and praise the Lord!

. . . . . . . . . . . . . . . . . . . . . . . . . . . . . . . . . . . . . . . . .

*Dear Lord, I give thanks to You, for You are good*
*and Your love endures forever. Amen.*

## DAY 291

# THERE'S NO PLACE LIKE GRANDMA'S

*"The eternal God is your refuge, and underneath are the everlasting arms."*
DEUTERONOMY 33:27 NIV

"There's no place like Grandma's," ten-year-old Ben piped up. "I can hardly wait to see what fun she has cooked up for us today!" he told his mother as she was driving him there.

Though Ben's room overflowed with souvenirs from theme park vacations, Grandma offered no such extras. What she did share was her time, home, encouragement—and fun!

"After I have a bad day," Ben continued, "Grandma hugs me and says, 'Ben, you're still going to grow up to be a wonderful man.' I feel better then."

When Ben arrived at Grandma's at the same time as two cousins, Grandma hugged the boys and ushered them into the kitchen, where she was making flour paste. She smiled and said, "We're making piñatas today! When they're dry and done, we'll fill them with candy and toys!"

The unanimous response: "Hooray!"

Like Grandma's investment in her grandsons and her provision of a refuge through good days and bad, God believes in us and gives us safe places to rest.

God's refuge of strength and protection has stood unchanged for millennia. He's worth our trust. Though the world pulls us to trust in money, careers, or causes, all become shaky investments of time and effort. But trusting in God never fails. He provides the solid foundation that stands for all time—and is a safe place always. Just as at Grandma's, God supports and encourages us inside hugs from His strong arms.

*Lord, each day, help me seek and find Your plans for me.*
*Send me into the world in Your strength. Amen.*

# DAY 292
# TRUST AND LEAN

*Trust in the L*ORD *with all your heart and*
*do not lean on your own understanding.*
PROVERBS 3:5 NASB

This verse contains two commands—trust in the Lord and don't rely on your own understanding.

Do you trust in God? You can rely on God because He is truly trustworthy—He has the strength to sustain, help, and protect you and an incomprehensible love for you that cannot be broken or grow stale. You are not bringing your prayers before someone who is powerful but fickle, or one who is loving and good but weak. You pray to a God who is all-powerful but also good and loving. Therefore, you can be confident that your life is placed firmly in His hands and His control and that He considers it precious.

How often do you lean on your own understanding and strength instead of God's? You are remarkably less capable of controlling your life than God is. Instead of trusting yourself, someone who doesn't know the future and certainly can't control it, lean on the all-powerful God who knows each step you will take. Relinquish all your anxious thoughts to His control. Trusting God with your future is far more productive than worrying about it. So lean on Him and trust Him with *everything* in your heart. He will sustain you.

* * * * * * * * * * * * * * * * * * * * * * * * * * * * * * * * *

*Lord, forgive me for not trusting You as I should. Forgive*
*me for leaning on my own understanding instead of relying*
*on Your infinite wisdom and strength. Thank You that these*
*commands You give me are for my greatest benefit. Amen.*

# FRIEND AND INTERCESSOR

*"My intercessor is my friend as my eyes pour out tears to God."*
JOB 16:20 NIV

Job was a man in need of a true friend. You have probably heard about the suffering of Job. (If you haven't, read the first couple of chapters of the book of Job—but be prepared for a shock.) The story of Job is about a man full of grief and hurt, a man allowed by God to be tested. He was surrounded by so-called friends, who perhaps meant well, but whose words weren't exactly helpful. About them Job said, "You are miserable comforters, all of you!" (v. 2), and he was right.

We have a better friend and comforter than any person we could find on earth. We have Jesus. Jesus is always there for us. Jesus speaks to God on our behalf. Can we imagine a better person to stand up for us? Jesus "pleads with God as one pleads for a friend" (v. 21).

And what does He plead? When we repent of our sins, He pleads for our forgiveness. When we have been hurt, He pleads for our restoration. When we stand before God to be judged for our worth, He stands in for us and says, "I make this one worthy."

It is good to have friends in high places. It's better still to have a friend willing to bring us up with Him.

. . . . . . . . . . . . . . . . . . . . . . . . . . . . . . . . . . . . . . . . . .

*Dear Jesus, thank You for pleading for me. Amen.*

# DAY 294
# EVEN IF HE DOESN'T

*"The God we serve is able to deliver us."*
DANIEL 3:17 NIV

Shadrach, Meshach, and Abednego, followers of the one true God, refused to worship Nebuchadnezzar's idol. They knew what would happen to them for disobeying the king's orders, and they still refused, saying, "If we are thrown into the blazing furnace, the God we serve is able to deliver us from it, and he will deliver us from Your Majesty's hand" (Daniel 3:17 NIV). They definitely had confidence in their God.

But that wasn't all they said: "But even if he does not, we want you to know, Your Majesty, that we will not serve your gods or worship the image of gold you have set up" (v. 18). "Even if he does not."

Have you been praying hard for something to happen recently? Something you really care about? Are you able to pray those words too: "God, even if You do not. . . "?

. . . . . . . . . . . . . . . . . . . . . . . . . . . . . . . . . . . . . . . . . .

*Help me, Lord, to believe even when things don't go my way. Amen.*

# JUST LOUNGE AROUND AND LISTEN TO GOD? WHO HAS TIME?

*After the earthquake came a fire, but the L*ORD *was not in the fire. And after the fire came a gentle whisper.*
1 KINGS 19:12 NIV

Susan greeted the couple as they entered the home improvement store: "What can I help you find?"

"We need patio furniture for our second home here," the wife began. "We have a big yard."

"Great! We have comfortable furniture here that is just like your dining and living room! It's weatherproof! Because you have the space, have you considered one of these colorful hammocks? Just kick back and enjoy!"

"We don't have time to lounge around," the husband responded. "We're just too busy with two homes, commuting, and work. What we need is a patio table and six chairs for when the kids and grandkids come up."

Susan thought about the work and time involved in big meals for lots of company. When would they be able to relax?

Susan reflected on the patio trend in home magazines. Even with garden makeovers focused on creating a pleasant retreat, spaces were furnished with two, four, or six chairs—never just a hammock or space for one.

With today's pace, we are pressured to do more and more multitasking. What's missing is time to think, reflect, appreciate, and listen to God—alone.

Being able to hear God's voice—even in a whisper—is one key to keeping close to Him. We just need to take the time to relax and enjoy His company and our own.

*Lord, thank You for coming to me in a whisper at times. I will take time to listen. Amen.*

# DAY 296
# ACKNOWLEDGE GOD

*In all your ways acknowledge Him, and He will make your paths straight.*
PROVERBS 3:6 NASB

When do you acknowledge God? Do you acknowledge Him when things are going well by thanking Him for the blessings in your life? Or maybe when things aren't going well, you realize that you need His help.

This verse commands you to acknowledge God in *all* your ways. When things are going well, praise Him, because everything good comes from His hand. Have a grateful heart, and look for ways to bless others with the bounty that God has given you.

When things are not going well, pray to Him; pour out your heart to Him (Psalm 68:2). He loves you in ways that you cannot even comprehend. He wants you to come before Him. Even in the deepest grief, still praise Him—He has loved you enough to die on your behalf, securing your salvation so you can spend eternity with Him. That is something that no circumstance can take away.

When life feels mundane and meaningless, acknowledge that He has put you where you are for a reason and that He will not waste your time or your talents. Worship Him while you wait for the next step in life.

God promises that when you acknowledge Him in all your ways, He will make your paths straight. What a comfort that He will guide you and lead you on the path you should take.

. . . . . . . . . . . . . . . . . . . . . . . . . . . . . . . . . . . . . . . .

*Lord, I acknowledge that You are sovereign and loving in the circumstance that I am in right now. Continue to lead me down a straight path. Amen.*

# DAY 297
# MY SOUL TO KEEP

*"Let the little children come to me, and do not hinder them,*
*for the kingdom of God belongs to such as these."*
MARK 10:14 NIV

Some of the best prayers you will ever hear may come from the lips of a child. Children speak to God as if they were speaking to their teacher or their grandpa or their dog, Fido. They use the words that come naturally to them and don't try to sound fancy or serious.

Children innocently reveal all their secrets and sometimes the secrets of others. They come clean about every size of mistake or wrong they ever did or that was ever done to them or by somebody near them. They empty their little souls of all their burdens. Perhaps that's what makes them so bouncy.

Children will pray about the ridiculous and the sublime at the same time, sometimes even in the same breath. They have no boundaries between them and their Father, no walls to break down, no veils to hide behind.

It is no wonder that Jesus asked for the little children to be allowed to come to Him. How refreshing it must be for God to hear the prayers of hearts and minds that have not yet been made world-weary. We might do well to shed our grown-up manners once in a while and pray with the children: "Now I lay me down to sleep, I pray the Lord my soul to keep."

*Dear Father, remind me that I am Your child still. Amen.*

# DAY 298
# GOD KNOWS

*"Do not be like them, for your Father knows*
*what you need before you ask him."*
MATTHEW 6:8 NIV

The "them" in Matthew 6:8 are an interesting crew. Jesus describes them in verse 7, saying: "And when you pray, do not keep on babbling like pagans, for they think they will be heard because of their many words." Jesus is telling the believers not to be babblers. It sounds like people were having trouble figuring out this prayer thing even way back then.

Jesus wants us to be less concerned with our style of prayer and more concerned with what we say and who we are saying it to.

The pagans go on babbling perhaps because they can't be quite certain who it is they are talking to or what it is they want their god(s) to do. But we have a Father in heaven who is holy and in control. We know who He is, and He knows us. And we do not have to use many words to make our needs known.

We do not pray to offer God information. We pray to offer God us.

. . . . . . . . . . . . . . . . . . . . . . . . . . . . . . . . . . . . . . . . . . . .

*Dear God, thank You for hearing my imperfect prayers. Amen.*

# DAY 299
# TAKING CHARACTER TO HEART

*"But the seed on good soil stands for those with a noble and good heart,*
*who hear the word, retain it, and by persevering produce a crop."*
LUKE 8:15 NIV

Character education is popular today. Schoolchildren are taught positive values such as responsibility, honesty, fairness, caring, teamwork, and helpfulness. But it's not because schools really care about each student's future. Nor is it because of the Bible's teaching and God's Ten Commandments. Character programs were first designed to reduce classroom discipline problems, drop-out rates, and juvenile delinquency. Our society wants caring, contributing citizens. The bottom-line motivation is monetary: it's cheaper than maintaining jails and inmates.

But God cares about individuals—each person—their future and their community contribution as well as their character path. His training program and hands-on challenges produce people who make a difference.

Consider Queen Esther, who confronted her husband, the king of Persia, to save her people. Or Mary and Martha, who shared meals with Jesus and His disciples numerous times (Luke 10:38). Or the woman at the well, who persuaded the entire village to meet Jesus (Luke 28). Or Mary Magdalene, who believed what she saw at the tomb and boldly announced Jesus' resurrection (John 20:10–18).

God's training helps individuals grow through helping others. It is the real deal. The legacy of God's character education stands for all time.

*Lord, make me a bold woman of character who invests time*
*and effort in those things that are precious to You. Amen.*

# DAY 300
# WATCH EXPECTANTLY

*But as for me, I will watch expectantly for the Lord;*
*I will wait for the God of my salvation. My God will hear me.*
MICAH 7:7 NASB

In this verse, Micah has prayed to God and is now waiting expectantly for what He will do. How often do you pray without really thinking that God hears or cares? Or maybe you think your prayers are just too big (or too small) to matter to Him.

You pray to the sovereign and all-powerful God who loves you. This means you can pray big and often, and you can expect God to act. Obviously, we don't know how God will answer a prayer, because His ways are far above our ways. So watch expectantly to see how He will act in ways beyond your imaginings.

Wait for God. Too often we become impatient after we pray, wanting a quick fix or an obvious and direct answer. In this verse, we find that Micah was willing to wait for God to answer. While you wait, praise Him for what He is already doing in your life.

Your God will hear you. Be confident in this. God does not turn away from His children. He hears you and desires to give you good things. Next time you pray, be confident that the most high God is listening.

. . . . . . . . . . . . . . . . . . . . . . . . . . . . . . . . . . . . .

*Lord, thank You that You hear every one of my prayers.*
*I wait expectantly to see in what ways You will answer me. Amen.*

# DAY 301
# TEMPLE PRAYERS

*Don't you know that you yourselves are God's*
*temple and that God's Spirit dwells in your midst?*
1 CORINTHIANS 3:16 NIV

A lesson on the geography of God: God is where you are. You are where God is. You don't have to go to a special place to pray to God. You don't have to have an altar. You don't have to be in the high places. You don't have to be in a valley. You don't have to go to a church, a cathedral, a temple, or a synagogue.

As Paul told the Corinthians, you—not you by yourself, but the collective you—are the temple. We as the body of Christ are the gathering place where people can meet God. God's Spirit dwells among us, among the whole family of us. Not in one special person or exclusive place.

So when you want to pray, pray. Pray where you are, wherever that may be. In your car, on the street, in the woods, in your laundry room. Treat that time as set apart to God in your mind, though it is not physically set apart by a sign or walls or doors.

Be on the lookout for those who seek to destroy God's temple by setting up rules and regulations that God Himself never made. When you want to pray, pray. Where you are, wherever you go, whenever you happen to think of speaking to God. Your temple prayers can happen anywhere.

. . . . . . . . . . . . . . . . . . . . . . . . . . . . . . . . . . . . . . . . . .

*Help me, God, to protect Your temple—the body of believers. Amen.*

# DAY 302
## DO NOT BE DISCOURAGED

*"I have told you these things, so that in me you may have peace. In this world you will have trouble. But take heart! I have overcome the world."*
JOHN 16:33 NIV

Perhaps your prayer life feels a little like gazing out at the calm surface of the sea, but all the while you're thinking that your mighty supplications should be building and frothing those waves up into a real storm of answered prayers. But even when the sea seems quiet—as if nothing is happening—the oceans are shifting and traveling all around the world. God is also moving, sometimes just below the surface where we can't perceive it, but He is ever working things for good.

Remember, God wants His children to have peace and hope. The Lord declares in His Word that He has plans to prosper you and not to harm you, plans to give you hope and a future (Jeremiah 29:11). The Lord also said, "In this world you will have trouble. But take heart! I have overcome the world."

Accept His comfort. Live His commands. Embrace His love.

. . . . . . . . . . . . . . . . . . . . . . . . . . . . . . . . . . . . . . . . . . .

*God, help me to be persistent in prayer even when I can't see the direct fruits of it. Don't let me give up on the power of communing with You. Amen.*

# DAY 303

# LOOKING BEYOND EARTHLY REASSURANCES

*Some nations boast of their chariots and horses,
but we boast in the name of the LORD our God.*

PSALM 20:7 NLT

David, the writer of this psalm, did not find his hope in things that came from this earth—things he could see with his own eyes or create with his own hands. He did not find it through a solution his mind could conjure. He had faith in the Lord, and that was enough. We can only imagine how comforting it would be to look upon our defending army during a time of war, but he chose to look beyond the army and instead fixed his eyes on the Lord.

Through any trial or pain, the Lord sees all, and He loves His people in a deep, unfailing way. Although a thousand may fall, our fate and lives rest in Him and Him alone. We cannot look to earthly things to predict our future, finances, employment, etc. God's plans far exceed anything we could plan, and if we trust and follow Him, we will end up in a place we never would have come up with on our own.

Breathe in. Breathe out. Rest and believe. It is through fixing our eyes on God and looking to Him for direction that we are reassured and can experience peace.

*Lord, please set my eyes on You. Help me not to seek reassurance through earthly things but to understand on a deeper level that You control all. You hold my heart and care about each step I take. My hope is in You alone. Amen.*

# DAY 304
# DESIRE GOD

*Whom have I in heaven but You? And besides You, I desire*
*nothing on earth. My flesh and my heart may fail, but God*
*is the strength of my heart and my portion forever.*
PSALM 73:25–26 NASB

Do you ever look forward to meeting God in heaven? He is waiting for you there to welcome you home once your pilgrimage on earth is done. You can look forward to that extraordinary meeting. But God is not a distant being who is looking down on you from the sky, aloof and unreachable until the next life. He is present and active in your life now and offers you a relationship with Him. The psalmist who wrote these verses says that apart from God, there is *nothing* on earth that he desires. What an amazing perspective and remarkable passion. Do you have that same desire for God—believing that nothing on this earth could please you if it is devoid of Him? God will be your focus and all-consuming passion in heaven, so start on the trail of eternity now by putting Him first in your life and committing to spend time with Him and in His Word.

Even when your heart, body, and emotions fail you, God is your strength and will be for eternity. He is the only One in whom you can have a rock-solid faith and who will never fail you even through death.

. . . . . . . . . . . . . . . . . . . . . . . . . . . . . . . . . . . . . . . . . . .

*Lord, grant me an all-consuming desire to know You here on this earth. Amen.*

# DAY 305
# HOLLOW

*See to it that no one takes you captive
through hollow and deceptive philosophy.*
COLOSSIANS 2:8 NIV

Perhaps more than ever, there is a jungle of ideas out there in the world, and all are easily accessible through the internet, on television, on the radio, and even shouting from billboards. Many of these messages are hollow—they are full of pictures and colorful presentations, captivating in their entertainment value but lacking substance.

Yet these messages can easily distract from the truth.

The best way to guard against this distraction and the temptation to become entangled in ungodly thinking is to immerse yourself in God's Word. You can do this by reading the Bible, of course. Yet you can also do this through prayer. In prayer, you have direct access to the plan and will of God. Though God may not speak to you through a burning bush or give you tablets of stone, through consistent submission of your will to His and through the daily disciplines of faith, you can become familiar with the thoughts and reasons and plans He has for living in His kingdom—and for your particular path.

Don't let your mind be filled with fluff and cloudy thinking. Put your trust in God and let Him fill you up.

* * * * * * * * * * * * * * * * * * * * * * * * * * * * * * * * * * * * * * * * * * * *

*Dear God, help me to be able to discern what is true and what is not. Amen.*

# DAY 306
# THAT VOLATILE LIQUID

*"Therefore I tell you, do not worry about your life, what you will eat
or drink; or about your body, what you will wear. Is not life more than
food, and the body more than clothes? Look at the birds of the air;
they do not sow or reap or store away in barns, and yet your heavenly
Father feeds them. Are you not much more valuable than they?"*
MATTHEW 6:25–26 NIV

Women tend to be like vats of worry. We toss everything imaginable into that emotional, messy brew. You know what I mean—the many frets that we distill down when we choose to hand-wring through our days and toss and turn through our nights. Then we pour that volatile liquid into spray bottles, and we hose down our friends and family with it.

Jesus asks us if we can add a single hour to our life with worry. We cannot. Jesus also says that the birds are cared for and that we are much more valuable to Him than they are. So, what are we to do?

We can pray.

It's real. It's powerful. And our friends and family will thank us!

. . . . . . . . . . . . . . . . . . . . . . . . . . . . . . . . . . . .

*Father, remind me that You're in control. I place
my burdens and fears in Your capable hands. Amen.*

# DAY 307
# SEEKING ADVICE

*The Lord says, "I will guide you along the best pathway for your life.*
*I will advise you and watch over you. Do not be like a senseless horse*
*or mule that needs a bit and bridle to keep it under control."*
PSALM 32:8–9 NLT

There is a key word in this passage: *advise.* The Lord says He will advise us and watch over us. But what if we don't take the time to ask for His guidance? How many times have we been sidetracked, lost, and confused simply because we never asked for the Lord's advice?

In the hurried lives we live, it's easy to fall into a routine and switch over to autopilot. Our calendars are teeming with activities and deadlines, and all too often we simply enter "survival mode." You could say that we become similar to the mule in this scripture—putting hardly any thought into our days and simply being guided by chaos and distraction.

God has more for us. If we take the time to seek out His counsel, He will advise us. He will guide us along the best pathway for our lives and watch over us. He will give us purpose, and our lives will be filled with adventure and divine encounters.

. . . . . . . . . . . . . . . . . . . . . . . . . . . . . . . . . . . . . . . . . .

*Lord, thank You for opening my eyes to the reality that You desire to*
*guide my life. Forgive me for being so busy, and help me to slow down*
*and seek Your counsel. I want to walk this journey of life with You. Amen.*

# DAY 308
# ROOTED AND GROUNDED

*And that you, being rooted and grounded in love, may be able to comprehend with all the saints what is the breadth and length and height and depth, and to know the love of Christ which surpasses knowledge, that you may be filled up to all the fullness of God.*
EPHESIANS 3:17–19 NASB

Pray these verses over yourself. Pray that God's love would ground you and make you secure. Pray that the roots of His love would reach deeper and deeper into your heart, leaving no room for fear, guilt, or sin. To be rooted and grounded in His love is to fully understand that He is for you and that He desires you to walk more closely with Him.

Pray that you would be able to comprehend the love of Christ that surpasses knowledge. What an interesting oxymoron to think that you could understand something that surpasses understanding. His love for you is so overwhelming that you *can't even imagine* its breadth and length and height and depth. Pray to comprehend even a fraction of His love for you so that it will transform your life.

Pray that you would be filled up to all the fullness of God. Being filled up to the fullness of God leaves no room for anything else. That God would desire to condescend to fill us up with Himself is awe-inspiring. Ask Him to do just that.

. . . . . . . . . . . . . . . . . . . . . . . . . . . . . . . . . . . . . . . . . . . . .

*Lord, ground me in Your love. Help me to comprehend Your overwhelming love for me. Fill me up to overflowing with Your Spirit. Amen.*

# DAY 309
# BLESSING

*"The LORD bless you and keep you."*
NUMBERS 6:24 NIV

Sometimes the simplest prayers are the ones that make a difference.

This particular blessing of the Israelites from Numbers 6 has been quoted countless times—in weddings and funerals, as toasts at dinners, as memory verses for children, and so on. People have heard it so many times, in fact, that they probably don't even recognize it as a prayer anymore, and chances are they don't have the faintest idea where it is from.

Yet this simple prayer has given comfort and peace to many hearts. It has put smiles on people's faces and made busy people stop for a moment to listen and hear the Word of the Lord (even if they didn't realize it).

The Lord first gave this prayer to Moses to tell Aaron and his sons, the priests of Israel, how to bless the Israelites. After telling him the words to say, God says that this is the way the priests will "put my name on the Israelites" (v. 27). It was like a tag on the people saying "This nation belongs to God."

There's a lot of strength and goodness in repetition—especially in a reminder of who God is and who we are to Him.

"The LORD make his face shine on you and be gracious to you; the LORD turn his face toward you and give you peace" (vv. 25–26).

. . . . . . . . . . . . . . . . . . . . . . . . . . . . . . . . . . . . . . . . . . . . . .

*Lord, thank You for prayers that span generations. Amen.*

# DAY 310
# THE VOICE OF HEAVEN

*Jesus answered, "I am the way and the truth and the life.*
*No one comes to the Father except through me."*
JOHN 14:6 NIV

The world never seems to be in sync with what God wants for us, dreams for us. We get the idea that what the fallen earth has to offer is more fascinating and glorious and irresistible. Yet how can that be, when people fail us and everything that *can* fall apart *does* fall apart? When even the kings and queens of this earth are destined to the same lonely and hopeless end without divine assistance?

There are no answers in this earthly dust, only in the voice of heaven. We should look up to our hope—for it lies in Christ and Christ alone. He is life, not death. He is the most fascinating and glorious and irresistible hope there ever was or ever will be. This could be our heart praise as dawn arrives and as the sun sets.

. . . . . . . . . . . . . . . . . . . . . . . . . . . . . . . . . . . . . . . . . .

*God, You are the answer to the riddles and the problems*
*of life. You are the salve for my sin-sick soul. Amen.*

# DAY 311

# A PERSISTENT LOVE

*"O Israel," says the Lord, "if you wanted to return to me, you could.*
*You could throw away your detestable idols and stray away no more."*

JEREMIAH 4:1 NLT

Reading the Bible can be scary at times, as we see God threaten to destroy entire nations. All throughout Jeremiah, the Lord speaks of the punishment that is about to befall His people. He goes on and on about the destruction that will come to their cities and families. And yet He continually says things like "If you return to me, I will restore you so you can continue to serve me" (Jeremiah 15:19 NLT).

God's love for us is vast and deep, and He offers more than second chances! Even though some may never decide to choose Him—and He must deal with them as He sees fit—He continually offers us the chance to return to Him. What wonderful news this is for us!

If you are feeling like you are past redemption, take heart! Read through the book of Jeremiah, and be reassured that He desires you. Use a highlighter to mark every time He offers redemption. As you do this, you will begin to see that He ultimately desires for you to be with Him.

. . . . . . . . . . . . . . . . . . . . . . . . . . . . . . . . . . . . . . . . . . . .

*Lord, I am amazed by Your love for me! Every day You are ready*
*and waiting for me to trust only in You. Father, I choose to do so*
*today. Thank You for not giving up on me and for giving me second*
*chances. May I walk in confidence of Your great love today. Amen.*

# DAY 312
# PROMISES

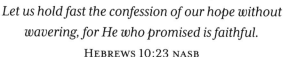

*Let us hold fast the confession of our hope without*
*wavering, for He who promised is faithful.*
HEBREWS 10:23 NASB

In this life, you can have endurance and hope because your God is faithful to keep His promises. The Christian life would be hopeless if God were not faithful and trustworthy. But He will absolutely keep His promises. You can (and do) bet your life on that.

God has promised to complete and perfect the good work He has started in you (Philippians 1:6). He will never leave you or forsake you (Hebrews 13:5). He has promised that He will wipe away every tear from your eyes and that in heaven there will no longer be any mourning or crying or pain (Revelation 21:4). He will never allow you to be separated from His love (Romans 8:38–39). He promises that He will come again and that you will be with Him forever (1 Thessalonians 4:16–17). He assures you that no one can take you from His hand (John 10:29).

These are just some of the promises God has made. These aren't just nice sentiments. These are things that God will, without question, bring to pass. He does not break His promises—He will do what He has said He will do. You can put your hope in these promises, knowing that you won't be disappointed.

. . . . . . . . . . . . . . . . . . . . . . . . . . . . . . . . . . . . . . . . . . . . . . .

*Lord, in a world where promises are so often broken, thank You*
*that I can trust that You will keep Yours. What beautiful promises*
*You have made. I put my hope firmly in their fulfillment. Amen.*

# DAY 313

## PRAYING FOR THE PERSECUTORS

*Bless those who persecute you; bless and do not curse.*
ROMANS 12:14 NIV

If you've ever been the target of ridicule, ever been bullied or humiliated, or ever been hurt by someone simply for what you believe, you may find Paul's instruction to be difficult to swallow.

It's all well and good to say bless your enemies, but how do you actually do that? Are you supposed to bring them gifts? Do you take them dinner? Should you subject yourself to weekly beatings?

Possibly. (Well, not that last one.) You can find more clues about how this actually works in the surrounding words. "Be devoted to one another in love. Honor one another above yourselves. Never be lacking in zeal, but keep your spiritual fervor, serving the Lord. Be joyful in hope, patient in affliction, faithful in prayer. Share with the Lord's people who are in need. Practice hospitality. . . . Rejoice with those who rejoice; mourn with those who mourn" (vv. 10–15).

You are to act toward your persecutors as you should to those you love: Honoring them above yourself, serving them, sharing with them. Rejoice with them when good things happen, and mourn with them when bad times come their way. Show them how you find joy in hope and how you bear the suffering they inflict on you; pray for them faithfully, asking God to soften their hearts and to help you find a way to love them.

. . . . . . . . . . . . . . . . . . . . . . . . . . . . . . . . . . . . . . . . .

*Dear Lord, give me words to pray for those who*
*have hurt me, and help me to mean them. Amen.*

# DAY 314
# COMFORTABLE

*Praise be to the God and Father of our Lord Jesus Christ, the Father*
*of compassion and the God of all comfort, who comforts us in all*
*our troubles, so that we can comfort those in any trouble.*
2 CORINTHIANS 1:3–4 NIV

Everyone has their favorite sources of comfort. When a workday hasn't gone well, a rather large bill has arrived, a fight has occurred, or a loved one is suffering, people reach out for a security blanket in the form of a person, place, or thing. Humans need a tangible reminder of safety, peace, and strength.

God loves us so much He feels our worries, bears our troubles, and reaches out to us through His words and His songs and His reminders of love that come in all the little ways He knows will suit us best. He comforts us through the hands and feet of others who embrace us in hard times.

*Lord, help me to be a comfort to others in the ways You comfort me. Amen.*

# DAY 315
# LET GOD REIGN!

*Oh, how great are God's riches and wisdom and knowledge! How impossible it is for us to understand his decisions and his ways! For who can know the Lord's thoughts? Who knows enough to give him advice? And who has given him so much that he needs to pay it back? For everything comes from him and exists by his power and is intended for his glory. All glory to him forever! Amen.*

ROMANS 11:33–36 NLT

It's easy for us to believe that we carry the world on our shoulders. We tend to believe, though we may not admit it, that we alone make the world turn. We convince ourselves that worry, finances, or power will put us in control. But in truth God is the One who controls all.

What a blessed peace awaits us! As you go about your day, rest in the assurance that God, not you, is in control. God understands every feeling you experience, and He can comfort you. God knows the best steps for you to take in life, and He is willing to guide you. He is above all and knows all, yet He is not out of reach.

Set your eyes firmly on the Lord, and He will care for you.

* * * * * * * * * * * * * * * * * * * * * * * * * * * * * * * * * * * * * * * *

*Lord, please let this truth sink deep into my heart today so that I may live in joy and peace. Please guide me by Your wisdom and provide for me according to Your riches. I praise You because You are good! Amen.*

# DAY 316
# LET YOUR FIRE BURN

*Our God is a consuming fire.*
HEBREWS 12:29 NKJV

The Holy Spirit is often referred to as a fire. Each believer's heart carries that flaming light of God. Just as heat boils out the impurities in elements such as gold, so the Spirit burns in our hearts both to refine and to fuel the work He has called us to do.

Paul admonishes believers not to quench the fire (1 Thessalonians 5:19), but many restrict it from growing so there is barely a glow in the coals of their bellies. They fear that the flames might actually spread and purify their hearts, compelling them to give up their darling sins—the ones that aren't hurting anyone, the ones that stay hidden.

So when the heart is convicted of sin or called to mission work or challenged to change, it's easier to smother the Spirit with logic and justification and keep the coal neither hot nor cold but comfortably lukewarm.

Henry Blackaby wrote, "If the Spirit speaks to you about God's will for you, and if you refuse to take action, a time will come when the Spirit's voice will be muted in your life."

Is it time to remove the bushel that has hidden your light so long and trust the winds of God's Spirit to fan the flames? Fuel the fire with prayer, obedience, and meditation, and watch in amazement as God transforms you into what He's always wanted you to be.

. . . . . . . . . . . . . . . . . . . . . . . . . . . . . . . . . . . . . . . . . .

*Father, let the fire of the Holy Spirit blaze and spread
among Your people so that we burn with passion for
Your Word and the coming of Your kingdom. Amen.*

# DAY 317

# WHATEVER

*Whatever happens, conduct yourselves in*
*a manner worthy of the gospel of Christ.*
PHILIPPIANS 1:27 NIV

The washer dies midcycle. The cat throws up right before company comes over. Nobody's socks match, and it's ten past time to go. The roof is leaking, but you don't have insurance. You can't seem to stop fighting with your spouse. Debt is piling up with no end in sight. You just found a hole in your favorite sweater.

There are lots of times when you won't feel able to conduct yourself in a manner worthy of the Gospel. You may not feel able to conduct yourself in a manner worthy of anything useful at all. You'd rather just curl up in the dryer and permanent press yourself to death, or at least take a long nap.

Yet Paul's words were not directed to individuals going through life alone. Paul's words were to the body of believers. He urges them to be "striving together as one for the faith of the gospel" (v. 27).

In times of trouble and opposition, you don't have to go it alone. It can be scary to share your problems with others. But in order to live in a manner that reflects the Gospel of Christ, at some point you've got to let go of your personal fears and lean into the body for protection, care, and support. You've got to love one another and be loved.

* * * * * * * * * * * * * * * * * * * * * * * * * * * * * * * * * * * * * * *

*Dear Lord, I'm having a rotten day. Help me*
*to be a good witness for Christ anyway. Amen.*

# DAY 318

# COMMANDING PRESENCE

*Trouble and distress have come upon me, but your commands give me delight.*
PSALM 119:143 NIV

The word *commands* is not generally seen in a positive light.

Yet God commands. When people come into His commanding presence in prayer, they do find comfort. Why? Because when the foundations of your life are shaken, you want to hold on to something that is real, that is true, that will not and cannot be moved. The law of the Lord is that. Moreover, His law is *good*.

The more you meditate on His Word, the more you'll be convinced of this. Use the laws of God in your prayer time, and you will be forced to think about others, to consider what it means to really live in community, and to put others before yourself. In that process, the sorrow and trouble that are weighing you down will not disappear but will be put in proper perspective and thus become a bit lighter load.

. . . . . . . . . . . . . . . . . . . . . . . . . . . . . . . . . . . . . . . . . . . . .

*Lord, thank You for the comfort You bring us in Your law. Amen.*

# DAY 319
# REJOICE!

*Always be full of joy in the Lord. I say it again—rejoice!*
PHILIPPIANS 4:4 NLT

Do you feel like life is a fifty-pound backpack? Life can get "heavy" if we aren't careful, with everyday worries wearing us down and making us exhausted. Even small decisions tend to grow in our minds to be more important than they really are. Big decisions can completely take us over so that even the most wonderful news becomes tainted.

Look away from the cares of this world! Rejoice in what the Lord has done! Instead of lending every thought to the troubles at hand, praise God for the ways He has provided in the past and doubtless will again in the future!

Begin to count your blessings, and feel the weight lifting off your shoulders. Feel the freedom you have to enjoy your life. Enjoy your home and the comfort it brings. Enjoy your family, pets, and things you have. Allow yourself to fully feel the joy that comes with the first snow, the first warm breeze of spring, or the first rays of sun in the morning. There are so many wonderful things to enjoy even as you read this!

Life is complicated, yes. But it should never be allowed to rob you of the joy the Lord provides. "I say it again—rejoice!"

. . . . . . . . . . . . . . . . . . . . . . . . . . . . . . . . . . . . . .

*Lord, You are so good! Teach me Your ways and show me Your faithfulness, that I may be full of joy because of You. You created this earth to be enjoyed, and enjoy it I shall! Amen.*

# YOUR CHILD'S SALVATION

*"Ask, and it will be given to you; seek, and you will find; knock, and
it will be opened to you. For everyone who asks receives, and he
who seeks finds, and to him who knocks it will be opened."*
MATTHEW 7:7–8 NKJV

When John Spurgeon returned home from a ministry trip, he found the house quiet except for the voice of his wife from behind the bedroom door. She was pleading for the salvation of all their children but especially their strong-willed firstborn son. The young man she carried such a burden for later became one of the greatest preachers and evangelists of all time, Charles Spurgeon.

We spend so much time disciplining our children for social behavior and so little time in prayer for their souls. A relationship with God can't be earned by good works or a sweet disposition. It can't be passed down through bloodlines or learned like a language. Salvation is a gift from God.

Jesus said in Matthew 21:22 (NIV), "If you believe, you will receive whatever you ask for in prayer." So we must ask the Giver to grace our children with His endowment of salvation. Don't take it for granted that because kids are raised in a godly home or go to a Christian school they will have a personal relationship with Christ. Instead, sincerely, humbly, and relentlessly pray to God, who is generous in His gifts and waits for a people who are desperate for His work in their lives.

. . . . . . . . . . . . . . . . . . . . . . . . . . . . . . . . . . . . . . . . . . . . .

*Dear Lord, fill my children with Your Holy Spirit. Give them the desire
to love You, serve You, and honor You all the days of their lives. Amen.*

# DAY 321

# PRAYING FOR THE GOSPEL

*Join with me in suffering for the gospel, by the power of God.*
2 TIMOTHY 1:8 NIV

One of the most important Christian duties is to tell others about Christ—to spread the Gospel message. This is a primary goal, not because doing so will gain us points in heaven or a better pew position. It is a fulfillment of the two commands that Jesus said all of God's law hangs on—to love God (by working to expand His kingdom) and to love others (by telling them about the love of Christ).

You may not be called to spread the Gospel in another language in a country far away. Yet you can help those who are. You can pray for them. You can ask God for their protection. You can ask God to give them courage and boldness. You can ask God to give them wisdom—to know when to speak and when not to, when to stand out and when to blend in.

Though you may not be called to deliver the Gospel in foreign lands, you may be surprised to find yourself an ambassador for God in your own community. Just because a place is blessed with a church on every block does not necessarily mean all its residents understand the message of love and grace that the Gospel carries with it.

Pray for an opportunity every day to share the Gospel or to support those who do.

*Dear Lord, help me to spread Your good news around the world. Amen.*

# DAY 322

# HOW BEAUTIFUL IS THY NAME!

*All flocks and herds, and the animals of the wild, the birds in the sky, and the fish in the sea, all that swim the paths of the seas. LORD, our Lord, how majestic is your name in all the earth!*
PSALM 8:7–9 NIV

When we experience an alpine walk along a misty trail or take in the moon's reflection on a still, blue sea, when we hear the thunderous roar of a lion or the voice of the wind through swaying palms, don't we feel a sweet ache in our hearts to be thankful—to Someone?

God's creation is indeed full of beauty and wonder, and we should take great pleasure in His handiwork. We should explore His world. We should see with new eyes each morning.

As Christians, we do not worship creation, but we instead worship the One who is the Creator of such magnificence. A thankful heart full of praise is a form of prayer. Shall we thank Him and praise Him today?

Lord, our Lord, how majestic is Your name in all the earth!

. . . . . . . . . . . . . . . . . . . . . . . . . . . . . . . . . . . . . . . . . . .

*Creator God, thank You for the beauty and wonder of Your handiwork. Give me grateful eyes to see it every day. Amen.*

# DAY 323
# WAITING

*Wait patiently for the LORD. Be brave and courageous.*
*Yes, wait patiently for the LORD.*
PSALM 27:14 NLT

Waiting is rarely easy. Waiting means that something we desire is being delayed—postponed—and we don't know when it will arrive. It can be even harder when we are waiting for news that could be terrible—news that could change our lives for the worse.

Isn't it interesting that David linked being brave and courageous to this act of waiting? He is telling us that even though we don't know the timing or outcome of whatever it is we're waiting on, we should be brave in the face of it! We should not cower in a corner but move forward with courage! He also says to wait *patiently*. Here are some other words for *patient*: *calm*, *composed*, *enduring*, *uncomplaining*, and *understanding*. Waiting is not a passive thing! There is a call to action during this time.

There is good in waiting. Take this opportunity to lean into God. At first you may find that spending time with Him is hard because you feel like He is keeping things from you. But soon you will find that waiting on God is one of the most rewarding things you could ever do.

* * * * * * * * * * * * * * * * * * * * * * * * * * * * * * * * * * * * * * * * *

*Lord, through faith in You I can be brave in facing the unknown and I can move forward with courage. Help me to be patient as I trust Your timing and Your ways, and help me to lean on You more and more. Amen.*

# DAY 324

# WAITING ON GOD

*Let us not become weary in doing good, for at the proper
time we will reap a harvest if we do not give up.*

GALATIANS 6:9 NIV

Theologian John Owen wrote, "For the most part we [Christians] live upon successes, not promises—unless we see and feel the print of victories, we will not believe."

The Christian walk is about faith. Hebrews 11:1 (NKJV) describes it as "the substance of things hoped for, the evidence of things not seen." Faith is trusting God to keep His promises even while we wait.

It's easy to depend on God when all is well, but hard times may cause doubt whether God really is good. However, if you cling to God's promises, you will experience tremendous growth. Grapes don't grow overnight. They slowly ripen, attached to the vine for sustenance. Likewise, Jesus said, "I am the vine; you are the branches. If you remain in me and I in you, you will bear much fruit" (John 15:5 NIV).

In the Old Testament, God called David to the throne, but King Saul refused to abdicate and attempted to kill his successor. David had many opportunities to kill Saul, but he spared him because he trusted God. David wrote, "Indeed, none of those who wait for You will be ashamed" (Psalm 25:3 NASB).

No matter what you're facing, sustain yourself in the Word and in prayer. Trust that God will bring you through this season, and don't give up. In God's time, He will deliver you.

. . . . . . . . . . . . . . . . . . . . . . . . . . . . . . . . . . . . . . . .

*God, give me wisdom as I wait for You to carry out Your will,
and give me peace knowing that You will work it out for my good. Amen.*

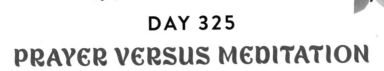

# PRAYER VERSUS MEDITATION

*Rather, he delights in the teachings of the LORD*
*and reflects on his teachings day and night.*
PSALM 1:2 GW

On the topic of prayer versus meditation, there needs to be clarity. When the Bible speaks of reflection or meditation, it is not referring to meditation that encourages its participants to empty their minds. This type of meditation is at the heart of yoga and other spiritual practices within non-Christian religions.

An empty mind is not a way to spiritual understanding but an invitation to what's unholy. During our quiet times, let us think on good and lovely things. Let us focus on God's Word, His truths, and His ways.

We shouldn't succumb to a desire to be trendy in our faith over a desire to please the one true God. While other religions and ancient traditions seem inviting—with their alluring promises of harmony and enlightenment—remember that biblical wisdom teaches us to beware of false prophets, to use discernment through the power of the Holy Spirit, and to weigh everything in light of God's holy Word.

Never does God encourage us to empty our minds. It is an increasingly popular spiritual practice, but don't be deceived—it is not biblical. Instead, these rituals are another attempt by the enemy of our souls to direct us away from the truth—from the power of real prayer.

Let us focus on what is biblical, what is holy, what is everlasting.

* * *

*Lord, help me to pray and study Your Word*
*in a way that is pleasing to You. Amen.*

# DAY 326
# BETTER TO ENDURE

*"He cuts off every branch in me that bears no fruit, while every branch that does bear fruit he prunes so that it will be even more fruitful."*
JOHN 15:2 NIV

How many times have we met children who haven't been disciplined by their parents, who've been given whatever they wanted, whenever they wanted, without any sensitivity to what they really needed? Not a pretty sight. Later, they end up being such miserable adults that they may even miss out on what they were destined to be.

The Lord wants the best for each of us—and the best sometimes requires that uncomfortable d-word. *Discipline.* But wouldn't it be better to endure God's occasional pruning than the devil's persuasions and praise? The Lord wants more for us than we can even imagine for ourselves.

Thank God today for His corrections, for they are full of mercy and love. They are beautiful.

· · · · · · · · · · · · · · · · · · · · · · · · · · · · · · · · · · · · · · · · ·

*Dear Lord, thank You for always desiring what is best for me even if it sometimes requires painful discipline. Help me to trust Your sovereignty and love. Amen.*

# DAY 327

## UNFAILING LOVE SURROUNDS US

*Many sorrows come to the wicked, but unfailing love surrounds those who trust the LORD.*

PSALM 32:10 NLT

When you read this verse, what is the first thing that comes to mind? Maybe that evil people will face many sorrows, but you will be surrounded by the Lord's unfailing love. You will be surrounded with love because you are a good person and far from evil! Right?

But what if this verse is saying something else? As we read through the Bible, we see that we are all wicked. "No one is righteous—not even one" (Romans 3:10 NLT). No one is *good*. That is, except through the grace of God. Maybe, then, this verse is saying that many sorrows will come to the wicked—to humankind—but those who choose to put their trust in the Lord, in Christ Jesus, will be surrounded by His unfailing love. Those people may face trouble because they are still in a world full of fallen people, but they will not face it alone.

No matter what you may be facing, let this be your anthem. Let this be the promise you hold close to your heart. Let it be a verse you recite to yourself as you fall asleep at night. "Many sorrows come to the wicked, but unfailing love surrounds those who trust the LORD."

. . . . . . . . . . . . . . . . . . . . . . . . . . . . . . . . . . . . . .

*I have this promise to hold on to. Lord, remember me. Remember how I put my trust in You and seek You day and night. Surround me with Your unfailing love, that I may walk through this life knowing that I am secure in Your hands. Amen.*

# DAY 328

## STANDING OUT IN A CROWD

*Be kind and compassionate to one another,*
*forgiving each other, just as in Christ God forgave you.*
EPHESIANS 4:32 NIV

In a world of billions of people, we sometimes feel like one tiny grain of sand in a desert full of dunes. We long to rise up, to stand out—to achieve greatness. But we don't have to write a bestselling novel or win a gold medal in the Olympics or become president of the United States to stand out in the crowd. It's as easy as one simple word. . .*kindness.*

The impact of one kind deed can change a life forever, even if we only offer a sincere smile. Kindness has a ripple effect that can keep on flowing around the world. We might never know the full impact of our kind deeds. Yet God knows.

Paul's letter to the Ephesians tells us to "be kind and compassionate to one another, forgiving each other, just as in Christ God forgave you."

But you might argue that kindness is not easy in a world that is becoming increasingly hardened and cruel. You're right—kindness isn't always easy. But it is good, just as God is good. We are to be compassionate and forgiving and kind because Christ has done the same for us.

Praying for a kind heart is a great way to start the day—it's beneficial for our own spirits and for every living soul who comes our way.

. . . . . . . . . . . . . . . . . . . . . . . . . . . . . . . . . . . . . . . . . . . .

*Jesus, mold me into a greater likeness of You. Give me*
*supernatural stores of patience and compassion. Amen.*

## DAY 329
# EXPECTATION

*"Ask and it will be given to you; seek and you will find; knock and the door will be opened to you. For everyone who asks receives; the one who seeks finds; and to the one who knocks, the door will be opened."*
MATTHEW 7:7–8 NIV

When we call on the Lord for help and mercy, we can come into His presence with expectation. In His Word He promises to hear our prayers, to open the door to us, to give us what we need. The Gospel of Matthew goes on to say, "Which of you, if your son asks for bread, will give him a stone? Or if he asks for a fish, will give him a snake? If you, then, though you are evil, know how to give good gifts to your children, how much more will your Father in heaven give good gifts to those who ask him!" (vv. 9–11).

Of course, the gifts that the Lord chooses to give us might be wisdom or forgiveness or peace or joy. These gifts may not be material, but they are timeless. So, like a child on her birthday, come to Christ with anticipation of good things of delight, and wonder!

* * *

*Father, thank You for all of the wonderful gifts You've given me. I have hope in Your loving provision. Amen.*

# DAY 330
# WRESTLING WITH PRAYER

*I am praying to you because I know you will answer,*
*O God. Bend down and listen as I pray.*
PSALM 17:6 NLT

Do you ever find it hard to pray? It can be difficult to believe that God would take the time to listen to our honest plea, and so we rarely try. Oftentimes, when we do muster up the courage, we feel as if no one is listening to us. It is only the still air and our pained hearts.

Our society of computer screens and internet searches makes it even harder for us to pray. Praying takes time and effort and then forces us to wait on God for an answer. This is rarely a sought-after option when we have answers available to us just clicks away. Although it is good to seek wisdom from others, God ultimately desires that we come directly to Him. This passage states it beautifully: "My heart has heard you say, 'Come and talk with me.' And my heart responds, 'LORD, I am coming' " (Psalm 27:8 NLT). There is an invitation.

Both of these passages from Psalms are wonderful ways to open up in prayer, as they reaffirm our faith and remind us of the truth that God does listen and care. If you are in dire need of answers or simply a connection to the Father, go directly to Him.

. . . . . . . . . . . . . . . . . . . . . . . . . . . . . . . . . . . . . . . . . . .

*I am praying to You, Lord, because I know You will answer.*
*Bend down and listen as I pray and present You with my*
*requests. I have felt Your invitation, and so I come. Amen.*

# KEEPING UP WITH THE CHRISTIAN JONESES

*"Come to Me, all you who labor and are heavy laden, and I will give you rest."*
MATTHEW 11:28 NKJV

Christians have a lot to do. There are so many needs in the world, from spreading the Gospel and feeding the poor to teaching children the Bible and remaining in prayer.

But somehow our practice of the faith has morphed into a jam-packed schedule of women's meetings, Christian sporting events, and committees. It's almost an unwritten rule that good Christian people must load their schedules with good Christian stuff to do, especially during the holidays.

John Wesley said, "I have no time to be in a hurry." He has a point. With all the hurrying around, the precious limited time we have each day isn't allocated toward the actual works of God. It's taken up with busyness.

Consequently, our families are strangers, our hearts are unfulfilled, our minds are stressed, and our Bible reading and prayer life are shallow.

God isn't impressed with a clean house or schedules marked with every church event for the next six months. He wants our hearts, minds, and souls, and He wants us to be obedient to share His love with all people throughout our lives. It's not complicated.

If you find yourself unable to keep up with the fast-paced Christian life, then be at peace and say no sometimes. What matters is the condition of our hearts, not the number of Christian acquaintances we have or the number of Bible studies we attend.

- - - - - - - - - - - - - - - - - - - - - - - - - - - - - - - - - - - - - - -

*Lord, help me see the difference between the life of a Christian and the heart of a Christian, and help me discern when my life is misaligned. Amen.*

# DAY 332
# A SUPERNATURAL REALM

*For our struggle is not against flesh and blood, but against the rulers,*
*against the authorities, against the powers of this dark world and*
*against the spiritual forces of evil in the heavenly realms.*
EPHESIANS 6:12 NIV

Since we have a keen familiarity with our material world, it's hard to imagine a supernatural realm that exists beyond the borders of our sensory experiences. But the Bible says that there is much more to this life than flesh and blood. More than what we merely see with our eyes.

There is a spiritual domain as well, and it's as real as the rocks and the trees and the clouds—and us. Yes, this can be a dark world, and we struggle against the spiritual forces of evil, which include Satan and his emissaries. If you are truly honest with yourself, you know in your spirit that this is truth.

So, how can we deal with such evil? In Ephesians it reads, "Stand firm then, with the belt of truth buckled around your waist, with the breastplate of righteousness in place, and with your feet fitted with the readiness that comes from the gospel of peace" (vv. 14–15).

We can stand firm and love God.

We can live by His Word and His truths.

And we can pray like there is no tomorrow.

*Holy Spirit, help me to always be aware of the spiritual forces in this world. Give me the strength and power to face them. Amen.*

# DAY 333

# A TREE PLANTED BY THE WATER

*"But blessed is the one who trusts in the LORD, whose confidence is in him.*
*They will be like a tree planted by the water that sends out its roots by the*
*stream. It does not fear when heat comes; its leaves are always green.*
*It has no worries in a year of drought and never fails to bear fruit."*
JEREMIAH 17:7–8 NIV

The streams have dried up. The land is barren. Rain is only a memory. The cicadas may be the only thing left singing. Have you ever experienced this kind of serious drought? If you have, it is unforgettable. Drought is a brutal force of nature—an unforgiving taskmaster. That is the way of the world. It will steal your strength until you are weak and vulnerable and fruitless.

Yet prayer can build up our trust in the Lord. He is our strength in a harsh and desolate land. If we faithfully spend time with Him and His good Word, we will be like that tree in the book of Jeremiah. We will be that tree planted by the water that sends out its roots by the stream. A tree that does not fear the heat or a year of drought. It's the kind of tree that will never fail to bear fruit.

. . . . . . . . . . . . . . . . . . . . . . . . . . . . . . . . . . . . . . . . . . . . .

*Lord, when I'm feeling lost and dried up, give me the strength to turn to You*
*with outstretched arms and to have faith in Your goodness and love. Amen.*

# DAY 334
# OUR DAILY BREAD

*"Give us this day our daily bread."*
MATTHEW 6:11 NKJV

A young woman gazed out her window as the morning sun just began to touch the snow-covered peaks of the Colorado Rockies. Her thoughts could hardly be collected and organized, and so she just stared and prayed, "Lord, give us today our daily bread." Her husband was in a job where he was criticized daily and treated like dirt. Each day felt like Russian roulette, as they never knew if their cars would get them to work or not. Money was tight. Their grocery budget was minimal. Being new to the area, they had no one to turn to.

*"Give us this day our daily bread."*

Each day, the Lord answered this prayer. He gave them what they needed, whether it be patience, mental or physical strength, food, or faith. A bill never went unpaid. A stomach never went hungry. A body never went unclothed. The Lord provided all their needs.

Eventually, slowly, their situation began to improve. They were able to buy a new car, she picked up more hours at work, and he found a new job. A community began to form around them. Looking back, she remembers it as one of the best years of her life. It was a year she walked closely, intimately, with her Savior.

* * * * * * * * * * * * * * * * * * * * * * * * * * * * * * * * * * * * * * * * * * *

*Father, I ask today that You would give me today's bread. Fill me with what I need to make it through the day, that I may praise Your name forever. Amen.*

# DAY 335
# WHAT YOU *CAN* CONTROL

*Seek the Lord and His strength; seek His face continually.*
1 Chronicles 16:11 nasb

Many women struggle with control. Intentions of loving concern often result in overbearing anxiety rooted in fear. Max Lucado wrote, "[Fear] turns us into control freaks. . . . When life spins wildly, we grab for a component of life we can manage: our diet, the tidiness of our home, the armrest of a plane, or, in many cases, people."

Fear in parenting takes many forms—guilt, worry, manipulation. Fear imagines every terrible future possibility, but God is Jehovah-Raphe, the Healer. Many things will happen out of your control, but these may be the circumstances God uses to make your children strong, faith-filled adults prepared for good works.

Concerned moms have not been rendered helpless, however. There are two things we can do that will result in fruit.

First, plant seeds of God's Word. Use scriptures in your decor and in lunch box notes. Read Bible stories and sing scripture-rich songs.

Second, pray. Jesus said we should pray like a man who bangs on the door of a reluctant friend. "Because of your shameless audacity he will surely get up and give you as much as you need" (Luke 11:8 niv). Be a prayer warrior for your children. Pray for their salvation and their callings.

Through prayer and the Word, you will go from living in fear to resting in God's sovereignty, from anxiety to thanksgiving.

- - - - - - - - - - - - - - - - - - - - - - - - - - - - - - - - - - - - - - -

*Dear Lord, You have promised to answer my prayers, and I know I can trust You. Thank You for listening to me and for the comfort of Your sovereign will. Amen.*

# DAY 336
# YOU ARE NEVER ALONE

*He took Peter and the two sons of Zebedee along with him, and he began to be sorrowful and troubled. Then he said to them, "My soul is overwhelmed with sorrow to the point of death. Stay here and keep watch with me."*
MATTHEW 26:37–38 NIV

The night is a hundred shades of black, and it has nothing to do with nightfall. Your spirit is crushed, and you feel utterly abandoned. Sometimes life is that dark—it can feel that hopeless.

It is a great comfort to know that you are not alone in the midst of life's horror. Jesus grew up here on earth, and He must have known many of the usual trials and triumphs of a childhood. Yet when He became a man and faced His divine destiny, Christ knew the black flood of suffering—pain and anguish we cannot even imagine. He said, "My soul is overwhelmed with sorrow to the point of death." Jesus' agony was so very great He sweat drops of blood.

When despair comes to you, be comforted in the knowledge that Jesus knows torment as deep and lonely as the darkest reaches of hell. In your hour of need, He will hold you in the palm of His hand because He understands like no one else. Because He loves you. He always has loved you—enough to die for you.

When you pray—know this truth—you are never ever alone in that dark night.

. . . . . . . . . . . . . . . . . . . . . . . . . . . . . . . . . . . . . . . . . . . .

*Father, in times of great despair, shield and sustain me. Be my hiding place and my source of supernatural comfort and peace. Amen.*

# DAY 337

# A NEW HEART

*"I will give you a new heart and put a new spirit within you; I will
take the heart of stone out of your flesh and give you a heart of
flesh. I will put My Spirit within you and cause you to walk in
My statutes, and you will keep My judgments and do them."*

EZEKIEL 36:26–27 NKJV

Sue accompanied her husband, Bill, to a follow-up appointment with the cardiologist following a heart procedure a few months earlier. The nurse checked his blood pressure and took an EKG; then the doctor came in for a visit. After talking with them for a few minutes, he said, "Everything looks great, perfect in fact. It doesn't mean the AFib won't come back, but let's continue with the medication you're taking. It's good for your heart and will help protect you." They left the doctor's office feeling good about Bill's condition.

Before we met Christ, each of us had serious heart problems. In short, we needed a heart transplant. Our heart was sinful, self-centered, and full of carnal desires. God saw our need and provided the necessary operation. He promised us a new heart and a new spirit. He removed the heart of stone and gave us a heart of flesh, one that would respond to His touch. He placed His Spirit within us to teach us to follow His statutes. As we do, He will give us the good report we need to hear from the Great Physician, who performed the surgery.

· · · · · · · · · · · · · · · · · · · · · · · · · · · · · · · · · · · · · · · · ·

*Father, give me a heart of flesh touched by Your
Spirit and receptive to Your voice. Amen.*

# DAY 338
# CHOOSING FAITH

*Be still in the presence of the LORD, and wait patiently for him to act. Don't worry about evil people who prosper or fret about their wicked schemes. Stop being angry! Turn from your rage! Do not lose your temper—it only leads to harm. For the wicked will be destroyed, but those who trust in the LORD will possess the land.*

PSALM 37:7–9 NLT

Our faith is tested when life doesn't go the way we expect it to, when people who aren't following God prosper, and we seem to be an afterthought. At times we even go so far as to blame God for the things that are going wrong.

Even though it seems like the wicked are prospering and we are sitting on the sidelines, our daily grind is not in vain. Each day we are faithful is another seed planted. It may take time for it to grow, but grow it will. There will be a harvest.

Faith sees the facts but trusts God anyway. Faith is forcing yourself to worry no longer but to pray in earnest and leave the situation in His hands. Faith is choosing to trust and rest in His plan rather than fret about what could happen. We must choose faith even when we don't feel it. It is through choosing faith that we please God. Choose faith, and see what He will do.

. . . . . . . . . . . . . . . . . . . . . . . . . . . . . . . . . . . . .

*Lord, despite what logic or the world tells me, I choose now to let my worries go and have faith in You. I trust that You will take care of every need, and I lay down all my burdens at Your feet. Amen.*

# DAY 339
## WITH ALL YOUR SOUL

*"Be zealous."*
REVELATION 3:19 NASB

Tasha's son was saved at youth group and shared the Gospel with her. She was so amazed at this news that she couldn't wait to hear more. She eagerly entered the church with great expectation.

The music moved her. The message challenged her. The excitement was all over her face. She looked around at the Christians who sat stoically around her and asked herself, "Am I missing something? Is this how Christians are supposed to act?"

Why is it that Christians have no problem screaming for their favorite football team or dancing at a pop concert, but in the church with the greatest news on earth, the majority of us sit complacent and unmoved?

Jesus said we should worship God with all our heart, soul, mind, and strength (Luke 10:27). But for some reason, many have cut out the soul in worship. They will worship God with their mind and mean it with all their heart. But the emotional expressions that start in the depths of the soul are suppressed.

Every Christian should have the experience of seeing the congregation from the choir loft. The blank stares and emotionless participation are glaring. As Puritan Samuel Ward wrote, "Christian zeal is a spiritual heat wrought in the heart of a man by the Holy Ghost." Perhaps if the fire of zeal were practiced, it would spread and bring revival.

*Dear Lord, let zeal for Your Word and Your glory well up in me*
*beyond all other loves in my life. Bring conviction to my heart*
*no matter who's watching. Burn a fire in my soul. Amen.*

# DAY 340
# THOSE WHO BRING GOOD NEWS

*How, then, can they call on the one they have not believed in? And*
*how can they believe in the one of whom they have not heard?*
*And how can they hear without someone preaching to them?*
*And how can anyone preach unless they are sent? As it is written:*
*"How beautiful are the feet of those who bring good news!"*
ROMANS 10:14–15 NIV

In our modern world, there has been much concern about the carbon footprint we leave behind as humans. When God created our earth, He did indeed ask us to be good stewards of His beautiful world, but over the years, our priorities have shifted. We now focus more intensely on the needs of our planet rather than the needs of people and their souls.

As Christians, when we leave this earth and come to meet our Maker face-to-face, He won't be as concerned about whether we recycled as much as whether we obeyed His mandate of sharing the Gospel. Did we spend our days worrying about our carbon footprint or more of our time dealing with the eternal imprint that we were able to leave by sharing the good news of Christ?

Let us always pray for opportunities to share the mercy and love of our Savior with people of all nations—whether it's our neighbors overseas or simply our neighbors across the street.

* * * * * * * * * * * * * * * * * * * * * * * * * * * * * * * * * * * * * * * * * *

*Lord, remind me of my calling as a Christian. Equip me with the*
*words to say, and give me the boldness to carry out Your plan. Amen.*

# DAY 341

# GOD MAKES US BEAUTIFUL

*For the LORD takes pleasure in His people;*
*He will beautify the humble with salvation.*
PSALM 149:4 NKJV

Standing in front of a magazine rack can be depressing if you believe everything on the front covers. Women in skimpy clothes with long, flowing locks and perfect figures adorn most periodicals. The article titles are just as daunting: "How to Have the Body of Your Dreams in 30 Days," "What Men Really Want in a Woman," and "Lose 10 Pounds in a Week." Their information on how to be beautiful and be the perfect woman tempts a lot of women into buying the latest issue, thinking it will solve their problems.

The world's definition of beauty is a far cry from God's. We were created in His image, made in His likeness. There's nothing wrong with trying to lose weight, buying a new dress, or getting our hair cut. We all want to look and feel our best—but not by the world's standard. Trying to measure up to others leads to disappointment and low self-esteem.

As God's children, we are made beautiful through Him. It's not a physical beauty like the world lauds. It's an inner loveliness that comes through knowing Christ. We take on a beauty the world can't understand or achieve. To those who know us and love us, we are beautiful women because of God's Spirit within us, radiating a beauty beyond human imagination.

- - - - - - - - - - - - - - - - - - - - - - - - - - - - - - - - - - - - - - -

*Lord, give me an inner beauty through Your Spirit,*
*that I might bring You glory and honor. Amen.*

# DAY 342
# A HEART OF FAITH AND HONOR

*"He lifts the poor from the dust and the needy from the garbage dump. He sets them among princes, placing them in seats of honor. For all the earth is the Lord's, and he has set the world in order."*

1 SAMUEL 2:8 NLT

This is just a part of the prayer that Hannah, mother of Samuel, prayed as she left her son to live with Eli the priest and serve the Lord all his life. Samuel was her firstborn, a child she desperately prayed to God for, and she fulfilled her promise and left Samuel in the care of Eli.

Have you ever considered how hard it was for her to pray this prayer of praise to God? She finally had a child, but she was committed to her promise to offer him in service to the Lord. She would not be the one to raise him and experience all of his "firsts" in life. And yet she prayed this prayer that does nothing but honor the Lord. Even if there were moments when she wished she hadn't made such a promise, she praised Him. "My heart rejoices in the Lord! The Lord has made me strong" (v. 1).

We can learn so much from Hannah in the short space she is written about in 1 Samuel. She honored the Lord above all else and trusted His ways. May God give you a heart of courage that honors Him and strengthens you.

* * * * * * * * * * * * * * * * * * * * * * * * * * * * * * * * * * * * * *

*Dear Lord, thank You for hearing my prayers and remembering me in Your faithfulness. May I be like Hannah, who fervently pursued and honored You. Amen.*

# DAY 343

# YOUR GREATEST DELIGHT

*His delight is in the law of the LORD, and in His law he meditates day and night.*
PSALM 1:2 NKJV

What are your heart's desires? To be happy? To find purpose? To be loved? There is a way to satisfy those longings without fail. Psalm 37:4 (NASB) says, "Delight yourself in the LORD; and He will give you the desires of your heart."

Many Christians expect God to provide their desires, but they don't want to delight in Him. They treat their relationship with God as a duty, a desperate plea for help, a religious lucky charm, a daily dependence, but a delight? That requires far too much time and energy.

A relationship without delight is like a marriage with no passion or friendship. Yes, you can perform the duties of married life, but it will become a prison. Nehemiah 8:10 (NASB) says, "Do not be grieved [by the words of the Law], for the joy of the LORD is your strength." We should love and serve God not to avoid His wrath but rather out of gratitude and awe.

When you live this way, you will find the delights of your heart. Albert Schweitzer wrote: "Your life is something opaque, not transparent, as long as you look at it in ordinary human ways. But if you hold it up against the light of God's goodness, it shines and turns transparent, radiant, and bright. And then you ask yourself in amazement: Is this really my own life I see before me?"

. . . . . . . . . . . . . . . . . . . . . . . . . . . . . . . . . . . . . . . . . .

*Lord, let our relationship be one of pure delight. Even though I'm grateful for Your works, I'm most grateful for You. Amen.*

# DAY 344
## WHAT IS PARAMOUNT?

*"Again, truly I tell you that if two of you on earth agree about anything they ask for, it will be done for them by my Father in heaven. For where two or three gather in my name, there am I with them."*
MATTHEW 18:19–20 NIV

Calling out to God anywhere and anytime is appropriate, and yet one scenario we should never forget is to pray along with other believers. When two or more gather in the name of Christ, the Bible says God will give us what we need. If we come into alignment with His will, then our requests will take on a righteous and heavenly scope. Within His plan and surrounded by godly people, our petitions will become focused on what is truly needed rather than every whim of our hearts.

Only God can know what we truly need. What if we were to beg Him for a big house in a gated community, but that lifestyle would cause us—little by little—to become so fashionable and self-centered and exclusive behind those gated walls that we could no longer do His will or even wish to do His will? Only He can know all the wiles of Satan. Only He can know all the ways we might be tempted to fall into sin. Therefore, seeking God's will for our lives is not just a helpful suggestion. It is paramount.

. . . . . . . . . . . . . . . . . . . . . . . . . . . . . . . . . . . .

*God, even when life doesn't go my way, help me to trust in Your plan and remember that You know the desires of my heart. Amen.*

# MAKING GOOD DECISIONS

*Trust in the Lord with all your heart, and lean not on your own understanding;*
*in all your ways acknowledge Him, and He shall direct your paths. Do*
*not be wise in your own eyes; fear the Lord and depart from evil.*
PROVERBS 3:5–7 NKJV

Everyone goes through tough times, and having to make important decisions during those dark days only adds to the pain and frustration. Marilyn wanted to do the right thing in regard to a failing relationship, but she worried she would make a mistake she'd regret. She went to an older Christian friend for advice. He listened and talked with her, but in the end, he said, "You need to decide, but only you can do it. No one can make it for you."

Marilyn knew her friend was right. She began praying earnestly about the situation, relying on God for wisdom and courage. Some days were still hard, and she didn't know which direction to take, but she continued to trust God and wait for His help. When the resolution came, Marilyn knew God had intervened and worked things out for the best.

When we learn to trust the Lord and not our own limited understanding, He will direct our paths. The secret is to trust Him with all our heart and acknowledge Him. God is personal for each of us. He wants to be included in our decisions and our daily lives. No matter what we face, He knows how to resolve it. Whatever you need, trust Him.

*Father, give me Your wisdom and understanding.*
*Help me to rely on You and not myself. Amen.*

# DAY 346
## FOCUSING ON TODAY

*Don't brag about tomorrow, since you don't know what the day will bring.*
PROVERBS 27:1 NLT

What do you have on your plate today? What about tomorrow? Do you remember those plans you have next week? And that trip you have later this month? What about the work thing you have next year?

If we take an honest look at this verse, we see there is no point in worrying about tomorrow, just as there is no point in worrying about next year! *Nothing* is set in stone. Even today is a fluid river of moments, susceptible to change.

We will find that we can be happier in life by simply taking each day as it comes. If we are not focused on our calendar of events and instead decidedly focused on each moment of *this* day, we will have the ability to enjoy moments that otherwise would have passed us by. The hilarious thing your child just said that bubbles into laughter. The sweet message from your husband that warms your heart. A lunch date with a friend that encourages your soul. These are all moments we can revel in and enjoy rather than thinking about the next thing on the list or schedule.

Today, let's keep our focus on only the events of *today*. We will find fulfillment, laughter, and a reduction in stress if we refuse to borrow the worries of tomorrow.

*Lord, thank You for encouraging me to live life moment by moment.*
*Help me to recognize the blessings that abound in each day. Amen.*

## DAY 347
# BE THE SPARK

*"As surely as I live. . .I take no pleasure in the death of wicked people.*
*I only want them to turn from their wicked ways so they can live."*
EZEKIEL 33:11 NLT

The Great Awakening was triggered by the evangelist George Whitefield, who spent "whole days and even weeks. . .prostrate on the ground in silent or vocal prayer." He said, "[Prayer] is the very breath of the new creature, the fan of the divine life, whereby the spark of holy fire, kindled in the soul by God, is not only kept in, but raised into a flame."

How many believers say they will pray for a situation when all they really do is think about it? Could it be that when we say, "I'll pray for you," we really mean, "I will hope for your sake that things get better"?

God said, "If My people who are called by My name will humble themselves, and pray and seek My face, and turn from their wicked ways, then I will hear from heaven, and will forgive their sin and heal their land" (2 Chronicles 7:14 NKJV).

Prayer for revival should be a daily activity for every Christian. It takes no special talent, no magic words. Prayer doesn't require strength, youth, health, or wealth. You can maintain an attitude of prayer during car trips, meals, or whenever the thought crosses your mind. It is a contrite heart that God loves, and He's waiting for the day His people cry out to Him in desperation. Today, be the spark that starts the fire.

. . . . . . . . . . . . . . . . . . . . . . . . . . . . . . . . . . . . . . . . . . . .

*Lord, pour out Your Spirit on Your people,*
*and bring revival to our land. Amen.*

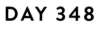

# DAY 348

# GENTLE AND HUMBLE OF HEART

*But God chose the foolish things of the world to shame the wise;*
*God chose the weak things of the world to shame the strong. God*
*chose the lowly things of this world and the despised things—*
*and the things that are not—to nullify the things that are.*
1 CORINTHIANS 1:27–28 NIV

Throughout the Bible, we see God selecting people for His tasks who might be considered by the world's standards to be very unwise choices. Yet God does not see people the way we see them. He may pick someone—whom the world despises because of a lack of wealth or fame or academic accolades or clever wit or worldly savvy—and raise her up to show a haughty society just how foolish their pride looks.

Matthew 5:5 (NIV) says, "Blessed are the meek, for they will inherit the earth." Jesus called Himself gentle and humble of heart. So, if you are feeling unfit for duty because you are humble and lowly by the world's standards, take heart. God loves the meek. If you feel you are lacking in a gentle and selfless spirit, just ask God for one, and He would be pleased to give it to you.

. . . . . . . . . . . . . . . . . . . . . . . . . . . . . . . . . . . . . . . . . . . .

*Father, thank You for loving misfits, outcasts, and sinners.*
*Cultivate in me a spirit of humility. Amen.*

# DAY 349
# KNOWING WHAT TO SAY

*"The Lord God has given Me the tongue of the learned, that I should know how to speak a word in season to him who is weary. He awakens Me morning by morning, He awakens My ear to hear as the learned."*
ISAIAH 50:4 NKJV

Sometimes it's hard to know what to say to a friend or loved one when tragedy strikes their family. We all know the usual trite lines like "Everything will turn out for the best" or "I'm sorry for your loss." And even though these aren't bad words, they do little to comfort someone in pain.

We are limited in our ability to comfort. We can sympathize with others, but unless we have experienced what they are going through, we cannot feel the depth of their pain or how it is affecting them. It's in these times that we need God's Spirit to help us be a comforter.

Isaiah writes that the Lord gave him a tongue so he would know how to speak the right word to someone who was weary. We can apply this scripture to our own lives and ask God to give us the right word to speak to the one needing comfort. If we allow Him, God will awaken our ears to hear His voice every day. Then we can speak God's words and bring a measure of comfort to a hurting individual. When we give His word to someone, it will be the right one.

. . . . . . . . . . . . . . . . . . . . . . . . . . . . . . . . . . . . . . . . . . . . .

*Lord, open my ears to hear Your message of hope and speak it to someone in need. Amen.*

# DAY 350
# AN EVER-FLOWING SPRING

*"The LORD will guide you continually, giving you water when*
*you are dry and restoring your strength. You will be like a*
*well-watered garden, like an ever-flowing spring."*
ISAIAH 58:11 NLT

It's easy to fall into the trap of looking to earthly things to restore us. Instead of immediately looking to the One who made us and knows every detail of what we need, we often look other places. The Lord is our water when we are dry. He restores our strength. As we look to Him, we will become like a lush, well-watered garden. Fruitful. Energetic. Growing.

This is one of those verses to keep close to your heart during a busy season. When it feels like your next day of rest is far off, this is a promise to cling to and draw strength from. Every day, as often as you can, make space for quiet moments with the Lord. A few moments can give you everything you need. Even as you fall asleep at night, this passage can be one you recite to bring you into a peaceful rest.

The Lord will restore you as you choose to take time to meditate on His Word and sit in His presence. When you are seeking out the right Source, you will find you can make it through even the most rigorous of weeks.

* * * * * * * * * * * * * * * * * * * * * * * * * * * * * * * * * * * * * *

*My eyes are set on You, and You restore me. As a gentle rain brings life to*
*the driest soil, so Your very presence and love bring life to my soul. Amen.*

# THE HIDDEN BLESSINGS OF GRIEF

*Truly, O God of Israel, our Savior, you work in mysterious ways.*
ISAIAH 45:15 NLT

The 2013 Morgan Fire was sparked by target shooting, an innocent accident that destroyed 3,111 acres on Mount Diablo, California. But the following spring, rare "fire followers" burst with color, covering the mountain. The last time they were seen was half a century ago. For botanists and naturalists, viewing this phenomenon was a once-in-a-lifetime opportunity.

The death of a loved one can be like a wildfire. You don't know what parts of your life will turn to ashes and what parts will survive. Many may feel everything is lost, but just like the fire followers, God brings beautiful things from ashes.

Grief can be difficult during the holidays. The pain of loss has a way of resurfacing when the temperatures cool and the days get shorter.

Philippians 3:13–14 (NASB) says, "Forgetting what lies behind and reaching forward to what lies ahead, I press on toward the goal for the prize of the upward call of God in Christ Jesus." We will never forget the significance of those lost, but we can press forward to see how God will use the influence of their lives and deaths to make us stronger believers.

Take some time this season to reflect on the unexpected treasures you have found through grief. God has brought you through this trial for your good and His glory. Don't let the sadness blind you to the beautiful display of flowers on your mountain.

. . . . . . . . . . . . . . . . . . . . . . . . . . . . . . . . . . . . . . . . . .

*Father, the grief in my heart is still tender, but I trust You
to work everything together for my good. Open my eyes
to see my own personal fire followers. Amen.*

# DAY 352
# LESSONS FROM THE PAST

*"While I was fainting away, I remembered the LORD."*
JONAH 2:7 NASB

Corrie ten Boom once said, "Memories are not the key to the past. They are the key to the future."

This year may have been filled with beautiful nostalgia, or you may have come face-to-face with tragedy. Don't block out the bad memories and avoid the pain; rather, assess where you are. Consider the devastation of your dreams, and seek the parts of you that are still alive.

Just as the farmer's land must be turned over and fertilized to make ready for a new crop, God is using each event in your life to make your heart ready to bear spiritual fruit.

Give thanks for all the blessings—and for suffering. Pray and believe in faith for what God has planned in your future.

For those who have hurt you, consider how you may return a blessing for Christ's sake. For those who have abused their power, pray for them. For those you have offended, seek the best way to make peace and find forgiveness.

Romans 8:28 (nlt) says, "God causes everything to work together for the good of those who love God and are called according to his purpose for them."

When we reflect on our lives, it isn't for the sake of self-pity or shame but to exercise our faith. You will be amazed as you watch God unfold His promises.

· · · · · · · · · · · · · · · · · · · · · · · · · · · · · · · · · · · · · · · · ·

*Father, never let me forget the blessings You have given to*
*me and my family, and bless me with the grace to move*
*beyond the pain that lingers in my past. Amen.*

## DAY 353
# GOD NEVER FAILS

*Then Moses said to them, "No one is to keep any of it until morning." However,*
*some of them paid no attention to Moses; they kept part of it until morning,*
*but it was full of maggots and began to smell. So Moses was angry with them.*
EXODUS 16:19–20 NIV

In Exodus, we find that the Israelites went against God's command and gathered more manna than what they needed for each day. It was obvious that the Israelites didn't trust the Almighty. Even though they had witnessed wondrous miracles, they assumed God would forget about them, so they took precautions.

How is that different from the way we treat God today? We desire the security of a bigger bank account and more space in our homes than we can use. We want more clothes than we can wear. More food than we can eat. We want assurances for the future. If God wants to come alongside our plans and our stockpiling, well, all the better.

God wants us to prayerfully trust Him to supply our needs. We must work, yes, but we shouldn't get ahead of God. Just like the Israelites, He wants us to know that walking alongside Him is the safest place to be. The wisest place. The securities and promises of this world ring hollow. Banks close and kingdoms fall.

God never fails.

* * * * * * * * * * * * * * * * * * * * * * * * * * * * * * * * * * * * * * * * * *

*Lord, help me to find my security in You and not*
*in the fickle, fleeting things of this world. Amen.*

# HOLD YOUR TEMPER

*A hot-tempered person stirs up conflict,*
*but the one who is patient calms a quarrel.*
PROVERBS 15:18 NIV

For the third time in a week, Jane called her internet provider hoping for a solution to her problem. Internet service had been sporadic for several days, and she hoped to reach someone who could give her some answers.

The person on the other end of the line sounded young and inexperienced, but Jane decided to give her a chance. As they discussed the problem, the technician tried several ideas to get the service working again but to no avail. She finally offered a solution that would require Jane to pay a fee of $150. Jane felt angry the company would require a large fee in light of the fact she was already paying a monthly fee and not receiving good service. The longer they talked, the more stressed and upset she became. But in spite of the frustration she voiced to the other person, the girl remained polite and helpful.

Jane felt like giving the service technician a piece of her mind but knew it wouldn't solve anything. With God's help, she remained calm in spite of the stress she felt. They ended the call by wishing each other a good day despite the failure to resolve the situation. Even though Jane still didn't have an answer to her problem, she was glad she had not spoken in haste and made the situation worse.

* * * * * * * * * * * * * * * * * * * * * * * * * * * * * * * * * * * * * * * * *

*Lord, keep me calm in the face of anger and trouble. Help me*
*not to quarrel even when I feel justified in doing so. Amen.*

# DAY 355

# HE KNOWS YOU

*How precious are your thoughts about me, O God. They cannot
be numbered! I can't even count them; they outnumber the
grains of sand! And when I wake up, you are still with me!*
PSALM 139:17–18 NLT

Did you know that you have a history with God? Your relationship is ever growing, ever changing, and He knows you. He knit you together in your mother's womb. He's watched as you've grown up. He's seen every good day. Every bad day. Not a moment passes that He's unaware of what you're up to.

And He still loves you. When you live in relationship with Him, covered by the sacrifice of Christ, He doesn't see the things you've done wrong. Don't walk into this day feeling the weight of your failures and imagining there is no way He could continue to love you. He does love you even through the worst of times. Sending His Son while we were still sinners is proof of that love.

So instead of coming before Him full of shame and with a heavy heart, come before Him in humble thankfulness and confidence that He loves you so much. When you come before Him, He is pleased to see His daughter—spotless and whole. He is willing—and desires—to have a deep and thriving relationship with you.

. . . . . . . . . . . . . . . . . . . . . . . . . . . . . . . . . . . . . . . . .

*Lord, I can never fully understand the grace with which You love
me. I am forever amazed and filled with joy. Let our relationship
grow deeper through this day and the days ahead. Amen.*

# DAY 356
# A WORK IN PROGRESS

*I am confident of this very thing, that He who*
*began a good work in you will perfect it.*
PHILIPPIANS 1:6 NASB

With each turn in life, whether it's a job change, a new baby, an empty nest, or a major move, you may be asking, "Who am I now?" We all feel disjointed or lost sometimes, but somehow in our desire for calm, we forget that the answer to that question is an ever-changing one.

The words to the old Sunday school song sum it up: "He's still working on me to make me what I ought to be. It took Him just a week to make the moon and the stars, the sun and the earth and Jupiter and Mars. How loving and patient He must be. He's still working on me."

God is not finished defining who you are. Like a child asking, "Are we there yet?" at each new mile, trying to rush the journey is futile. You won't fully know who God created you to be until the end. As John so beautifully expressed, "Beloved, now we are children of God; and it has not yet been revealed what we shall be, but we know that when He is revealed, we shall be like Him, for we shall see Him as He is" (1 John 3:2 NKJV).

So the real question is not "Who am I?" but rather "How is this new stage in my life making me the woman God is calling me to become?"

*Father, help me find beauty in each stage of my life,*
*knowing that each one is part of Your ultimate plan. Amen.*

# DAY 357
# COME INTO HIS PRESENCE

*Even though I walk through the darkest valley, I will fear no*
*evil, for you are with me; your rod and your staff, they comfort*
*me. You prepare a table before me in the presence of my*
*enemies. You anoint my head with oil; my cup overflows.*
PSALM 23:4–5 NIV

When you wake up in the morning, do you feel like your spiritual tank is on empty or, at best, you're running on fumes? The world has plenty of soul-fuel of every kind, but it's like putting water into a gas tank. You can open the garage door to drive away, but the car won't take you where you need to go.

God says if we come into His presence, He will give us rest. He will give us peace that passes all understanding—something the world cannot give, cannot even comprehend. He will lead us beside quiet waters, giving us comfort in times of trial. We will fear no evil when He is near. He will refresh our souls and guide us along the right paths. When we make Him our daily Shepherd, we will lack for nothing.

In fact, when we're in His presence, we'll find that our spirit's cup will overflow—with joy and love and strength for the day.

Prayer.

It's the best soul-fuel money can't buy.

*Father, help me to make fellowship with You my top priority. You are the only*
*true source of peace, joy, and fulfillment in a world full of counterfeits. Amen.*

# DAY 358

## DRESSED TO THE NINES

*Put on all of God's armor so that you will be able
to stand firm against all strategies of the devil.*
EPHESIANS 6:11 NLT

Have you ever left your house feeling as though you had forgotten something and weren't completely ready to face the world? Maybe you left home without putting on the belt that matches the dress you're wearing or traveled to an out-of-town conference without the proper shoes to wear. It may have been something as simple as forgetting to put on your watch or lipstick. Whatever the case may be, you feel underdressed and incomplete because of the missing item. You feel as if everyone is looking at you, which makes you feel self-conscious and keeps you from being your best on those days.

Paul wrote to the Ephesians, and to us, that it's important to put on the whole armor of God. This is our spiritual wardrobe. He lists the various pieces we should wear every day in order to stand against the devil and his tricks. We cannot afford to forget even one item. Why? Because the missing piece makes us vulnerable in that area. The enemy knows to attack us there. Each day, we must equip ourselves with the armor God has given us, from the breast-plate of righteousness to the sword of the Spirit. Before you start your day, be sure you're fully dressed. Don't allow the devil to keep you from feeling confident and being at your best for God.

- - - - - - - - - - - - - - - - - - - - - - - - - - - - - - - - - - - - - - - - - - - -

*Lord, help me to realize the importance of wearing the armor
You have provided and to never leave home without it. Amen.*

## DAY 359

# THE BATTLE IS REAL, BUT SO IS OUR REFUGE

*Keep me safe, O God, for I have come to you for refuge.*
PSALM 16:1 NLT

Have you ever had days, weeks, or months when this was all you could pray? Or maybe in the heat of the battle, in the intensity of the chase, the thought of running to Him for safety never even crossed your mind. Perhaps you believed this was a battle you could win on your own! And yet with each swing of your sword, you felt your strength fail.

Life is hard, and it's okay to admit that. The enemy we face on a daily basis is cunning and unrelenting. How wonderful it is that David looked to the Lord for his protection. And it wasn't protection in a spiritual sense—David's very life was at stake! He prayed to the Lord to keep him safe.

Maybe it feels like the Lord is far away—too intangible to be sought out for emotional strength, much less physical needs. My sister, He is not too far. He is a physical God who is able to keep you secure. He is ready and waiting to be your refuge. Whether your need is tangible or emotional, go to Him.

. . . . . . . . . . . . . . . . . . . . . . . . . . . . . . . . . . . . . . . .

*Lord, I come to You for refuge. Open Your doors to me and take me in. Keep me safe from the enemy who pursues me day and night. Let me hide myself within Your fortress, where You will keep watch over me. Amen.*

# GOD IS NOT A "PRIORITY"

*Whatever you do or say, do it as a representative of the Lord Jesus.*
COLOSSIANS 3:17 NLT

If most Christians listed their priorities, they would probably put God at the top, followed by family and friends and then other significant areas, but is that really where God belongs—at the top of a list to be compartmentalized and checked off?

Our relationship with God shouldn't be treated as a priority but rather as the essence of everything. God should be the center of marriage, parenting, business practices, thought life, television viewing—everything.

Acts 17:28 (NKJV) says, "For in Him we live and move and have our being." Even something as mundane as mealtime should be done for God's glory (1 Corinthians 10:31).

When the patriarch Jacob awoke from his dream about angels descending on a ladder, he declared, "Surely the LORD is in this place, and I did not know it" (Genesis 28:16 NKJV). A. W. Tozer commented, "Jacob had never been for one small division of a moment outside of the circle of that all-pervading Presence. But he knew it not. That was his trouble, and it is ours. Men do not know God is here. What a difference it would make if they knew."

God's presence is with you when you buy groceries, drive your car, put your children to bed. What are you doing to honor Him through these mundane tasks? The time for God is not first thing each morning; it's every minute of every day.

* * * * * * * * * * * * * * * * * * * * * * * * * * * * * * * * * * * *

*Lord, I want everything in my life to be saturated with Your character
and Your Word. Teach me to consider You in all my ways. Amen.*

# DAY 361

# A WORLD IN PERIL

*For our struggle is not against flesh and blood, but against the rulers,*
*against the authorities, against the powers of this dark world and*
*against the spiritual forces of evil in the heavenly realms.*

EPHESIANS 6:12 NIV

If you've ever faced evil—and we all have—you know how it looks. It is ugly and terrifying. However, it might also be just a little bit enticing. It makes one shudder, but at the same time, it might make us take a peek around the corner for just one more look.

We are in a spiritual tug-of-war, and like in a real battle, the enemy and his dark battalion are intent on destroying us, especially the part of us that matters the most—our very souls.

Our world is in peril. What can we do? Perhaps it is time for us to be like the title of that beloved hymn "Rise Up, O Saints of God!"

The book of Ephesians gives us a warning—almost like a battle cry—when it says, "Therefore put on the full armor of God, so that when the day of evil comes, you may be able to stand your ground, and after you have done everything, to stand. Stand firm then, with the belt of truth buckled around your waist, with the breastplate of righteousness in place" (vv. 13–14).

In this deadly spiritual battle for our souls, which side do you stand on? What prayer is on your heart in these perilous times?

- - - - - - - - - - - - - - - - - - - - - - - - - - - - - - - - - - - - - - - -

*God, help me to stand firm in Your truth and light.*
*Shield me from Satan's lies. Amen.*

# DAY 362
# LET GOD FIGHT FOR YOU

*"O our God, will You not judge them? For we have no*
*power against this great multitude that is coming against us;*
*nor do we know what to do, but our eyes are upon You."*
2 CHRONICLES 20:12 NKJV

Sue was called as a witness in a robbery. Never having been involved in anything of this nature, she felt fearful of what might happen when she saw the young man who had robbed her. He was only fifteen, but he had an adult accomplice who had recently been released from prison. Would the perpetrator recognize her, and would he or his accomplice take revenge on her for testifying against him? She wanted to be brave, but fear threatened to paralyze her. She knew her strength came from God and prayed for His help.

When she was sworn in, Sue took her place on the witness stand. The adult was being tried for his part in the crime, but the juvenile needed to be identified. The judge turned to Sue and said, "We're going to bring in a young man. If he's the one who robbed you, all you have to do is shake your head yes or no." When it was over, she felt great relief and knew God had been with her in the courtroom that day.

No matter who or what we face in life, God will be with us. He supplies the power and strength we don't have. If we allow Him to fight for us, we will have victory.

*Father, help us to keep our eyes on You, knowing the battle is Yours. Amen.*

# DAY 363
# WE WON'T BE SHAKEN

*I know the Lord is always with me. I will*
*not be shaken, for he is right beside me.*
PSALM 16:8 NLT

When crisis strikes, people often drift away from the Lord. Heartbreak doesn't heal overnight. As each day passes, another part of them either dies or regains life. Though they may believe nothing ever could have prepared them for such pain, the everyday choices they've made throughout life determine what they will be like on the other side.

Every day we have a choice to trust God and the opportunity to put things in His hands and look eagerly for the way He will work them out. Every day we are developing a relationship with Him. We are choosing whether we will invest or neglect. Build up or break down. Draw closer or walk farther. It is how we handle ourselves in our daily lives that determines the amount of faith we'll have when a crisis comes.

Maybe our hearts will still break, but we will know who to turn to. We will trust and believe when everything is dark, because we have walked many roads with Him. We know His character. We know He is good. We know that though we don't understand, *He does*. And because He does, we can rest in His love. We don't need to know the reason, only that He is with us.

. . . . . . . . . . . . . . . . . . . . . . . . . . . . . . . . . . . . . . . .

*Though darkness surrounds me, I know the Light. I know that You are*
*always with me. I will not be shaken, for You are right beside me. Amen.*

# DAY 364
# THESE SACRED WORDS

*One day Jesus was praying in a certain place. When he finished, one of his disciples said to him, "Lord, teach us to pray, just as John taught his disciples."*
LUKE 11:1 NIV

Imagine being taught how to pray by God Himself? What an inspiring event in history. Did the disciples comprehend the majesty of the moment? Did they know these sacred words would transcend time, that they would virtually crackle the air like lightning every time they were spoken, and they would contain enough supernatural power to alter every human heart? Surely they must have known the awesome significance of that holy lesson on prayer.

Here is Jesus' prayer as it appears in the Gospel of Matthew:

*"Our Father in heaven, hallowed be your name, your kingdom come, your will be done, on earth as it is in heaven. Give us today our daily bread. Forgive us our debts, as we also have forgiven our debtors. And lead us not into temptation, but deliver us from the evil one." (Matthew 6:9–13 NIV)*

There are many right ways to pray, but isn't it a joyous thing, an awesome privilege to be taught how to pray by the One who made us? The One who longs to be with us? Who wants to someday take that conversation you're having with Him right into eternity?

. . . . . . . . . . . . . . . . . . . . . . . . . . . . . . . . . . . . . . . . .

*Lord, thank You for teaching me how to pray. Please give me more discipline in my prayer life. Make my communion with You more essential to me than food. Amen.*

## DAY 365

# THE GIFT OF PEACE

*"Peace I leave with you; my peace I give you. I do not give to you as the world gives. Do not let your hearts be troubled and do not be afraid."*
JOHN 14:27 NIV

Watching the news every day is enough to make anyone uneasy and restless, especially if the news stories are happening nearby. People disappear every day, children are abused, and cities are torn apart by rioting and looting. There seems to be no end to the evil that abounds in every city and town across our country. How can anyone live in peace under those circumstances?

As Christians, we can have peace even in the face of all the tragedy happening around us. Jesus made a promise to His disciples and to us as well. He was going back to the Father, but He was giving us a priceless gift. He gave us His peace. The world can never give us the peace that Jesus gives. It's a peace that we, the recipients, can't even understand. It's too wonderful for our minds to grasp, but we know it comes from Him.

Whatever is happening in your world, Christ can give you peace. None of the problems you're facing are too big for Him, whether it's trouble in the city where you live or pain in your own home. He is saying to you, "Don't let your heart be troubled about these things, and don't be afraid."

. . . . . . . . . . . . . . . . . . . . . . . . . . . . . . . . . . . . . . . . . .

*Jesus, I ask for Your peace to fill my heart and mind.*
*Help me not to be afraid of the problems I'm facing. Amen.*

# SCRIPTURE INDEX

# DAILY INSPIRATION FOR A WOMAN'S SPIRIT!

## Choose Joy for Morning and Evening

This book includes a morning and evening 3-minute devotion for every day of the year. You'll discover an abundance of comfort and inspiration in the daily, just-right-sized readings that will help you grow ever closer to the Joy-Giver Himself.

Flexible Casebound / 978-1-63609-372-7

## 365 Encouraging Prayers for Morning and Evening Journal

This daily devotional prayer journal is a lovely reminder to bring any petition before your heavenly Father. Hundreds of just-right-sized prayers touch on topics that will resonate with your heart.

DiCarta / 978-1-63609-338-3